Praise for *Reclaim the Moment*

"Greg's perspectives on focus are essential for a world in which we are pulled in every possible direction."

—**Jocelyn Hamilton,**
President, *Marco Ophthalmic*

"Edgy and incisive and full of ideas and insights, *Reclaim the Moment* is a roadmap for those looking to improve their business and their life."

—**Joseph C. Davis,**
Managing Director and Senior Partner, *Boston Consulting Group*

"In the thirty years that I've known Greg and his work, he has always inspired with both rapid-fire intellect and deep laughter."

—**Richard Birkenhead,**
Partner / Creative Director, *DBOX*

"Our business is rooted in solid relationships. Greg gets it. He offers ideas to strengthen true connections."

—**Brian Kendrella,**
President, *Stacks Bowers Galleries*

"Whether he is singing in a punk band, giving an inspiring keynote address, or sharing his accumulated insights in this book, Greg Bennick's passion for growth and change is infectious. With wisdom and grace, humor and vulnerability, Greg shows what we do matters and how our lives can matter even more. Staying true to ourselves, developing focus and creativity, and cultivating compassion for self and others helps us *build a better now*. Through gripping storytelling informed by insights from philosophy, sociology, psychology, and literature, Greg moves us from pessimism to possibility, ready to take the risks necessary that lead to more intentional, fulfilling lives."

—**Ross Haenfler,**
author and Professor of Sociology, *Grinnell College*

"*Reclaim the Moment* is a masterclass in balancing life's seriousness with its lighter side. Greg Bennick, a former punk rocker and current juggler—because why not?—brings his humor to every page, turning deceptively profound insights into fun, and often funny, lessons. If you're looking to improve your focus, leadership, and overall outlook on life, this book offers the perfect mix of strategies and smiles. A truly inspiring and entertaining read!"

– **Bill Stainton,**
29-time Emmy Award winner, CSP, CPAE

"Building, cultivating, and retaining a cohesive team takes commitment and focus, and a clear plan that's actionable. Greg's book is full of tools that can be used by leaders to further develop themselves and their teams to be their best."

—**Shelley R. Schoenfeld,**
Chief Marketing and Client Services Officer, *GoMo Health*

"Greg Bennick has had a big life, from fronting a punk rock band to keynoting and juggling knives on stages across the world. In *Reclaim the Moment,* he brings his distinctive, gifted voice as well as his decades of experience entertaining, uplifting, and learning from people globally to some of our most impactful everyday concerns: productivity, connection, and focus. This book offers innovative insights for new ways to understand how creation is powerful, strategies for how we can turn mistakes into wins, and tangible approaches to how we can build a better now for ourselves and our organizations. It is an unforgettable, joyful, and indispensable read for anyone striving for more powerful human connection in our always-on world."

—**Dr. Heather Ashley Hayes,**
Assistant Professor of Communication and
Information Sciences, *University of Alabama*

"Greg Bennick's powerful book *Reclaim the Moment* was a wakeup call. What I found in this page turner was a thought blueprint for personal introspection and intentionality. *Reclaim the Moment* is a marvelous book, one you didn't know you needed to read—but you do."

—**David Avrin, CSP, GSF,**
author of *Ridiculously Easy to Do Business With* (*2024 Classified Press*)

"Knowing Greg's ability to energize and connect with an audience intellectually and emotionally like few can, it's not a surprise that *Reclaim the Moment* is cannon fire from the soul. This book is the product of that personal journey and is essential for galvanizing one's own experience."

—**Mike Gitter,**
Music Executive/xXx Fanzine 1983–1988

"Bennick's strategies and tactics will get you back on track when the world throws you off course."

—**Shep Hyken,**
CX expert, award-winning keynote speaker, and
New York Times bestselling author

RECLAIM
THE
MOMENT

GREG BENNICK

RECLAIM THE MOMENT

7 STRATEGIES TO BUILD A BETTER NOW

WILEY

Published by John Wiley & Sons, Inc., Hoboken, New Jersey.
Published simultaneously in Canada.

For general information on our other products and services or for technical support, please contact our Customer Care Department within the United States at (800) 762-2974, outside the United States at (317) 572-3993 or fax (317) 572-4002.

Wiley also publishes its books in a variety of electronic formats. Some content that appears in print may not be available in electronic formats. For more information about Wiley products, visit our website at www.wiley.com.

Library of Congress Cataloging-in-Publication Data:

Names: Bennick, Greg, author.
Title: Reclaim the moment : seven strategies to build a better now / Greg
    Bennick.
Description: Hoboken, New Jersey : Wiley, [2024] | Includes bibliographical
    references and index.
Identifiers: LCCN 2024013147 (print) | LCCN 2024013148 (ebook) | ISBN
    9781394247684 (hardback) | ISBN 9781394247707 (adobe pdf) | ISBN
    9781394247714 (epub)
Subjects: LCSH: Organizational effectiveness. | Organizational change. |
    Teams in the workplace. | Leadership.
Classification: LCC HD58.9 .B449 2024 (print) | LCC HD58.9 (ebook) | DDC
    658.4—dc23/eng/20240418
LC record available at https://lccn.loc.gov/2024013147
LC ebook record available at https://lccn.loc.gov/2024013148

Cover Design: Paul McCarthy
Printed and bound by CPI Group (UK) Ltd, Croydon, CR0 4YY

C9781394247684_280624

To my parents, Dian and David, for a lifetime of unconditional love and for always believing in me.

Contents

Preface   *xi*

Setting the Stage: Lying to Yourself Is Dangerous   *1*

Chapter 1   There's a Madness to My Method   19

Chapter 2   A World Changer's Guide to Life   43

Chapter 3   Mickey Mouse, a Thunderstorm, and Anarchy   55

Chapter 4   BELIEVE IN THE POSSIBILITY
              OF KINDNESS to Escape the Trap of Pessimism   69

Chapter 5   KEEP YOUR EYES ON THE KNIFE to Resist
              the Allure of Distraction   87

Chapter 6   CULTIVATE A REVOLUTIONARY
              MINDSET to Break Free from the Deception
              of Defeat   123

Chapter 7   LEAP INTO THE DARK to
              Embrace the Possibility of Success   139

Chapter 8   ENGAGE WITH LAUGHTER to Connect
              Amidst the Weight of the World   161

Chapter 9   BUILD RELATIONSHIPS
              to Outsmart the Dread of Isolation   179

Chapter 10   START A REVERBERATION EFFECT
              to Build a Better Now   201

Acknowledgments   229

About the Author   231

Index   233

Preface

THIS BOOK IS about amplifying your life, regaining your focus, and transforming your world.

Note that I said *your* world. Not *the* world. When we think of trying to transform *the* world, it might be romantic and exciting, even awe-inspiring. But it is largely unrealistic. Existential writer Franz Kafka made this clear when he wrote if it's you against the world, *bet on the world.*[1]

Perhaps not the most inspiring sentiment, but what he wrote makes sense. You, versus the entire world, doesn't offer the best odds. This doesn't mean giving up trying to make improvements to where you work or how you live. But it does mean thinking in terms of *better* rather than *perfect*, and working in stages toward making the improvements you want to manifest. This mindset is the *think global, act local* of personal and organizational development.

Taking care of *your* world is more accessible and easier to define. It is a world that you have ownership of, and for which you hold

---

[1] Franz Kafka, "The Zürau Aphorisms," *The Aphorisms of Franz Kafka*, ed. Reiner Stach (Princeton University Press, 2022), 106. Translated from the German, "Im Kampf zwischen Dir und der Welt sekundiere dir Welt," or "In the battle between you and the world, second the world."

responsibility. We are developers and designers of our lives and contributors to the lives of those around us. Your world is where you work, create, and expand. You have a vested self-interest in keeping your world in order, and helping it grow.

To reclaim the moment is to regain your focus from a place of feeling stuck, overwhelmed, or underdeveloped, all of which are too common today. These ideas are about getting back on track.

If you're reading this book, it means that you care about growth and expansion. You consider where other people and their psychological well-being fit into that process. It means that you want things to be better in your business, your potential, and your outlook.

To *take care* of your world includes stewardship over your projects and approaches to them, and having a willingness to risk, shift, and change in order to improve the things you want to be better. It means embracing discipline and putting in a little (or more than a little) extra effort so that your relationships, potential for leadership, clarity, and pathways to the future can be better than they are today.

Because let's be realistic, while we want improvement and stronger connections, it is often easy to lose faith in possibility, especially these days. In the last few years life has often felt out of control. Socially, we are forging new norms at a feverish pace. Our desire for success outpaces our stamina. Frustration feels like it is increasing. Our world seems more selfish and, at times, even mean. We are pitted between what we want and a social framework that leaves us behind even as it drags us forward. Self-esteem is in a battle on many fronts, including our online identities, which both are, and are not, who we are. People feel disconnected – ironic in a digital world. We seem intensely ego-driven and ruthless in our judgment of one another. We are overwhelmed with input. We are too greedy and shortsighted. We feel stressed, disoriented, ineffective, and unsure.

These aren't trends with limited effects. Globally, the planet is suffering, and I'm referring to the literal earth. We take out our rage on where we live, because we aren't wise enough to think about the consequences of our actions and reactions. Our selfishness has real effects. In case you're someone who doesn't believe in science, here's a quick news update: the warming of the earth and the effects on its health are real.[2] Have you noticed more people mentioning that the weather in their city wasn't as hot years ago, or that there was less rain, more rain, or noticeable changes having taken place over time? Anyone notice that summers these days always seem to include wildfires? I certainly have.

The effects on us aren't just that we are hotter in the summer or colder in the winter. Everything ties in and around itself. The changes we are experiencing affect our emotional and psychological health. They influence customer behaviors, too. We feel the impacts of retail shifts due to disruptions in supply chains and changes in energy sources. Emotional imbalances, social unrest, and environmental upheaval intertwine and the trickle down from this is becoming a flood. Our shortsightedness and disconnection from ourselves and our loss of focus, both in business and in life, is extending beyond our capability to manage. This leads to even more arguments and upheaval, and the cycle begins again. Things feel, to say the least, a bit out of control.

My mind often slips into hopelessness.

In January 2024, as I was finalizing the edits to this book, I took a month off in Thailand to recenter after I finished the first 99 percent or so of the text. I was in need of experiences rooted in compassion, as focus and clarity often accompany them.

I spent ten days between Malaysia and Myanmar in the Andaman Sea, living on a scuba boat with a predominately Thai crew, and spending a good part of each day in the water and under the surface. Scuba is like deep meditation, plus fish. In the water, a world within our world offered lessons in focus and reflection that supported the ideas in this book.

While the reefs I saw were vibrant, I was told that they were no longer as vibrant as they had been. The water was getting warmer evidently, year after year. The new temperature levels were impacting life under the surface. The dive leader, who had been diving the waters for decades, commented that in addition to the impact the climate has on the ocean, people wanting selfies underwater were

---

[2] Intergovernmental Panel on Climate Change, *Climate Change 2022: Impacts, Adaptation and Vulnerability. Contribution of Working Group II to the Sixth Assessment* (Cambridge University Press), 37–118, https://www.ipcc.ch/report/ar6/wg2/chapter/technical-summary/ (accessed March 2024).

disregarding the natural landscape. Coral is often kicked and broken and sea life is disrupted so that people can get that perfect photo under the surface. He was seeing a lack of focus amidst tourists, a self-centeredness and vanity. It was a priority shift that was having wide-ranging effects. I started thinking that the world might be out of balance, but people's imbalances were driving that. The impact was real.

We spoke on the boat one night as the sun was setting over the horizon. "The world is doomed," he said. He added, "The only hope is that it wipes us clean and starts again with a new kind of human."

I sat by myself on the deck under the stars after he went to bed and thought about that for a good long while. *A new kind of human.* What would a new kind of human look like, sound like, or act like? How would a new kind of leader lead? What would a new kind of communicator say? What could a new kind of teammate contribute?

I realized that I don't agree that the only hope for the future is that humans are wiped clean. For if that is the case, then why write books in the first place, or become better leaders or communicators, or wake up in the morning, or eat vegan coconut ice cream, or love our kids and partners, or do most anything?

The work to transform our world starts with humans. It doesn't end with them. We need a ramping up of what it means to be human, not a diminishment of it.

It struck me that this is the world as it is. We have built it up, we have fouled it up, and we have done so not just in terms of nature or kicking coral. Our way of treating one another is out of line. Our systems are off balance and off course. Our selfishness and greed are utterly ridiculous. The wreckage of humanity, both psychological and physical, has been strewn across the land, and an hour of desperation is at hand. We have reached a point of reckoning. Our inching toward accepting meanness and cruelty without judgment and our propensity for, and acceptance of, violence has begun to spin out of control and has led us off the proverbial rails. Our lack of focus and our acceptance of it as normal has started to shift us in ways that are off course from where we could be if we worked to shift back to center. We need to get back on track in many ways.

Our ability to be managers of people, effective teammates, inspirers to others, and supporters to them has taken a serious hit. We have so much to learn about focus, leadership, communication, teamwork, ambition, compassion, and our own potential. We have given in to our base desires without consideration for the impact that they have on others.

My friend's words were a deep condemnation, rooted in despair to a certain degree. But the ocean gives all sorts of lessons. One of them is about space and how one might experience it. Amidst vastness, what is one's place in it? What can you affect and change when the world is so immense?

If it's you against the world ...

As I sat on the deck of the boat, looking out over the Andaman Sea, with 360 degrees of horizon around me, and immensity on a seemingly incalculable scale, I realized that we can either believe we are doomed and hopeless because we decide that the issues we are facing at work or in life are too overwhelming ... or we can get active and creative about how we treat both our world and others in it. We can try new things, do some deeper self-work, and hear some new perspectives. We can move beyond however we've gone astray and commit to being better. We can regain our focus. We can reclaim this moment.

We can decide to build a better now, and from there build the future that we want and need.

With that in mind, in these pages we will be committing to the idea that change for ourselves and the systems we have developed is indeed possible. Opportunities abound for our experiences to get better.

Thomas Hardy, in a celebrated poem called *"In Tenebris II,"* described a path toward a future that requires asking hard questions. He said that "if a way to the Better there be, it exacts a full look at the Worst."[3] Translation: if we want to build a better future, we have to build a better now, and we need to take a hard look at what's wrong first and foremost.

Solutions, or a determined shift in direction, start with looking deeply at situations, standards, and systems that need to change. That look at the worst while hoping for better can lead us to what we want to improve. It starts with not being satisfied with what is, and from there, wanting something more.

---

[3] Thomas Hardy, *The Complete Works of Thomas Hardy* (Prometheus Classics, 2019).

When people ask me what I speak about, I often say I offer strategies for increased focus and peak performance. But it's more than that. I speak about creative strategies for world changers who want to make solid advancements and operate at a peak level.

This is a book for those who want to build better systems, better businesses, better mindsets, and better selves. It is for those who want to take care of themselves and their team, and ultimately, to not give up, and instead to embrace hope and explore the possibility of change.

This book is ultimately for those willing to do the work to be *that new kind of human.*

Setting the Stage:
Lying to Yourself Is Dangerous

"You can't fight what gives you life. That's treason."[1]

– Naked Raygun, "Treason"

WRITING THIS BOOK almost killed me.

That's not a statement about my work ethic, which wavers between laser-focused and distracted by everything. It's a literal statement about me, in the early process of figuring out how to write this book, almost becoming actually dead. Good times.

I seem to have a habit of getting hit by cars. I wouldn't recommend it. There are countless other hobbies you might like better, from coin collecting to baking. But for a while I was seemingly really good at being in the exactly wrong place at the exactly wrong time.

To be clear, not getting hit by a car is actually very easy. I could draw you a diagram, but instead I will just describe it simply: When a car is coming at you, gently step approximately 3 feet to your left or your right of the car. Your choice. You can't go wrong either way.

---

[1] Naked Raygun, "Treason," written by John Haggerty and Pierre Kedzy, Track 1 on *Understand?* (Caroline Records, 1989), 12" vinyl.

The idea is to let the car pass without directly impacting your body and causing you to be seriously wounded or dead. It is simple in theory. At least it is for most people.

It was my fault really, looking back. Strange things happen when we aren't honest with ourselves. Have you ever gotten off track because of a lack of focus, and then only later realized just how far you'd strayed? This is happening more and more, everywhere I look. I can definitely relate, because a few years ago I was so off track that I decided I wanted to compromise my ideals and totally sell out.

That's not something I do. In retrospect, how I came to that decision makes sense in a way, even if it was a terrible idea and completely went against everything I believed in. The world has a way of piling on influences and ideas until we can barely navigate which come from within, and which have been thrust upon us from elsewhere. The cumulative effect of this mayhem is that we end up completely discombobulated and making bad choices, disconnected from what we truly want. Choices about career, desires, partners, what we eat, and where we put our attention all get affected. And more.

It often isn't even major turning points that cause the shifts in course. All it takes is having an unstable base, and then even small influences, little tweaks to our minds, maybe the slightest allure or suggestion, and a cascade or domino effect begins, which has much larger impact later.

We are like sponges with the potential to absorb the worst of everything. For me, when I ignore my heart and listen too much to what people say instead of what I might tell myself, I end up spiraling out of control like Darth Vader (spoiler alert) as he spins away at the end of *Star Wars*. Once down that path for long enough, I find myself already deeply committed to goals that don't make any sense. It is as if that mode of being off track becomes my new reality, one that I never wanted in the first place, and it becomes so normal itself that I don't even question it.

> Losing focus impacts possibility and negatively influences your *now*...

I find at times that I become influenced by too many different angles, and too many different voices, telling me that this little decision or that one is right. Once I am past a particular fork in the road, something else convinces me that this way or that way is best. Eventually I am miles away from center, having made wrong decisions at half a dozen forks and listened to everyone other than myself. I am on the other side of the map, and I didn't even want to be on this particular road in the first place.

Focus is a challenge when everything is massively appealing, or made to look like it is.

At the time of my (almost) selling out, the world had presented itself to me in the form of other people's successes. It seemed to me that people – I wasn't exactly sure who, but it felt like everyone *except* me – were making a lot of money and I wasn't. That's easy to think all the time when everyone online looks so cool and has so many toys and vacations and all the right everything, and you still have last year's phone model. You know, the one with the camera that has one less lens than the camera on your friend's phone? How embarrassing.

At the time, algorithms had placed an idea in front of me, making it seem that there was an easy solution. The algorithms do that. They figure out what you don't want and can't really afford, and then present it to you in such overwhelming and insidious ways that you can't help but want it, or want to buy it.[2] And you will do anything to get it.

For me, the algorithm gods had decided that I should write a self-help book.

The self-help concept is rooted in the idea that we are attracted to people who seem to have more than we do or who know more than we do. When somebody who seems to be in perfect condition and has an unbeatable process for being a human being describes that experience to us, it is no wonder that we immediately are attracted to them and want to be like them. Thus, the self-help industry, thus the profit margins.

---

[2] Lee Raine and Janna Anderson, "Code-Dependent: Pros and Cons of the Algorithm Age," *Pew Research Center*, February 8, 2017, https://www.pewresearch.org/internet/2017/02/08/code-dependent-pros-and-cons-of-the-algorithm-age/.

I think that was the allure for me, both to be perceived of as having my life together and to reap the benefits of that facade. This, even though decades ago I wrote on my band's well-known record (at least in our small subset of a particular microcosm in the punk world) that "I am incomplete, damaged and imperfect. This world is not divided between saints and sinners. Forgive me for being human."[3] The point of the lyric was to invite the idea that we can all have flaws and still be very much alive, and thriving, regardless.

Self-help relies on a constant longing, wanting, never getting, overextending, and looking outside of oneself. It demands that I always feel that I am less than, that you have something I want, and – because I am not willing to literally steal it from you – that I have to follow and worship you to acquire some version of it for myself. Self-help is the ultimate profit-yielding manifestation of knowing that there are people coveting thy neighbor's stuff that we've been warned about for the last few thousand years in a globally successful work by another publisher.

I started to notice self-help books everywhere. You know how it goes. When you get something in your mind, even something seemingly inconsequential, you start to see it all over the place.

Believe in the Possibility of Kindness

Be kind with yourself and with those around you.

Say *yes* in your mind before you say no.

Know that kindness is up to you.

Around that time, I went to Southern California for a vacation. I mentioned to a friend there that I wanted to cash in and sell out. It was like I had momentarily, completely, thoroughly lost my mind. In this moment, all I could think of was money and buying airplanes and eating off of plates made of gold. I figured writing that kind of book would be the way to do it.

---

[3] Trial, "Saints and Sinners," written by Greg Bennick and Timm McIntosh, Track 11 on *Are These Our Lives* (Panic Records, 2008), 12" vinyl.

It was like someone buying a guitar expecting that the next day they will be asked to join Metallica. And that this would happen not because they have brilliant abilities for music inside them and are worthy of the role but because they dream of being onstage listening to all of the cheering. It's the question I was asked when I decided to go to acting school in my early twenties: Do I see myself in the theatre or do I see the theatre within myself? Chasing a payday is backward. It is never the way to create or to operate. History is filled with stories of individuals who had their careers thrown off track or destroyed as a result of chasing success down that errant path. Creative process and developmental process for business have to be rooted in deeper values than just profit.

I am not sure exactly what inspired me with the idea of writing that kind of book. It definitely wasn't motivated by any authenticity or connected to a sense of purpose as the book you're reading/listening to in this moment. At the time, I didn't care what my book would be about. It didn't matter that the content meant anything to me, or for that matter that it meant anything to anyone else – the goal was simply to fill my pockets deeply with unfathomable riches.

What a terrible idea. To position myself as someone with problems solved rather than more genuinely as someone who is a work in process like anyone else. But at the time, my perspectives and perceptions were skewed.

It is no surprise then that my friend looked at me quizzically when I brought up this idea. Selling out had never been my path, and he knew that. The very idea had caught him off guard, and he immediately asked me a critical question: "Have you ever actually even read a self-help book?"

I had to admit that I hadn't. He wisely suggested that I go to a local bookstore to have a look at some in order to see what they were all about. I think in retrospect he was trying to dissuade me by having me realize for myself, once I got to the store, that the entire genre often feels like chewing a giant piece of flavorless gum. Without a doubt, there are some incredible self-help books, but that's not what I was necessarily looking for. I was looking for the easiest one I could emulate.

The thing is, I misread the moment and took my friend's suggestion as encouragement, and off I went to the local Borders Books, may they rest in peace.

I walked into the bookstore and felt unusual from the start. It was like I didn't belong. It wasn't because I don't like books, but rather because I was there for suspicious reasons. I wasn't there to honor books. I was there to undermine them. Books are the repository of our knowledge and are to be respected. Amidst glowing rectangles on our wrists, desks, and in our pockets and cars, books offer very tactile, enduring, and powerful experiences. They are a force of their own.

But I was there not for the force. I was there to add to the proverbial dark side.

I had a sneaking suspicion that I was in the wrong place and on the wrong path, but I chose to ignore that faint but clear voice, which is never a good idea. After all, I was there to cash in, not think. I walked up to the cashier's desk in the front of the store and asked the woman behind the counter where the self-help section was. She pointed and offered a half smile, as if she could see right through me. Or maybe she just hated her job. Either way, I followed her directions directly across the store to where an entire wall of self-help books awaited.

I'd seen this particular wall from the outside of the store many times. You see, the highway through Mission Viejo, California, I-5 south, runs right along and above where this bookstore was situated. As one drives south on the highway, you can see the bookstore down below beneath the road to your right, at the bottom of a steep embankment. It was as if the bookstore was in a little valley, nestled seventy feet down on the valley floor and up against the road. It was strange to be inside the store now, on this side of the wall, and on this particular errand.

Keep Your Eyes on the Knife

Focus your attention on the one thing that is the most mission-critical.

Distractions will always be there, increasingly so as time goes on.

Your productivity is connected to your ability to prioritize.

I walked over to the self-help wall and sat down in front of it. I had a 180-degree view of books. I sat cross-legged and looked up at the sea of help and realized that any problem I might have faced in that moment had a solution within arm's reach. Too much to eat? Solved. No one to love? Solved. Not enough friends? Solved. It was a one-stop cure-all, we've got all the answers and you don't, social club. And I not only wanted a ticket to get in, I wanted the club to be renamed after me.

I noticed a book by Tony Robbins. Well, that was a familiar name. He'd definitely been successful in inspiring people and as a result, manifesting piles of money. I pulled the book off the shelf and started to flip through it. I wasn't even sure what I was looking for. Perhaps a wink directly from Tony in the margins that said, "Hey buddy. It's me. Do exactly what I did and we will race yachts together soon." There was nothing of the sort. I didn't even consider that maybe Tony actually had something really valuable to say, as he actually does for countless people. As I flipped through the book, I found myself thinking, "What am I doing here?" I pondered that question for a few moments as I put the book back on the shelf.

I decided to shift a few feet to my left and reposition myself along the wall. There I saw a book jumping out at me: *50 Self Help Classics.* I picked it off the shelf, and realized that it not only had Tony Robbins, but forty-nine other gurus who were ready to tell me how I had to be living my life. Maybe, I thought, this fifty-pack of experts was a better deal financially on a dollar per book or dollar per guru basis. I sat there for a moment and thought about it.

And then there was an explosion.

In an instant I was covered in a pile of books and shelves, choking on dust and totally disoriented. I couldn't see and couldn't breathe, from what I thought at first was chemical warfare, or maybe something worse. I turned to my right and saw through the dust that the entire wall had exploded.

My first thought was a terrorist attack, perhaps perpetrated by someone who hated sellouts and who therefore had specifically targeted me. My second thought was that I knew Tony Robbins was powerful but that this was ridiculous.

To say that there was an explosion isn't even loud enough. I had no idea what had happened. After a few moments of coughing from the dust (third thought: "Asbestos, I'm dying early now. Thanks, Borders Books."), I rolled over and got up and looked back at the self-help wall.

Just a few feet away, almost exactly where I had been sitting when I took the first Tony book into my hands, I saw something that didn't quite make sense.

Rather than seeing a wall of books each telling me how my life would be so much better for $29.95, there was the front end of a pickup truck where the bookshelves had been. It was thrust through the wall and was halfway into the bookstore. Yes, you read that correctly.

> **Bookstores can be hazardous to your health.**

We pieced together later, that evidently the truck's driver had lost control on the highway and had careened over that embankment at seventy miles per hour and flown down the hill, crashing through the wall of the bookstore exactly where I had been sitting. Had I still been looking at that first book by Tony Robbins and thinking through all the ways that I could make my billions inauthentically with him as my guru and guide, I would have caught that truck right in the face.

I stood up, and as I did, I heard the driver say, "I'm alright. I'm alright."

His reassurance aside, he had actually not been my first concern. Fortunately, no one else in the bookstore was injured, either. The driver was later found to not be intoxicated, and thankfully, also was not terribly wounded. He had a broken nose and a broken leg, but otherwise was fine. As I stood there in that first moment, listening to him call out from inside the truck and let shoppers know that he was fine, I reflected on the moment, ears still ringing, confusion reigning supreme, with Tony Robbins and his forty-nine friends clutched in my hand.

The entire situation was bizarre but what I did next fully enhanced the weirdness. Logic would dictate that I should have dropped the book and gotten out of the store immediately.

Instead, without thinking, I took the book and walked across the room to the cashier I'd spoken to when I'd first walked in. I looked at her blankly. She looked at me blankly. She was completely in shock and staring over my shoulder at the truck that was sticking through the wall of her store. I said to her calmly, "Hello." She replied, emotionless,

"Hello." I said, "I'd like to buy this book, please." And she replied, "OK." I might have been a bit in shock. The cashier rang me up like an automaton.

> ### Cultivate a Revolutionary Mindset
>
> **See defeat as simply the next step of your process.**
>
> **Imagine possibilities at every turn even if they require breaking the rules.**
>
> **A revolutionary thinker considers options that are new, unusual, and challenging.**

I walked out into the parking lot with my new purchase. Once outside, I called my dear friend, former professor, and life mentor John Wilson. John is the greatest genius you've never heard of. John is the one I turn to when I need to make sense of the world or something unexplainable going on in it.

Case in point, a year prior in Laguna Beach, California, while trying to catch up to someone I was *way* overextending emotionally to reach, I'd been almost run over when a car screeched to a halt. I'd rolled up onto and over the hood while passersby screamed, and fell into the street. Thankfully, I was largely uninjured except for a sore back, a weird hip, a partially damaged ego, and some pain in my heart. At the time of that accident, I had called John too once I was released from the hospital. John had a bit of sympathy, but he'd also rightly criticized me for going against my better judgment and against myself and literally running after someone across a busy street filled with cars. Smart, that John.

As I stood there covered in bookstore dust, he listened closely to every detail of my story. He didn't say a word. Once I was finished, I heard him take a slow deep breath. I knew I was about to get my head handed to me.

"Let me get this straight," he said. "Last year you were lying to yourself about your relationship with someone and a car ran into you. And tonight, you were about to lie to the world about who you are, and while you were inside a bookstore, a truck almost ran you over?"

I reflected for a moment and said, "Yeah. That's about right."

John said, "Greg, you'd better renegotiate your deal with the universe."

I knew exactly what he meant.

Leap Into the Dark

Get started today on the thing that seems impossible.

We might not yet see the end, but we'll never get there without a first step.

Dive fully into the Creative Sine Wave.

He was talking about being myself and approaching the universe with integrity. This, instead of trying to be something I'm not. He was talking about getting my head together and working to reverse my course before I got too far off balance. He was warning me about being on a trajectory I didn't want to be on, and desiring things I didn't really want, in order to acquire a sense of satisfaction that wasn't going to materialize.

You can sink your teeth into whatever vision you want, but if it is insincere, the universe always bites back.

I told John that from this moment forward I would renegotiate the deal. I told him I would rework how I approach the precious few moments in my life I have. I would get serious about focus. I would redefine the potential I enjoy to live fully before I disappear from this mortal coil into the ether.

Well, that's what I thought at least. What I actually said was, "You're right."

John agreed with this, reminding me that the less I am honest with myself and the less I value the time I have in the world and how I approach the moments in my life, the more the universe would send me warnings to stop doing exactly that. And given that these warnings were in the form of cars, he politely suggested that it was in my best interest to start listening.

We hung up. I brushed as much dust as I could from myself. I looked down at the book in my hands, a book that remains unopened to this day, but which I still own. I have it framed on the wall. It is a symbol first and foremost, after all.

It's a symbol of me being completely disconnected and off center. Of being inauthentic. It's a symbol of being dishonest with myself and a reminder about where that can lead. It's a symbol of how important it is for me, for us, to stay true to what we want, to our vision, and how in a moment, we could lose it all.

I realized that when we are off track, and spiraling out of control, we need to center ourselves and reclaim the moment before we become too far lost and lose sight of our goals, or worse. We can transform and elevate but only when we make these moves with integrity.

> **Imagine living as if every moment matters, because it does...**

We want something more. We can feel disillusioned, overwhelmed, off center at times, and confused. We are often unable to navigate the maelstrom that the world and society have placed before us and thrown us into. Of course, "the world" and "society" is *us*. We have contributed to and participated in the chaos we are trying now so hard to navigate. That's part of *a double bind*. It is when two opposites exist at the same time, and in this case was the path of doing one thing while contributing to the opposite of it. That's what happens when we are off center, like my mission to the bookstore, and we ignore the voice in our minds which says, "Stop. Go back. Turn a different way."

To want something more and to go after it requires reclaiming the moment from the double bind. If we want to build a better now, for ourselves or for anyone else, it starts with techniques and strategies that can bring us back to center when we have been thrown, or more accurately, when we have thrown ourselves, off course. Being able to envision what we want is one thing, but being able to take steps toward it requires being grounded first. These strategies can help.

I shook the dust off and I started living the rest of my life. I thought about how I could remind myself about what I really wanted even when allure was everywhere. I started thinking about how I could bring myself back to center when I'd spiraled away from where I knew I wanted and needed to be.

When our foundation is centered, we can make solid choices and create the reality we want from there. For me, it often starts with patience with myself, and then coming up with words to reframe my position. Our words create the world, bringing into reality abstract ideas that otherwise would jumble around in our heads without form or direction. So, for example, why wouldn't we aim toward clarity as a baseline and once we have that established, move forward from there. The strategies in this book can help us take that first solid step.

Imagine an archer aiming for a target. Now imagine that same archer aiming for a target while their friend is tickling them, and someone else is throwing paper balls at their head. Life sometimes feels like that with too much happening at once. These strategies help keep that arrow pointed at the target amidst the distractions and give our intentions the best possible shot at a bullseye. Our ideas and inspirations matter, and yet they are likely to miss the target entirely when we ourselves aren't grounded in this moment.

Now, instead of pursuing self-help gurus, when I am feeling discombobulated, I use the strategies in this book to get back on track.

Engage with Laughter

Laughter is a tool you can use to uplift yourself and those around you.

Think of laughter as fuel for productivity.

A shared laugh will drive your team forward.

From that moment forward, I took John's advice. I renegotiated my relationship to being more sincere with myself, and to rediscovering focus and intention in order to refine my direction and my now. We all could benefit from doing that.

Since then, I have paid very close attention to the people in my life from whom I draw inspiration in terms of what they do, and more importantly how they do it. The thought leaders, creatives, and businesspeople. There is an entire network of them. More often than not, their success comes by way of their integrity and devotion to ideas.

They are clear about what they are doing. They aren't wandering into bookstores trying to be something they are not. They spend their time doing things that are aligned with who they actually are.

I'd like to share two examples of that integrity: one from a business that has seen exponential growth, and one from an extremely successful journalist/writer.

Overcast Merch Inc. (https://overcastmerch.com/) started small. My friend Wolfe Bailey started the company as a T-shirt screen printing company, operating in the basement of his rented home in Seattle, Washington. Shortly afterward, my other friend Andrew Doyle relocated to Seattle and they became a two-man operation. They had synergy and were a perfect combination.

Their mindset about business was determined by a pact they made with themselves to serve their clients first and foremost with integrity. The approach was simple and direct: Provide excellent quality, at good prices, with good customer service. This bucked the traditional concept that when choosing between quality and price and service, one can choose only two of the three. Bailey and Doyle worked on all three fronts, choosing to work with people they liked, and doing so honestly and fairly.

They faced issues as the popularity of the company grew. How could they provide for the number of clients who were attracted to that triumvirate of quality, price, and service? Would they sell themselves out or stay true to their ideals?

They had to take some massive risks and expand. They moved to Southern California, and began a process of expansion, utilizing new decoration methods, and expanding their services, offerings, and hiring to make up for the demands on their time. But they stayed true to their values.

After a decade, Overcast has grown to a massive operation, employing 100+ full-time employees with offices stretched across the United States, Canada, throughout Mexico and the United Kingdom. They serve major touring bands with a global footprint. Overcast has set up production and eCommerce solutions across the world. National and regional companies as well as countless small businesses print merchandise and hard goods of all kinds with Overcast.

When I asked Bailey how he grew and about his approaches to business and integrity, he said:

"I've learned a lot over the years, far more than I could have ever imagined. The journey started from the idea of printing some tees in my basement for both my friends' bands and at the time mine. This seemed like a "good enough" deciding factor for starting a print shop. All of it has far surpassed any idea, goal, thought or desire I could have possibly dreamed of. In the beginning I didn't have a clear idea of what Overcast was to be. I knew I wanted to continue to work in music, and I had always enjoyed a challenge. I "knew" a multitude of reasons that I wanted to do the shop in some sort of capacity but it took time to find our groove, and to really be able to dissect what the DNA of what Overcast was, who we are and what defined us as a company. During those years and as time went on you are quick to learn that you can do worlds more together. We partnered with another shop, owned by Sam Liskey, and we aim to learn the uniqueness of each client we serve and cater to individually through the lens of a partnership – not just as a company that printed some shirts and says let me know when you need more."

Their company grew immensely because they stayed true to their ideas and their ideals. They didn't try to sell themselves out. If you keep your integrity intact, even as you grow in business, people will be attracted to you like a magnet. That's way better than cars being attracted to you like a magnet. Overcast Design and Print is proof of that pathway to success.

Let's switch gears to a different successful friend.

I first met national security reporter and journalist Spencer Ackerman when he was just a teenager. I was only a handful of years older, on tour with my band Trial, and Spencer would come to our shows in the New Jersey area. While the band members from the touring bands would stand around after the shows talking about politics, Spencer would approach and interject his ideas into the conversations. At first, we wondered who the upstart young kid was. Then quickly we realized that everything this upstart said was always more astute, insightful, and wise than anything we had to offer. By far.

Anyone who met Spencer knew that his life would be driven by ideas. We couldn't have foreseen what was to come. He surpassed us all. Within a couple years Spencer had graduated college and was working for *The New Republic*. Within another handful of years, he had amassed impressive credits including writing for *The Nation*, *Wired*, and *The Guardian*. In 2014, he won a Pulitzer Prize for his work.

Spencer is the real deal. His book *Reign of Terror* was named a best nonfiction book of 2021 by both *The New York Times* and the *Washington Post*. I asked Spencer about the challenges of staying true to his vision. He said, "Remember that journalism is about other people's stories, not your own. Someone trusted you enough to tell their story. That's a responsibility you choose to either honor or betray – and it's your actions, not your intentions, that determine that choice."

There's a focus there which we can all learn from. For Spencer, his work isn't about his own advancement; it is about service to the subject of his story. He extends his energy outward and the world is drawn toward it. His clarity and alignment with his values is tremendous.

If we want something more, we can have it when we focus. We want more both in our work and in our lives. The idea of wanting more is not about dissatisfaction but a desire for improvement and refining. It has become a personal slogan for me, a mantra in a way, about wanting things to be better. To want more is a sign of devotion, inspiration, and excitement about experiencing our potential.

One of the first steps I took, as a speaker and sharer of words, after my bookstore experience, was deciding to be honest with myself about what I wanted to say, and what I wanted to share, both onstage with my keynote presentations and offstage. I took a very long time to figure out what mattered to share. That was true for these pages as well. This is why, over the last bunch of years, as I have done countless presentations, when people would ask me if I have a book available, I'd say "no" again and again. In part because I've been refining my ideas. But also, because I am convinced that if I write a book before I am authentically ready, a car will make me die.

We'd be better off taking a step back to reassess, than steps forward knowing the path isn't right.

Build a Better Now® is about shifting perspectives to gain clarity in the moment. It's about wanting something more and shifting our perspectives to get it. When I feel off center, I revert to one of the strategies in this book and live it. This helps bring me back to center. It gives me a feeling of being grounded and able to achieve that something more, instead of wanting, longing, or hoping for that which others have. These are moments that otherwise would have been lost, and me along with them. Instead, they are potential that I regain. That improves my now, and lets me shift into what our real work is: creating space for possibility in order to build, develop, and grow.

The bookstore near-death experience offered a clear example that when you step forward toward a bizarre future from a *now* that is off center, every step you take will be potentially fraught with peril. The thing is, we've all had bookstore moments. The moment in your past where something wasn't quite right, and you knew it, but you did it anyway. There is information there, and learning to be had from it, but I'd prefer being ready to make a different choice in the first place.

Along the way in these pages, we will read about believing in the possibility of kindness, sharpening our focus, developing relationships, taking creative risks, laughing, cultivating a revolutionary mindset, and then letting our inspiration reverberate. These are ways to maximize this moment so that we can build from it the experiences, the life, the team, the community we want. Remember, this isn't a self-help book, as those things can evidently get you killed. Instead, these are helpful tools to change our mindset and gain clarity in an increasingly complex and existentially unsure world. I realized that I want to fill the moments in my life with as much clarity and genuine meaning as possible.

Develop Relationships that Matter

We are defined by way of our relationships with others.

Disconnection is not inevitable.

Relationship is a force multiplier.

Realizing this only took almost getting hit by two cars, a global pandemic, chaos worldwide, deep personal work, and a wonderful amount of therapy. Highly recommended ... ten out of ten ... would weep again.

Since the bookstore, the results have been *really* good. I have been speaking to associations, corporations, conferences, special events, and conventions all over the planet. I wrote this book as a call to action for world changers and to build a team of like-minded people.

To prove the efficacy of these ideas, and to demonstrate how they truly do offer a solid path: I can offer that I have been sitting here in my loft writing for the better part of ten hours and so far, not even one car has even come close to crashing into the side of my head.

Something is obviously working.

This is a book of perspective shifts, some small, some massive. Consider this a roadmap for those who envision themselves as having something significant to offer, maybe something important to say, and yet who feel stuck or off center. When we listen to the clutter of the world rather than the clarity within us, we set ourselves up for frustration. These strategies help me get back on track and regain clarity, because I too want something more than just chaos or clutter.

Start a Reverberation Effect

You can be the catalyst for the change you want to see in the world.

We might not see immediate results from our efforts but we have to believe in them regardless.

We can initiate or be a part of a reverberation with lasting impact.

For me, to build a better now is not about perfection, it is about advancing out of feeling stuck or overwhelmed so that I can get back to feeling alive and being effective once again. Perfection is overrated. Voltaire supposedly said that *perfect is the enemy of the good*. I think perfect is the first ingredient you reach hungrily for if you're cooking up a mental breakdown. It's unattainable. Let's strive for truly, incredibly, amazing. We just got a high five from Voltaire from beyond the grave.

Hopefully, the new perspectives here will help guide you through this bizarre world we've all managed to create together so that you can make deeper connections with others, expand your own creative self, shift your mindset when you need it most, and take the leap to be engaged with life rather than be an outside observer. From there, as a result, we can move forward with ideas, products, systems, and connections to impact the lives of those with whom we work and live.

This is a guide that doesn't involve the wall of a bookstore, and instead is one which hopefully leads you away from being in that bookstore, for the wrong reasons, and with a voice that's not your own, in the first place.

1

There's a Madness to My Method

"I believe in process. I believe that having a really difficult process is more valuable than a good outcome."[1]

– Tina Fey

THERE IS AN important gap I help fill when I work with organizations and individuals around the world. When clients contact me for help with problems, it is often because they want to more effectively reduce the space between what they *have* and what they *want*.

I craft keynote presentations, workshops, and trainings under the Build a Better Now® concept, to enhance individual performance and drive organizational success so that people can bridge that gap. That sounds fancy. What I do in simpler terms is to offer new perspectives so groups and individuals can embrace the challenges they face. I like to help inspire solutions centered around performance.

Problems I've helped clients address include:

Finding and sharpening our focus to gain clarity amidst an ever-changing world

Discovering new approaches to leadership and how to step into a listening role

---

[1] "Tina Fey on Top," Interview with Amy Poehler, *Marie Claire*, April 10, 2008.

Cultivating teamwork and methods to interact in ways that elevate and inspire

Strengthening communication and how to reach one another more effectively

Managing change (This is a big one recently, to no surprise.)

Navigating generational divides and how to work through shifting demographics

Juggling priorities and balancing these with work demands

Learning to use our voice for the greatest possible impact

Managing conflicts and developing better interactions with one another

Perspective shifts around these ideas help offer clarity, and this book is full of them. An outside perspective can help us see challenging situations in a new way.

In listening to people to get closer to the core of their problems, I've realized that many organizations and individuals are held back by issues around focus, validation, and people feeling meaningful. Groups struggle because without a collective sense of meaning and direction amongst a team of empowered individuals, teams find themselves scattered. When we feel thrown off track, the net result is that people feel silenced, small, and even meaningless. At the very least, they feel unable to lead, communicate, and manage at their best.

The strategy I end up speaking to and exploring most often is *focus*. We will read about this more when we talk about keeping our eyes on the knife in Chapter 5. The other strategies, about believing in the possibility of kindness, cultivating a revolutionary mindset, leaping into the dark, engaging with laughter, building relationships and starting a reverberation effect, all are important to explore. Focus, however – especially these days – is key for most individuals and organizations, given a world in which we find ourselves pulled in countless directions all the time. We want to be navigating, but instead it feels as though we are sinking. It often seems like we are barely staying afloat.

With that in mind, I see the gap I mentioned a few moments ago, between what we have and what we want, as one that is increasingly challenging to bridge.

Our nature is in constant opposition to the seeming realities of our nurture: A desire for safety and security has been corrupted and shifted into instilling in us a quest to find meaning through accomplishing, owning, acquiring, posturing, and dominating. We are solidly amidst the Anthropocene, and simultaneously feeling the weight of the commodification of culture. This leaves us feeling lost, and with a thirst for calm and security left dry by the deepening of an endless call for validation. This is a call that will never be answered through the channels we expect. It is a thirst that often causes us to disregard others in our frenzy to be satisfied. We've created quite a complex mess for ourselves, and as we will see later, it really is our doing.

I want to explore some ways to make a difference for ourselves around some of the issues I've described. Think of this chapter like side-stepping a car. The thirst might be real, but you can quench it through other means than what is expected of you. A few feet to the right or left and you're in really much better shape. For example, listening and connection will help you sidestep. Feeling that you matter will help you sidestep. Depending on how you spend your days, being grounded in the midst of emerging technologies, and staying ahead of the psychological curve that accompanies them will also help you sidestep. Sharpening your focus definitely will as well.

We need new leadership models now more than ever if we want to make collective advancements and to help others through challenges. Solid leadership is about effectively and efficiently filling the space between what we have, and what we want. But it goes further than that. People exist in a space between what they imagine and what they achieve. A leader inspires people to fill the space between what they are currently doing and what they *could* do. The best leaders inspire without leading people to succeed at the expense of others.

As a leader, a primary goal is to get the people with you from point A, across the gap of the unknown, to point B. The space in between, the undefined space without a roadmap, is where individuals, teams, and organizations can easily be pulled off track.

We need people to serve as better listeners because listening helps bridge that gap. The pandemic and its aftermath shook us to our psychological core globally and intensified already existing insecurities.[2] The aftermath will obviously echo for a generation in ways we have yet to understand. This does not help create a foundation of psychological and operational stability. At the same time, we seem to be walking an increasingly intensified, global, geopolitical tightrope of concern and tension.[3] The news is not great, and that's putting it lightly. The clouds of a perfect storm are brewing in which people feel upset, lost, frustrated, or simply off center.

We have more in common than we realize...

However, a saving grace of living in chaotic times is that there is a universality to the intensity we feel, and this offers an unexpected a glimmer of hope – and in turn, a bridge between us, from what we collectively have to what we want. Global upheaval draws us together in unusual ways even as we feel pulled apart. We have shared experiences from which to draw and to which we can listen. This offers us the potential to quench that proverbial thirst together, and to leap across the gap.

In the United States, part of the unification people feel is along the lines of wanting more than what we have and envisioning change as a possibility. People both want something more and also want to be part of manifesting it. For example, Pew Research cites that 84 percent of people see problems in the American political system, but along the

---

[2] M. Bonati, R. Campi, and G. Segre, "Psychological Impact of the Quarantine During the COVID-19 Pandemic on the General European Adult Population: A Systematic Review of the Evidence," *Epidemiology and Psychiatric Sciences* 31 (April 27, 2022): e27. https://www.ncbi.nlm.nih.gov/pmc/articles/PMC9069583/.

[3] "Top Geopolitical Risks of 2024," S&P Global, https://www.spglobal.com/en/enterprise/geopolitical-risk/#geopolitical-risk-faqs (accessed March 18, 2024).

lines of the tone and theme of this book, 63 percent said that they want to contribute and "care about making the political system work well."[4] That bodes well for those of us who want to see our world transformed, especially those who are willing to put in the time to forge alliances to make that happen.

Transformation – bridging the gap between what we can imagine and what we can actualize – is available to us beyond just the political. We can have it in terms of business, bettering our lives in general, and socially as well if we renew our focus and reclaim moments for ourselves rather than continually feeling swept away by tides beyond our control. Remember that idea about a little thing here, or a suggestion there, throwing us eventually entirely off course? That reclamation of moments is the foundation from which we can build a better now.

This feeling is cross-cultural and global, too. The *European Values Study* cites "a decline of civic life, a weakening of social bonds, and a loss of social cohesion"[5] but also notes the importance of *solidarity* as a core European value. People are imagining working together more effectively and manifesting effective, compassionate, and visionary leadership and inspiration for themselves on their own terms. They dream of and long for this amidst chaotic times. It is inspiring, especially during times when inspiration has been fleeting.

For anxious creatures in general, and I am talking about all of us, to have a world that feels out of control at worst or in upheaval at best is inherently discombobulating. Our stress points are manifesting and becoming entrenched in our day-to-day lives. Work, for example, feels like an obsession, and for many people it doesn't seem to be a completely fulfilling one.

---

[4] "Americans' Dismal Views of the Nation's Politics," Pew Research Center, September 19, 2023, https://www.pewresearch.org/politics/2023/09/19/the-biggest-problems-and-greatest-strengths-of-the-u-s-political-system/ (accessed April 21, 2024).
[5] European Values Study, EVS (2022). European Values Study 2017: Integrated Dataset (EVS2017). GESIS Data Archive, Cologne. ZA7500 Data file Version 5.0.0, doi:10.4232/1.13897. europeanvaluesstudy.eu.

The American Psychological Association reported that 65 percent of US workers identified that work was a "very" or "somewhat" significant source for stress in their lives.[6] That alone should make us all aware of changes that need to be made societally. It doesn't mean to quit your job, but instead the opposite in a way. This is the gap between the life we are living and what it could be. If we are going to spend our days at work, then our primary focus should be to make those days better. Much better.

If we are disconnected from how we spend our time, and in fact if how we spend our days makes us feel worse about being alive overall, then we have a clear marker for at least one place where we can put our energy for personal and social development. It strikes me that the value system upon which we have based our collective agreement about the world is inherently skewed if the very thing we spend most of our days doing is a stress point rather than one being nurturing or uplifting. We can do better than that. We have to.

We don't need facts or figures to know that social tension is high, and to feel the effects on us as individuals and as an interactive network. The question is what we are willing to do about it. I have learned, especially in the last few years but rooted in decades of exploring it, that building a better now starts with listening to ourselves and then connecting with others. To do so is a solid starting point for delving into effective personal and social development. We need this, both psychologically and socially, and especially during desperate times.

The pandemic isolated us, and at the same time gave us a unifying experience.[7] This is uncommon in history on the level at which we experienced it. Major events can draw the planet together and give us all a common referrable experience, but I can't think of another time in this generation when I could strike up a conversation with

---

[6] "Stress in America: Stress and Decision-Making During the Pandemic," *American Psychological Association* (October 2021), https://www.apa.org/news/press/releases/stress/2021/october-decision-making (accessed March 18 2024).
[7] Chinmayee Mishra and Rath Navaneeta, "Social Solidarity During a Pandemic: Through and Beyond Durkheimian Lens," *Social Sciences & Humanities Open* 2, no. 1 (2020): doi.org/10.1016/j.ssaho.2020.100079.

anyone on the planet about a shared experience and have a common reference point that was similar worldwide. In the United States, the tragic events of 9/11 came close, but realistically only remained a shared common experience for about a week before the entire experience became politically vindictive and polarizing rather than heartbreakingly personal.

The pandemic has been different. We were all in a similar boat during that first year. You could, then or now, go up to anyone and ask them, "What did you do during lockdown?" or "What was the pandemic like for you?" and we would all have a basis of familiarity from which to connect, regardless of the approach we took to it. There is immense potential here for connection globally, just in the concept that there are common bonds between us, and ones we often ignore, forgo, or deny.

Given even this single common bond, doesn't it seem like we should be working more actively to connect and understand one another rather than tearing each other apart? The polarizing nature of the world as it is makes that extremely challenging. We should be in active developmental process so that we are prepared to connect more readily on common points we share. I'd like us to be able to recognize those common points amongst the people with whom we work, live, and exist. This is entirely available to us if we are open to the possibility.

The question becomes whether we will succumb to the chaos and intensity or rise above it. To our community, to our businesses, for our customers, our friends, and for our world, we owe the fullness of our creativity, action, and connection. Our focus and direction need to be rooted in a deeper connectedness, and not just pinpointed on selfish aims. Reclaiming the moment from the chaos of the world allows us to rediscover our focus.

A real-life example...

The very best people I know in creativity and business listen and connect first and foremost. They have different metrics for success. Focus, listening, and connection become their brand. This is true in every industry from coin dealers to health care equipment manufacturers. You don't even need a product to market. All you need is to be in a space where you are centered and in which you have embraced a focus that is meaningful to you and be willing to share it with devotion.

I get inspired by people who have talked the talk, and who walk the walk. My friend Toni Okamoto Shapiro has created a mini-empire and has done that through focus. She started simply, blogging about inexpensive vegan recipes in 2012. The concept was deeply meaningful to her: Offer easy-to-make, simple-to-follow recipes that could be made at low cost and with high nutritive content as well as compassion. The market at the time was already flooded not only with vegan content but with cooking blogs and diet fads. I have been vegan since the only options to eat were brown rice, black beans, tofu, other kinds of beans, and soy milk, which tasted like, well, beans. Veganism has come light years since then, and it was groundbreakers like Toni who helped make that happen.

At the time, everyone had an angle, and they weren't afraid to share it. Veganism had been taking off for a while, and with the addition of social media, it was easy for anyone to be a presence. That said, Toni didn't just share things to eat. She remained on very specific brand. She stayed true to the core concept with which she most connected: to create inexpensive meals, with simple ingredients and recipes, that were accessible to the greatest number of people. People validated that vision and focus. They connected to it. This dedication drove her work through a sea of bland competition.

Today, Toni's marketing centers around her first book's title, *Plant Based on a Budget*, and she has amassed a devoted global community of over 630,000 Instagram followers, as well as having written three other cookbooks. Toni's work is an indicator that a clear vision, even if it is initially simple in scope, will resonate. Stay on brand. Listen to and connect with your constituency. People will be attracted to an idea they want, need, and understand, and in Toni's case, one that tastes delicious as well. She didn't need to market more effectively. She certainly didn't need to be something she wasn't. She simply presented herself more sincerely than the competition and won on the basis of speaking a culinary language that everyone could understand and appreciate.

She bridged the gap for people – recognizing the need and fulfilling it along a path in which she believed. Simplicity, ease, cost. That messaging cut through. Toni is a world changer. She measures success by how well her focus impacts her reach, and by the quality of the communication and interactions she has with her constituency.

Ideas to inspire…

You can make a difference, and you can make a change. You can make the difference between what someone, a group, or an entire constituency has and what they want. It takes reclaiming this moment from the chaos first. Once that's done, and once we have our focus and perspectives clear, we can expand from there. The gap between what we have and what we want to create sometimes feels like an endless chasm. But when we reclaim the moment for ourselves and focus, the better now we build is one in which we can cross that divide.

People need support, focus, and to be heard and validated more than ever. The world feels unsure, as the effects of global disruption of the normalcy we collectively agreed on before the pandemic continue to be felt.[8] The new normal feels very abnormal. People crave a sense of meaning, belonging and fitting in, and they want help bridging those gaps. You can be that person for them. Reaching across the divide between what is and what could be requires that we stay in process as we are in a continual state of improving and expanding our skills.

- Build = Create actively and with focus
- A = Not many, but only one
- Better = "Not perfect" is good enough for now
- Now = This very moment so you can launch from here

---

[8] MÉ Czeisler et al., "Mental Health, Substance Use, and Suicidal Ideation During the COVID-19 Pandemic - United States, June 24–30, 2020. *MMWR Morbidity and Mortality Weekly Report* 69, no. 32 (August 14, 2020):1049–1057. doi: 10.15585/mmwr.mm6932a1.

This is a journey. I am writing from the perspective of someone who makes his living from the development and the sharing of ideas in creative ways. This means that I know the difference between being in process and feeling unsure about where you're going, and being completely and wildly off track and inauthentic with yourself. One path eventually might just lead to success; the other likely leads to a truck smashing you in your face.

The first path is about realizing that development isn't always linear. But if you stay focused on your process and remain committed to perspective shifts and discovery of new ideas, you will arrive eventually or at least be much further along the journey. We will get into that in the chapter titled "Leap into the Dark."

The latter path, however, is another story. When we are unfocused and disconnected from who we are and what we want, all bets are off. We have a much harder time as a leader or teammate if we are off center. Helping people feel meaningful is a challenge when we can't find our center. We want to be able to help people bridge the gap, not fall into it ourselves.

Centering takes devotion to yourself amidst the chaos. The benefits and long-term result are worth the effort and will lead us to the more that we want. The strategies in this book will support you as you reclaim the moment, find your focus, hold your ground, and then expand into the world so that we can be bridges for other people and for the organizations we serve.

Some background to get us connected and on the same page...

Since we don't yet know one another, and since I'm certainly not a household name, I want to give you some background about my experience base and offer ideas around what we might learn from it. This way, you will have a sense of what I value and where my perspectives are coming from. My background is unusual and varied, maybe even weird at times. The lessons I've learned are ones from which you might find some benefit too.

I do want to offer a distinction first that there is a difference between who someone *is* and what they've *done*. I am not the things

I've done. From each example below, what is most important here is what it can offer to you in terms of ideas about ways to create bridges for others between what they have and what they want. Each of the following examples taught me lessons in how to build a better now.

The act of creation is powerful, and when you make something real that didn't exist before, you feel like a combination of a magician and a successful alchemist. We will talk about creative exploration in depth in Chapter 7. To create something from nothing and to try and gain a deeper understanding of people and their root motivations, I have been producing and writing films, specifically documentaries, since 2003. This includes the multi-award-winning exploration into human motivation, *Flight from Death: The Quest for Immortality*. The film looks at our inner fears, specifically around mortality, and how this manifests in terms of our treatment of one another. We created the film to get closer to the root of why people tend to behave violently toward one another even when psychologically it makes no sense to do so.

Director Patrick Shen and I took the film worldwide and won *Best Documentary* awards everywhere we went at film festivals. Gerry Krochak, who at the time was writing for *The Leader-Post* in Calgary, Alberta, Canada, said about the film's impact, *"If you see it alone, you'll be thinking about it for days. If you see it with a friend, you'll be talking about it for weeks."* This was exactly the response I wanted. The hope was to create a vehicle for ideas that matter in order to drive conversations globally about where we put our focus culturally, politically, and personally, and how those choices impact those around us. I personally brought the film to dozens of countries and had powerful conversations with people from all over the planet about the universality of human experience, why we mistreat one another, and how we can best coexist. We need these types of conversations more than ever. This was an ongoing lesson in teamwork on an immense scale.

Get out into the world and listen to others…

Reaching out beyond your immediate day-to-day surroundings expands your horizons and lets you see the world in a new way. To offer help where it is most needed and also to learn the true value of listening to others, in 2010, I responded to a request for help and started a nonprofit in Haiti (onehundredforhaiti.org) that works for Haitians to provide clean water for an entire region, sends forty kids to school from kindergarten through twelfth grade, helps farmers plant crops to feed hundreds of people, feeds the poorest 120 families in the region where we work year-round, provides internet for schools that otherwise wouldn't have it, and builds houses and roofs for families so that one of life's basic necessities (shelter) will be met. All of this is done on Haitian terms, meaning that I work for them. They don't work for me.

This relationship dynamic helps to continually remind me to have others maintain management and significant positioning rather than keeping those roles for myself. Leadership lessons have been all throughout this work. From working in Haiti, I learned about the power of listening and how that relates directly to the most effective type of leadership. The Haitians decide what is best for them. I am simply a support mechanism for that clarity. They know best what is best for them. As the founder and executive director of the nonprofit, I have learned that to be a true leader, one follows and listens first and foremost. On paper, I lead the nonprofit, but in reality, I am in service. What I bring to the table is a continued sense of the value of connection, and more than anything else, a devoted listening to the wisdom of those we serve.

There was a moment in this work when I hadn't yet learned that. We came up with what we thought was a brilliant idea. We started a program early on that we called "Moto Logistics." The idea was simple, at least to us. Haitians could get a moto, a motorcycle basically, on loan from us. We would provide the moto, and they would drive it by night as a moto taxi, carrying passengers around villages for a fee. They could use it by day for themselves. The fees they earned would be divided into a percentage for the driver as profit, a percentage for us to repay part of the loan over time, and a percentage for repairs. Brilliant, right? A program that paid for itself! Sure, except for the fact that the people who received the motorcycles were people with at best the equivalent of first-grade educations, who, while brilliantly devoted to their community, were unable to do the math required to divide up profits as we'd agreed.

In addition, we didn't think about the fact that if someone with little money suddenly has a handful of it from a day's work, they will be hard pressed to save a large percentage of it to repay us, save money for repairs, and not go ahead and spend the entire amount on food and survival today. Needless to say, the program was a success but not because of how we planned it to be. It was a success in learning humility and how not to impose one's plan and intention on others. We learned how to listen and to have our way guided by compassion and consideration of others first and foremost for all future endeavors and projects we undertook in Haiti.

What this means to you: Listen and lead from the standpoint of letting go of the desire to make decisions on behalf of others without their input and direction as well. And even more than that, be willing to shift direction when you realize that your course of action isn't serving your people, your customers, or your team well. This is a reclaim the moment lesson in leadership. You will be a far better leader for it.

Take what you feel inside of this room and break away...

Learning to stand and speak your mind and connect with other people is an incredible transformational tool. In order to explore the intersection of ideas, entertainment, and how they can positively impact and inspire groups of people, I've been inspiring laughter as a keynote speaker and performer (gregbennick.com) for global conferences, corporate, and association events, for decades. I have worked directly with some of the biggest organizations on the planet, some of the smallest and most devoted, and always with the most impassioned and inspired amongst them. When people want an *experience* at their event, they call me to make that happen.

As my career has grown, I have found that I am called most often to share fun ideas that elevate performance and specifically ones that enhance a feeling in people that they matter and that the work they do matters. These are high-performance lessons in problem-solving and performance for individuals and teams. From appearing onstage in high-pressure situations, I have learned that the most effective presentations are people-centric, meaning that even though the lights are on me, my focus is on the message, and what we are experiencing in the moment. This is a key takeaway, and we'll explore it more in Chapter 5.

When I am sincere onstage and focused on the audience as if I am truly in service to them, people respond exponentially more enthusiastically than if I am just going through the motions and delivering lines from last week's presentation. People crave sincerity, and one of the ways to deliver that is to share ideas that matter in a way that considers the listener's experience. Respect the audience, and respect the people with whom you communicate, and you will be someone who elevates and inspires, without doing much of anything beyond just being yourself.

But enough about me, let's talk about me for a while...

We have to get out of our comfort zone if we are ever really going to learn anything about ourselves and the world. To connect, inspire, and learn from others, I've pushed myself and toured as the singer in bands, speaking and singing in raw form about our inner psychological ambitions and conflicts. All of this touring took place as part of an art movement known as *punk rock*. Yes, I just italicized "punk rock" as if you're a 120-year-old who has never heard the term. Just covering all my bases here.

Yes, punk rock is an *art movement*, which sounds esoteric but it is accurate as a descriptor. In art, movements arise among like-minded creators, who share styles, techniques, and approaches (often with a shared or similar philosophy) over a number of years or even decades. We've seen and heard of many famous visual art movements throughout time such as Impressionism, the Bauhaus, Surrealism, and so on. In nascent form, and with music as a canvas, punk rock is similar.

I learned an immense amount from the genre, especially about personal transformation. Punk, at its best, is more than just screaming to a soundtrack. A phrase often used is that the genre, ideally, is "more than music," a reference to the ideas behind the lyrics, and the community organizing and collaborative elements with the social scene. Inherent in the genre is the idea that we can challenge ideas and create new ones, offering perspectives that reshape the status quo. This is applicable to anyone looking to build a better now. Throughout this book we will see examples of this that can help reframe both our work spaces and our personal lives in proactive, creative, and inspiring ways.

The years I spent touring around the planet in support of ideas outside the mainstream gave me chances to listen worldwide to the widest cross-section of people. I have gained deep knowledge cross-culturally about humans and how we think and act in similar ways. Notice that I said "we" not "they," as if the people I've met throughout the world are different than some version of "us." They aren't, because we are the same animal, and there are interwoven similarities everywhere amongst us. We speak similar truths, regardless of where we are from or what we have.

I've listened to people at the top of global industry and those who society would just assume as cast out. In working with people across the widest spectrum of society, from people in the jungles of countries politicians like to forget, to international teams collaborating about sustainability, to the individuals who built the technology that keeps us in touch, or engineered the airplanes that have made the world accessible for decades, I've gained a clearer picture of what people are feeling and are facing. Everywhere I have gone, speaking in dozens of countries for tens of thousands of people, I hear the same things when I engage people after I get offstage: *we want something more.*

I have heard it firsthand, from people in eastern Siberia, rural Haiti, throughout Rwanda and Africa, across the heartland of the United States, all over Europe, and in South America. We share core values that have woven threads of similarity. We want our kids happy, and our love strong. We want our health intact, our communities safe, and our families thriving. We want our finances secure, and our world to be calm. We are getting by but not yet thriving, and we want something more.

This book is part of the answer to that call.

Touring and meeting people from all over the planet has also helped at times to diminish unconscious biases by serving as a reminder that those threads of similarity between people, regardless of their backgrounds and so forth, are far stronger and more pronounced than the differences between us. The biases we bring to those we encounter can be limiting without us even realizing what is happening. We would be wise to remember that before we come to unconscious decisions. It is a process that makes us better teammates, better communicators, and far better leaders as well.

Find your voice and share it far and wide...

A world changer, from any walk of life, finds their voice, and uses it to support others and propel ideas. To help others grow, and to learn as much as possible about communication, I have served for multiple years as the first international speaking coach for the mainstage presenters at TEDxPerth Australia, one of the biggest TEDx events in the world. I have trained and coached speakers both in and out of TEDx, ranging from C-level executives unsure about their focus to individuals terrified of being in front of crowds. This work has been across all levels of business and innovation, helping when someone needs to find their voice and recognize their inner fire to find out what they want to say and how they want to say it.

This work has all been done with the intention of people sharing an idea or vision and inspiring others to do the same. Helping people bring ideas toward greater strength and clarity is what I do for presenters so that they can fulfill their goals and reverberate in the world. One can learn so much from a speech. And a speech delivered well, maybe even with laughter, can be life changing. We will take a closer look at laughter in Chapter 8.

As for my own TEDx talk from years ago, you can watch it on YouTube. What I like best about it is that the person who spoke right before me at TEDxPugetSound in 2009 was some unknown (at the time) business speaker named Simon Sinek. He shared a talk for the first time that day called "Start with Why." My talk over the years has about 30,000 views. His has about 20 gazillion, give or take. But yes, that's right. If you look him up, remember that the legendary business leadership strategist Simon Sinek technically opened *for me*. Thanks, Simon.

When I did my TEDx talk, the director of the event described her expectations for the stage and said simply, "Bring your 'A game,' and make no mistakes." No pressure! What you learn from TED and TEDx is that every word counts. I like to tell the TEDx speakers I coach that when you are in front of an audience, make each of the words you use drive toward the point you ultimately want to make. When we get specific with how we use our words, we elevate our power as communicators, and that inspires others to take action. We will hear more about this in Chapter 5.

"What's past is prologue..."[9]

To understand history is to know your present more intimately. To more fully explore history and how it relates to the present, and determine what lessons we can take from it, I co-founded The Legacy Project (thelegacyproject.com), a multiyear initiative to lead group trips to places around the world that have experienced social unrest or extreme trauma to understand restorative justice and reconciliation. Co-founder Dave Whitson and I led a group to Poland to study the Nazi occupation and the Holocaust to understand from survivors about terror that was everywhere but solidified by an occupying force. We spent three weeks in South Africa to hear from people across multiple ethnic backgrounds and from over a dozen different African countries to learn about the impact of state-sponsored apartheid and racism and terror. We lived for weeks in Rwanda to study the 1994 genocide and speak to government officials to hear about terror that was manifested in society. We went to Chile and Argentina to study how people reconcile terror that was invisible in terms of the death squads and their disappearances. We studied the First Nations residential schools in Canada and the USA, taking part in the Canadian Truth and Reconciliation Commission proceedings and inviting direct testimony

---

[9] William Shakespeare, "The Tempest," *The Riverside Shakespeare* (Boston: The Houghton Mifflin Company, 1974), 2.2.253. References are to act, scene, and line.

of witnesses to explore terror that was forgotten by history. You can read more about all of this at thelegacyproject.com and can engage and even find out how you can get involved in the future with a global network of education and conversation about how to best survive the most difficult of times.

Significantly, we learn other universal truths through reconciliation. A key takeaway of the work with The Legacy Project is realizing that the limits to what we think are irreconcilable differences are actually illusionary. We are limited in terms of what we can resolve in terms of differences with others only by our own ego and anger management. I have met people across the planet who have been through unimaginable horrors. I have sought them out to have deep conversations with them. They have experienced and survived some of history's most powerful traumas – from the Holocaust (I personally interviewed the barber to the former commandant of Auschwitz) to the genocide in Rwanda, where we talked to survivors and perpetrators about how they actually coexist afterward. In Chile and Argentina, we talked to people who had experienced loved ones deemed to be subversive disappeared by government forces. The stories are endless. But they are all rooted in a drive to survive. And that drive overpowers the need to right and wrong.

The core lesson and takeaway has been that we are limited only by our desire to push forward and to reconcile. We will learn more about relationships and how important they are to explore and nurture in Chapter 9. Even in the midst of history's most powerful horrors, people are able to find elements of restorative justice and reconciliation if they work toward those goals rather than toward revenge. We can learn a lot from that, especially amidst today's world where it is so easy to judge everyone else's actions. Yes, there is enough ego stroking online to go around for a lifetime of frustration to be justified. But if we hold reconciliation and progression as a primary directive rather than condemnation and judgment, it becomes possible to transform and really learn from the past as we step into a much better now.

> **On successfully working with systems to change them from within…**

In addition to the above, working on issues around municipal legislation taught me important lessons about working within the system to make substantial change. I worked once again with my friend Dave Whitson to write the law that changed the face of music in Seattle. The biggest 1990s music city on the planet had restrictive legislation that prevented all-ages music access and dancing for people in the city and effectively shut down the ability of promoters to put on live music events. Think *Footloose* combined with *Sleepless in Seattle*. A devoted group of us as citizen activists worked endlessly for years to change it. The restrictions on the music community were astounding, and access to the arts was severely curtailed.

The law, a draconian attempt to protect young people from supposed temptations leading to immorality, instead restricted access to music and the arts, and gave youth who wanted a healthy, creative outlet nothing to do. Ironically, it led to an underground music scene that was even *more* unrestricted and certainly out of the spotlight. All this took place during a time when the world was looking at Seattle as the most progressive and exciting music city on the planet.

We spoke regularly and met with city officials for years along with a group of devoted activists who together worked to overturn the Teen Dance Ordinance. Dave and I wrote the legislation – the All-Ages Dance Ordinance[10] – that replaced it.

That law is still currently on the books in the city of Seattle. We fought the law, but this time *we* won. This collective victory gave voice to an entire generation of people in Seattle, artistically, musically, and culturally. And that's not dramatic. The struggle for access to the arts and the work opposing the All-Ages Dance Ordinance was potentially a swaying factor in the mayoral election in Seattle in 2001 when a candidate who was a supporter of arts and culture Greg Nickels defeated anti-music, anti-community, Seattle

---

[10] "All-Ages Dances and Dance Venues," *Seattle Municipal Code*, Title 6, *Subtitle IV, Chapter 6.295*. Text of the "All-Ages Dance Ordinance," now retitled with its official name and municipal code number, can be found here: https://library.municode.com/wa/seattle/codes/municipal_code?nodeId= TIT6BURE_SUBTITLE_IVNELICO_CH6.295AESDADAVE.

City Attorney Mark Sidran.[11] The difference in voting numbers could be attributed to young people who finally had been given a voice. This altered the political course of the city in favor of arts, paving the way for the movement that today has helped prioritize art and music in Seattle.

This was an incredible lesson in the idea that if we have a clear vision, stay on brand, and remain true to it, we really can enroll others in that goal and together make it happen. It is possible to work within the systems in which we live to transform them. We can be world changers toward a unified goal, together. A team effort in Seattle made that happen and the effect has been long-lasting. Many people over the years have expanded on the original victory and transformed the city. It is incredible what can be accomplished when we reverberate from an original idea and share that inspiration with others. More on that in Chapter 10.

> **Expanding our field of vision inspires connections with one another...**

To try and more deeply understand people and their motivations globally across the widest range of backgrounds, I have gone out speaking on extensive solo tours. I've done spoken-word tours through twenty-seven countries, including the first-ever spoken word tour of all of Russia and Ukraine. I presented there in twenty-one cities, starting across Ukraine, and then from Kaliningrad in Russia, which is basically mainland Europe, to Vladivostok in the east, which sits on the Sea of Japan. I spoke about leadership, and perceptions Russians and Americans have of one another. I spoke about how those perceptions are rooted in propaganda rather than in fact. The number of times I would say in cities across Russia, "We all thought for years that you wanted to blow us up with nuclear weapons!" only to have Russians

---

[11] Kery Murakami, "Nickels Leads Sidran – Too Close to call," *Seattle Post-Intelligencer*, November 6, 2001, https://www.seattlepi.com/seattlenews/article/nickels-leads-sidran-too-close-to-call-1071006.php.

laugh out loud and reply, "What?! We were told *you* wanted to blow *us* up!!" cannot be counted. Talk about a group of people working as a team to bridge a gap! We laughed together amidst generations-old stereotypes, and came to deeper understandings of one another. This was an exploration of connection and teamwork on a global scale. You will find more on this in Chapter 9.

Ultimately, I don't just speak about these ideas. I do my best to go out and learn more about them. I had conversations like this to *hear* from people globally rather than just speak *at* them. I wanted to really get a sense of what people value worldwide. I have performed spoken events with translators and had audience feedback interpreted for me into more languages than I can remember. I didn't want to be limited by language as I sought to develop connections with the people I was meeting. I wanted to be able to understand, regardless of the language they spoke, what gave them a sense of meaning. Sometimes, reaching across a divide is an act of listening and of paying attention.

Engage, listen, respond...

Along those lines, in the turbulent late spring of 2020, my friends and I started the Portland Mutual Aid Network in Oregon, to provide food and survival supplies for unsheltered vulnerable people on the streets. We wanted to listen to the stories of people who were being cast aside as nonessential during the pandemic and protests. The structure of the group was nonhierarchical, consensus based, and rooted in community first and foremost.

We realized that people on the street were being silenced and forgotten and that we could be the ones to hear their unique voices and then take action. I came up with the motto, "Engage, Listen, Respond," and put it in place because people and their voices matter. What people on the street have to say matters, even if the news doesn't quote them. Listening to them matters. More on this project will appear in in Chapter 4.

We'd be wise, myself included, to bring this dynamic of perception and listening to all the areas of our lives that we are able. It goes back to what I was saying before about our unconscious biases and how they influence our thinking about others. Would you be more willing to listen to someone with a business card and a title of CEO, for example, before you heard the wisdom of a person you had met who was living on the street? If so, why? Might that person from the street have insight and perspective that you haven't encountered before? I have learned that they most certainly do. In fact, some of the most well-spoken and well-read people I have met in the last few years were people who had gained their knowledge and experience from a life path that society would typically be quick to disregard and worse, to discard.

Unconscious biases prevent us from deepening connections with those we might learn from, whether in extreme conditions like I have described, or in the workplace as we encounter them day to day. Stay open to the possibility that the person before you might just be the holder of vital and valuable contributions.

Let's imagine ourselves as world changers…

All of that said, the *what*, in terms of what I've done, and the who are different. The what I have done is the list of projects and approaches to speaking and taking action. The who is more general: I see myself as I hope you see yourself, as someone driven by a connection to a meaningful goal. I hope you see yourself as a potential world changer. World changers aren't necessarily trying to change the entire world as a primary directive. They are inspired first and foremost to change their own. They aren't driven by ego. They have a deeper calling. They don't have to be famous or powerful. They aren't necessarily someone as socially significant as the iconic Beyoncé or soccer star Cristiano Ronaldo or a captain of industry who lifts a finger and everyone's lives are immediately changed. A world changer is simply someone who believes that they have something valuable to contribute to the world, wants to share it, and takes action steps to make that a reality. They find new and creative ways to diminish the gap for people between what they dream of and what they can actualize. A world changer realizes that being present and grounded starts with reclaiming the moment and working to build a better now.

And before self-doubt starts to creep in, keep in mind that one of the most powerful qualities of a world changer is that they are willing to make mistakes. It is OK to make mistakes. What matters most is how you manage them or your mindset when they come up. Because they will.

One of my biggest mistakes in business was also my worst marketing fail of all time. I was just starting a new phase of my performing and speaking career when I was in my twenties. I thought I would start marketing to people with handouts at my performances. I decided on postcards. I designed what I felt was an epic postcard. It had my face on the front in the midst of performance. And on the back, it had perfectly worded text about what I offered to my audiences. It looked very professional. Who wouldn't hire me?

I was so sure of myself and confident that I was on the right track that I ordered 17,500 of these cards to start handing out the next time I was in front of a live audience. The cards arrived. That performance day came. Four hundred and fifty watched me onstage. Afterward, I told the audience I had souvenir postcards for everyone there. I was on top of the world as the crowds swarmed to take one. I think every single one of those people crowded the stage to get a card.

After they all left, a young boy stood in front of the stage. His parents were waiting for him in the back of the room. He was staring at the front of my card as if looking for something specific. Then he flipped it over and looked at the back of the card. Then he examined the front again. I looked down at him and smiled. He looked up and asked me a simple question, which ruined my week. "Mister? What's your name?"

What?! I was dumbfounded. Surely it was on the card, wasn't it? It wasn't. I was so busy typing excellent ad copy and coming up with the best possible photos that I had forgotten to put my name and contact information on the card. I rule.

The moral of the story is that we have to roll with our mistakes or else they will most certainly roll over us. A second moral of the story is to keep your focus or else you make ridiculous and costly mistakes.

We need to imagine the world a place that we can shift, mold, and adapt for the better. We can make that happen even if we aren't perfect along the way. Let's believe that our situation and also the conditions affecting others can be changed for the better, regardless of the past. Culture is replete with mistakes and missteps, and we should expect them, but when we make them, we should claim them for *ourselves*, and move on without getting mired in them.

A world changer recognizes that we have limited time and therefore maximizes moments and makes them meaningful. What a world this would be if everyone helped instill and inspire meaning in other people, rather than constantly critiquing them and cutting them down to look better themselves. You are someone who dreams of pushing limits and taking risks, preferring not to live with the status quo simply because it is the status quo. You envision and imagine that something more is possible.

To be a world changer and a *real* influencer:

- **Listen deeply to yourself and others.**
- **Strive to infuse others with a sense of belonging and meaning.**
- **Offer with generosity what you have to share.**
- **Realize that it is OK to make mistakes as you go.**
- **Seek out like-minded people and build a bond of trust with them.**

I'm like you. I believe that other people matter, and that ideas create possibilities. I know that it is possible for us to coach, train, lead, and follow others on a journey to personal and developmental, societal, business, and structural transformation. The journey begins with shifts of perspective in moments and decisions made to center ourselves amidst chaotic times.

The ideas and perspective shifts in these pages are a push in the right direction to regain a sense of clarity amidst a world filled with distractions. That clarity puts us in position to advance with a clear and powerful voice.

These ideas are how I return to center, reclaim the moment, and ready myself, so that I can then take steps to reveal and explore that *something more*. It all starts with being grounded. From there, you can refine what you want, how you want to communicate it, and move forward feeling like that new kind of human. Then you can build a team who will reverberate and transform.

OK. Let's dive in and start with the good news.

2

A World Changer's Guide to Life

"Is this sorrow, of which our impending being no more might be the foundation, the great wilderness?"[1]

— Ross Gay, *The Book of Delights*

LET'S ESTABLISH SOME ground rules before we get started. These are some core thoughts about what it means, from my perspective, to be human. I offer them not as a psychology lesson, but rather so that you will know where I am coming from throughout the rest of the book. That way, we can all agree – or agree to disagree – about some basic points that we all have in common. Reading through this, and staying open to the ideas here, will make you a better teammate, leader, and world changer. These ideas provide a sense of connection to others that is deeper than the superficiality of the world often allows.

Humans need a sense of meaning. We need to feel that we are valuable contributors to something meaningful, greater than ourselves, and that we matter amidst that process. That said, we are all insecure and frightened creatures, desperate for validation, hurtling toward uncertain individual ends with no roadmap to guide the way.

---

[1] Ross Gay, "Joy Is Such a Human Madness," *The Book of Delights* (Chapel Hill: Algonquin Books of Chapel Hill, 2019), 50.

Yes, you read me correctly. Just in case you think your eyes are failing you or the publisher tricked you with printing the wrong words, I will say it again: We are all insecure and frightened creatures, desperate for validation, hurtling toward uncertain individual ends with no roadmap to guide the way.

You're a creature. Deal with it.

Welcome, insecure creature. All of this is good news. Trust me on this. We are all in the same boat. In my opinion, being an insecure creature amidst other insecure creatures helps because it creates a level playing field.

Our news is good because it's a launching pad, and one we all have in common. We are fragile. We are *all* fragile. Fragile emotionally, and if you don't believe me, think about what taps into our feelings and gets a reaction. We think of ourselves as solid and strong and then one harsh comment and we crumble, or one baby lamb video and we melt. Or maybe that's just me. We are also fragile physically, and that one goes without saying. That a creature who can invent 3D printing, the blockchain, quantum computing, and professional wrestling could be killed by a falling rock or by slipping on a banana peel would be almost comical if it weren't tragic.

Knowing the core of our situation means that we have a solid foundation from which to work, speak, and act. There's nothing bad about the good news. It might not be as fluffy as good news you expect, but that's not a bad thing. It is still good. I promise. The reason it is good is that from my perspective, the way through the situation of our creatureliness is feeling that you are meaningful, that you matter, and that you're contributing to something valuable to the world while you're here. That might not prevent you from dying on a banana peel, but it will definitely make you feel better about the *possibility* of you dying on a banana peel. Our goal here is to make the journey more awesome, not to change the rules of the game entirely. Or to ban bananas.

This powerful sense we get from knowing that we are contributing is because people are reflective and self-aware. We can rationalize and get introspective. We can hold as meaningful the idea that we matter. And this is deeply empowering. When I say good news, it is because from a starting point of psychologically feeling potentially limited, we have incredible potential, and even more potential together.

The bad news gets much worse from there if we let ourselves slip in terms of what we, as insecure and frightened creatures, have the potential to do. We can really mess this existence up. We often allow ourselves to be swayed negatively by the overt, or subtle, suggestions of others, and then we react from there.

The world can be impossibly cruel and generally terrible, unfair, and unkind. We often, inadvertently, add to that terrible list. We can make one another feel silenced, stifled, immobilized. We often tear down before we try to build up. We diminish others, and make them feel meaningless and as if they don't matter. We help to create the issues we then work so hard to diminish, and we often do this without even realizing it.

We don't have to do that. We *choose* to, whether we realize it or not, and that is ominous. But we can make different choices. This book is about those different choices.

We can do more with the good news than we tend to. Because creatures are temporary and we don't get to live forever. As a result, we have to do the most we can with the time we have. And realistically, we don't have a ton of time, so we can maximize and celebrate what we do have rather than lament what we don't.

The problem is that people take that good news but don't do the work needed to develop themselves amidst it, and end up instead taking the easy way out, imploding on themselves by reacting to the bad news, and as a result lashing out at others, cutting others down or themselves, and generally bringing a storm of chaos to the world. Read that as *stripping others of their meaning* at the very least. We have the unfortunate potential, if we take the path of least resistance, to use our voices and privileges in destructive ways. In doing so we diminish and disempower others.

I am going to leave most of that side (the bad news) to other books and researchers to fill in the blanks. The bad news takes up way too much space in general. We see it, hear about it, and feel it every day, exponentially it seems in the last few years. Humans are often terrible at being human. We seem to not know the first thing about how to do this correctly and always seem to screw up the process.

> **You've got a vast mind, and a powerful voice. Use them to create some good in the world.**

We are here together in these pages to approach life from a different, and better, perspective. I want us to inspire others and help them feel meaningful. You must give yourself and them the best fighting chance for the future you want amidst a world and a mind that often work against us. You need to be telling yourself, rather than listening to the inner voices within yourself, about the life you want to create, and the moment you want to reclaim.

Can you imagine spending your entire existence dreaming of a better reality but not taking a single step to make it happen? You, your team, your business, your life, your relationships, depend on you building a better now for yourself and approaching the world with new perspectives. How else will the foundation for what you want to develop be built?

> **We need to be *telling* ourselves, rather than *listening* to ourselves, about the changes we want to create.**

Often, all it takes is one person taking action to motivate others to do the same. Influences and shifts and subtle suggestions from external sources don't have to be things which throw us off track bit by bit in a death through a thousand cuts. It can be the exact opposite, where our influences and suggestions lead us closer to our center. You break patterns, push yourself to explore new ideas, and refashion new routines where the old weren't working for you. Insecure, frightened creatures all have the potential to make changes this significant.

We can learn to disregard the small stuff and focus on the main tasks at hand. We can strengthen our perspectives on relationships, creativity, what it means to be a leader, and how to best listen to and amplify others' ideas. All while uplifting others instead of hovering over them, controlling them, or cutting them down.

If you can make that happen, you will have started a mini-revolution, and can share it from there with other insecure, frightened creatures.

This means that the strategies and approaches we take to get *to* this moment matter more than the roads we take *from* this moment. Insecure creatures often talk themselves out of the potential of what could come next.

"What if this or that or the other thing doesn't go as I planned?"

"What if I fall on my face?"

"What if I can't make this happen because I am too tall, short, big, oblong, smart, weird?" and so on.

When we build a better now, we are more ready and therefore more confident. We are clear about the good news. We are focused on what we are doing now to make things better, and the future is more filled with possibility than it is replete with potential failure. When we build a better now, the past was a steppingstone. When we build a better now, we are readying ourselves to create our future with intention. We do it from this moment, and the next moment, and the next. We let long-term plans be secondary to that process because if our moment isn't solid, our future holds more of a chance to not be solid as well.

> **Imagine the words you tell yourself as an ignition point, sparking potential again and again.**

To build a better now requires we take a continually hopeful look at a challenging human condition: We are individual pieces of consciousness, each with a face and a name, all wondering what purpose that face and name is supposed to have. This, while feeling and knowing that we can do better, create more effectively, and expand powerfully. We most definitely want something more.

I will add that a creature with a face and a name, who strives for meaning and purpose in a life that doesn't last forever, might never be perfectly satisfied. We don't have to change all of the rules of the game.

We can learn to live with some of them, and at other times bend and break them. That, my friends, is entirely and imperfectly OK.

I'd also love to feed you a line where I say that if you follow these strategies, the world, your business, your life and loves will all be flawless. They won't. And that is exactly where we need to be. The work we do on ourselves is continual and ongoing, influenced by wanting something more. That isn't a statement of futility. It is one of action.

When I was writing this book, I had someone tell me to take out anything that didn't make me sound like I had my life totally together so that I could come across as a guru. They wanted me to sound like I absolutely always have every single part of my life completely under control. They wanted me to create the image of myself as someone who was in demand because he wasn't vulnerable, flawed, or weak. Nothing sounds less interesting or less relatable. I'd rather be in demand because I make mistakes and work my way through and around them effectively. Perfection doesn't even sound fun. Those kinds of false heroes bore me senseless. The world needs less of them.

We are imperfectly perfect. Let's move forward from that place together.

The strategies and their exploration require some thinking, which is why there are smart ideas and substance throughout this book. They ask for reflection and focus, which is why there's personal connection. They ask for calm, which is why there are fun stories at times too. They most importantly ask for dedication and drive, which is why there's realistically motivational material throughout. "Realistically" being the key. Motivation without a grounding in ideas and a shared sense of reality is superficial and empty.

I will offer seven strategies next to help you reclaim moments in your life from a world that would just as soon leave you feeling that you have less, not more. We get one life. Let's make the moments of it count. So as not to bum you out completely, you can know that you get about two billion seconds in your life. That's the good news. The bad news is that you've used up a lot of them already. OK, enough with the bad news.

Some extra good news ...

This book helps us reclaim organizational and personal empowerment instead of feeling that we must always succumb to authority. We often feel *less than*, whether from the scrutiny of others, their comments, or possibly by way of someone else's condescension, often from those around us who themselves are off center too. Various modes of authority we encounter often throw us off track.

Power resides in each of us. Authority exists above us. Use your voice for empowerment.

While this might sound like a diversion, it is central to the theme. Power and empowerment are important topics when it comes to working to enhance ourselves and our teams. Let's take a second and explore the difference between power and authority. This is important to clarify because it plays directly into how you look at yourself and the people you work for, with, and the people you serve. It will also help you understand how you respond to them and their influence.

Oftentimes we use power and authority as somewhat interchangeable terms. Activists talk about the desire to *speak truth to power* (these words are often credited to Black Quaker leader Bayard Rustin as early as the early 1940s and then codified in a 1955 pamphlet of the same title by Rustin and co-authors[2]). Decades later, massively influential rap group Public Enemy told us to "fight the power" and made the statement iconic.[3] But I do want to make a differentiation so that we can contextualize and think about these two things differently.

Power is the sense of strength that emanates from within, and also the ability to inspire that in others. Personal power. Yours. Theirs. Power can be a feeling of worth and a feeling of potential all in one. Power also references an ability to guide or sway the behavior of others. It can be used for influence and to be uplifting, or it can be used in potentially difficult and impactful ways. When we exist in

---

[2] Stephen G. Cary et al., *Speak Truth to Power: A Quaker Search for an Alternative to Violence: A Study of International Conflict* (American Friends Service Committee, 1955), iv.

[3] Public Enemy, "Fight the Power," written by Carlton Ridenhour, Eric Sadler, Hank Boxley, Keith Boxley, *Do the Right Thing* (Motown Records, July 4, 1989), soundtrack, 12" vinyl.

a model of em*power*ment, the people around us will feel and sense it too, and they will be inspired to join us in the vision we have for the future. They will share in amplifying the voice we use to communicate that vision. We can create life and work spaces based on empowerment. Now far be it from me to argue with Public Enemy, especially because they brilliantly approached power sociologically from the standpoint of injustices and imbalances, but as a distinction for the point of exploration, I'd like to offer a thought about authority.

Authority is often different than power. Authority is centered on control. Sure, authority can be used effectively by creative business minds in terms of managerial control. But for the sake of this argument, we are not looking at Max Weber (writer on business theory – hard to read, approach at your own peril) and his perspectives about bureaucracy in the workplace.[4] We are talking about the humans within that workplace and how it feels and subsequently what it *means* to be there. When we exist amidst authority, our advancement and feeling of empowerment are entirely dependent on the graces of those above us. We might never feel like we are enough.

Authority becomes so intimately linked with power that we lose the ability to discern between the two. And yet in this one and only life we have, are we willing to give power freely with the promise that authority will provide for us? That sounds unsound to me.

We can be the catalyst of inspiration for ourselves and for those with whom we interact. These mechanisms of influence can be utilized in ways that are kind, creative, and supportive. You can be proverbially up a hierarchical chain and still not diminish the people who are, so-called, *beneath* you. You can imagine that relationship differently. It all comes down to how you conduct yourself, how centered you are, and how willing you are to infuse meaning in others. People can tell. If you're a jerk, people will see through the façade. If you're grounded and centered and supportive, people will see, feel, and be inspired by that too.

---

[4] Weber is well known and analyzed right and left, but a good synthesis of his ideas, dated as they might be conceptually, can be found here: Sean Peek, "The Management Theory of Max Weber," Business.com, https://www.business.com/articles/management-theory-of-max-weber/ (accessed February 4, 2024).

To decide to build a better now will find us on a mission to disengage our minds and hearts from authority while engaging them in positive manifestations of power at the same time. From there, we can share that power – and empowerment – with others, remembering that they want something more too. Part of that more is a sense that we matter. Once discovered and felt, a sense of mattering in the world is fuel poured over a fire of our potential. We can take that feeling and help to inspire it in others.

Even if it feels like things right now are out of control, unfocused, isolated, or unsure, we can bring all of that back to center. Remember that opening line about being insecure creatures? I'd like to dive into one last bit of wildly important smart stuff along those lines to help put that even further into context.

What we want, we must create. What we risk will be regained.

For the last couple decades, I have been delving deeply into the work of Austrian psychoanalyst Otto Rank. Rank examined in his critically important work *The Trauma of Birth* what it means to be a human born from nothingness and cast into a world we didn't choose.[5] It tells us a lot about who and what we are when we think of our lives as unexpected and turbulent from the first moment that we are cast into the light for the first time. We have a lot to manage right off the bat. Rank, for the historians amongst you, was a revolutionary thinker during his time.

Up until Rank, people had only Sigmund Freud's bizarre theories about our issues centering around lusting for our moms and wanting to kill our dads...and by "our" he meant men only, as he really didn't care much for women. Freud was bizarre.

Rank was Freud's protégé, and when Rank published *The Trauma of Birth*, it sent Freud into a state of upheaval because Rank's theory preceded Freud's in the human timeline. You didn't need a developed or messed-up relationship with your mom to be traumatized, suggested

---

[5] Otto Rank, *The Trauma of Birth* (New York: Harper Torchbooks, Harper and Row Publishers, 1973), 11.

Rank. You just needed, before all that even came about, to be born. That was enough.[6]

Drawing directly from Rank was an American social theorist and cultural anthropologist named Ernest Becker, who won a Pulitzer Prize in 1974 for his book *The Denial of Death* (by the time you read this book, I'll be writing my full biography about Becker, the first of its kind. I am admittedly very well-versed in his work and history). His book examined our creatureliness and offered an explanation and overview for what it means to be an animal with a reasoning and rational mind in a symbolic and overwhelming world. More to the point, he looked deeply into the psychological nature of a creature with abstract and limitless symbolic thinking, who is bound by an inner hourglass. We can dream, but when the sands run out, we keel over dead. Not fun.

But that was Becker's point: It is deeply troubling to be a creature who can imagine the infinite but be bound by physical limitations from within (when our health betrays our ambition) or from outside us (when we get any one of a million diseases, slip on that banana peel, are bitten by a spider, get hit by a truck in a bookstore, and so on). Becker felt that this was tragic at best. To his credit, he also recognized how ridiculous this all was. I mentioned it before, but how can we be so infinite in our minds and yet so limited in our lives?

But wait, there's more.

When I refer to us as a creature, I don't mean that you're a bear or a snail or Bigfoot. To be a creature is deeply meaningful. It is a badge of honor. It signifies and identifies what we are: animals. We are complicated weird and unusual animals. Not quite as furry or cute as most. Not as fast as some. But better jugglers, journalism professors, restaurant owners, coin collectors, and human resource managers than the others.

Being a creature gives us a level playing field from which we can all develop and grow. We aren't all the same, but we have core similar traits rooted in *what* we are that lets us examine how we can advance in this moment into *who* we are and then launch forward together with

---

[6] James Lieberman, *Acts of Will: The Life and Work of Otto Rank* (New York: The Free Press, McMillan, 1985), 201.

a degree of connectedness. And we can do so knowing that the people around us, close to us, near us, and even far from us, people we like, love, can't stand, are in a similar physiological and existential boat. This is really good news.

We are caught between want or want not, with no easy way out.

Being a creature isn't easy. It means we are temporary beings who can imagine the infinite. That in itself is an immense problem. For if we can imagine the infinite, what do we do with our limitations? For example, how do we deal with the fact that we will die, or that bad things will happen, or that we won't feel satisfied?

The answers are found in the act of constant creation and in sharing that with other people. We have to keep creating, growing, and being the very best creature we can possibly be (go ahead and roar if you like) in order to not fall prey to inclinations to react in negative ways toward one another. We can be sharing inspiration, meaning, and wonder with others. We can be uplifting our team instead of cutting them down. We can be offering products and ideas and services that support the condition in which we find ourselves. We can be world changers.

To what end does all this theorizing lead?

Being on a level playing field with those around us creates potentially strong team dynamics. Transformational ideas, even ones that are disruptive and new, can be heard and embraced more readily by an empowered team of individuals who themselves feel valued. We massively strengthen the bonds between team members if we feel that others are with us, instead of feeling like adversaries. You do not want your friends or your team to feel like they are less than, or in an adversarial position. As we've seen in this chapter, to do so is anti-human. We also can empower leaders with new perspectives that can drive development and progress forward in ways that honor the people they serve. We can listen as leaders instead of only hearing the sound of our own voices. We can inspire others to create and be generative in their thinking and then magnify those ideas, even if the original impetus was not our own. More on this in Chapter 10.

If that's not good news, then I don't know what is. Hopefully, the ideas here will help guide you through this bizarre world we've all managed to create together while we struggle for maximum life, enhanced meaning, and incredible experiences.

Not when. Not then. But now.

In order to balance the self-doubt, distraction, lack of self-esteem, failing confidence, and a general sense that things are out of control, which results from the bad news, we can use the strategies in this book and an awareness of the balance and connectedness brought by the good news as tools to step into the moments fueled by what we most value – to give ourselves the best fighting chance for the future that we want. From there, we can share it, describe it, communicate it, and do an incredible job of maximizing the time we have in the best possible way.

Seven strategies. Perspective shifts. Each with intention of maximizing potential, experience, profit (however you might define that, and remember it's not always rooted in money), depth, passion, and transformation. Bridge the gap between the hunger for what you want and the satisfaction of achieving it, and you'll find a deeper kind of profit. In this new model, you've traded your time and energy for a return far more valuable than the sum of its parts.

We are world changers after all, and we want something more. The point is, if you want to build a better future, you've got to build a better now.

So, let's connect by way of a feeling I believe will be familiar to you …

3

Mickey Mouse, a Thunderstorm, and Anarchy

"We have two lives, and the second begins when we realize we only have one."

– Some unknown wise human, though often
attributed incorrectly to Confucius

I FELT STUCK.

I felt stuck in my business. Even though it had been in place for years, I didn't feel productive because I couldn't seem to get focused, or convince the world that what I had to offer really mattered. If they did notice, they weren't letting me know in the way others seemed to be enjoying with their successes. I didn't feel that people were honoring my talents or, additionally, paying me what I was worth.

I felt stuck in my relationships, because I couldn't bring my full self to connection outside of myself when I wasn't satisfied within. Relationships are easy when they flow. And they flow when two people who are solid in themselves come together to walk a path at the same time. They are tricky when one person is a mess, or even when either person has misgivings about who they are and what they are all about. I often felt out of synch.

I felt stuck in life, the result of fighting myself constantly about who I felt I was *supposed* to be rather than who I *was*. It is easy to get distracted and disengaged when one imagines that everyone else has a better life than you do and you want to transform instantly and can't. Today, that's truer than ever. We can pose for the best selfies and offer the best smiles, but all the likes in the world can't hide the fact that we went back to feeling flat inside the second the selfie saved to a gallery in our phones, which is packed with attempts to capture just the right smile.

Stuck is an awful feeling. Productivity drops to near zero, and you feel terrible about yourself.

The closest I can come to describing how it felt for me to be stuck is to maybe bring up quicksand, or that awful moment during the holidays when you get a tiny piece of clear packing tape wrapped around your finger and can't get it off and it feels like a strait jacket and you want to scream because you feel like you're going to die. Or maybe that's just me.

Actually, the closest I can come to describing stuck is by bringing up Sisyphus, the mythologized and very much so doomed figure from ancient Greece.

Sisyphus had a rough go. As the story goes, due to having bad behavior in the eyes of the gods, and that's putting it lightly, Sisyphus was doomed for eternity to push a giant stone up a hill, only to have it then roll back down to the bottom. But wait, there's more! He then, cursed for all time, had to repeat this cycle again and again, forever. I've done some repetitive tasks in my time. But rolling a stone up a hill again and again for all of eternity?

The problem is, that felt like me. Never making the progress I wanted. I was constantly pushing too hard for too little return. Or I was pushing in the wrong direction and not having the results land where I wanted. I was lost in a story, the complexity of which was my own creation, and it seemed as though I was continually fighting against all of it. The frustration economically and personally was grinding and relentless.

This, if you haven't caught on yet, is not a fun place to be. There's no way you can find your voice or your place in the world amidst that, and there's little chance of recruiting others to your vision of what the world could be.

I was trying to make the future what I wanted rather than building right now better. It feels counterintuitive if you want to be somewhere better, but doing the work now matters most. To take the time to be present, to be ourselves, and to get grounded leads to that better future we want.

Sisyphus might have imagined that pushing that stone would get him to where he finally could take a rest. Bad news for Mr. Sisyphus. The gods wouldn't let him off that easily.

The thing is, Sisyphus was doomed. Cursed. Condemned. Eternity is not until Thursday at 3 p.m., or until the spring after baseball season starts. Eternity is forever. Sisyphus was in serious trouble, the result of his own misgivings and misguidances.

There is a huge difference between Sisyphus being stuck, like actually stuck, and you *feeling* stuck or not being able to *imagine* being unstuck. One is a curse from the gods. The other *feels* like a curse from the gods. But it isn't. If you find yourself rolling a stone up a hill again, you can make a different choice. Roll it faster. Roll it slower. Step out of the way and let it roll down the hill. You aren't cursed forever.

I quite like that idea of letting it roll down the hill. The thing you're pushing against only pushes back when you're in the midst of the fight. Let that stone roll past you and you can move on. That's a good one to remember.

But the thing about being stuck is that it doesn't feel in the moment like you can just let it go. When we are stuck, it feels like forever. The good news (yes, more good news) is that we have a choice as to how we approach that feeling of being stuck.

When you are stuck, nothing can be built. It felt like my feet were encased in cement, and that I still had a hill up which a stone needed to be pushed. Like I mentioned earlier, productivity drops to zero when we feel that we can't move forward.

When you take our jobs, families, lives, and all the pressures from outside to achieve, and the constant nagging to be like the Joneses next door but and also like every other family on every block in every town in every country in the social media world, the pressure and distraction is too much. It all compounds. We end up feeling like we are the ones pushing a stone up a hill, and yet like we haven't even begun the climb.

All this of course, while knowing somewhere deep in my mind that what kept me most stuck was me. I could try to escape by placing the blame on social forces and the influences (and influencers!) around me. I could accuse those nearby for keeping me always envious. I could put guilt on the difficulty of dealing with other people. But at the end of the day, I, as lowest common denominator amongst all of that, had to take the fall for the crime of inaction.

> **There is always a way through. What matters most is if you are willing to see it, recognize it, and pursue it.**

I don't need to tell you that you never know where valuable life lessons are going to come from. Believe it or not, my big life lesson in building a better now came from Mickey Mouse.

You see, I went to Walt Disney World only once. I'd put it off throughout my life because I invented a story in my mind that it was just for kids and that I wouldn't get anything out of it. When – years ago now – I finally visited this tidal wave of family entertainment, it was years ago, but the promise of salvation from the stresses of the world was real and I decided to give it a chance. The corresponding crowds who were there for that promise were immense.

The place itself was immense too. When you drove in, you knew you were in for a literally world-sized experience, because a tram would pick you up at the parking lot and take you and all your fellow travelers to the entrance and the attractions. When the parking space is that far away from the front door, you know the place and the promise on which it was built is gigantic.

At the end of the day, that same train would take you back to where you parked. On the day I went, it started getting cloudy in the afternoon, and by the time nightfall came and the nightly fireworks were going off, it looked like rain. The timing was perfect – we saw a great fireworks show and the rain held off. But as the crowds started to gather on the train platform for the tram to take us back to our cars, the rainclouds started looking more ominous, and the crowd started to get a little uneasy, watching the sky, watching for the tram, hoping to avoid the deluge. After a minute, the crowd on the platform started to get more and more packed in. We figured a train arriving was imminent.

That was wishful thinking. What actually happened was somewhat different.

It wasn't the train that arrived but the rain. A few drops at first. But then when the train wasn't on time, the increasingly packed throngs paid closer attention to the fact that the rain was getting more intense. It went from a sprinkle to an actual rain. The crowd began to get uneasy. The train was still nowhere in sight. People started to get nervous, then upset, then slightly frantic.

This was very un-Disney.

There wasn't any lightning, so we weren't in any immediate danger, but a minute or two turned into five, which feels like an eternity when you add on the apprehension that the skies are going to completely open up and shower you with Epcot-sized tears. And that's exactly what happened. It started pouring. The train still wasn't anywhere in sight.

By now, the crowd was up in arms, which manifested in everyone frustratedly grumbling a lot and saying nothing. After the now-soaked crowd got dumped on for a bit, we realized fully that something wasn't perfect in the happiest place on earth. The rain didn't let up. There were a couple hundred of us standing on that platform frustratedly confused. Then suddenly someone said something which changed my life. A voice from the middle of the group said...

"What do we do? Who is going to tell us what to do?"

It was a question without any possibility of an answer.

It wasn't intended to have an answer. It was spoken from a place of despair and from a mindset that there had to be someone, somewhere, with something to share that would direct us and save us and tell us exactly what we were supposed to do in order to get back to our warm cars and dry clothes and on our way back to television and our phones and the non-Disney rest of our lives with its less-expensive snacks.

No one is going to give you your voice. You have to find it yourself.

I was dumbfounded by her question. Was there no way for us to do this ourselves? If it was up to me, why wasn't I making the move to do anything? Why was I standing there getting soaked? Why was I standing there like everyone else?

The same applied to the rest of us. If it was up to *us*, then why were we all standing there in dumbfounded silence, letting ourselves get soaked?

I remember realizing that there was no plan behind the question and no process by which the problem would be solved. That's why what she said hit me so hard.

I was just as unwilling to step outside my comfort zone too, even if that step was somewhere out from under the rain. Were we waiting for an authority figure to direct us? Could we not empower ourselves to take action? Did I not have the creativity to figure out what to do? Could I not find a leadership voice and say *something* to help others? Even if the step we took was for us to all laugh at ourselves, couldn't we agree on any course of action at all?

I suddenly didn't care anymore about the rain. What I cared about was that hundreds of people, collectively banded together by a shared experience, and one decidedly seen as negative, couldn't together figure out what to do. This, when the problem was only rain.

We were most definitely, absolutely, critically, stuck.

We could have sent someone to get help. We could have fashioned rain protection out of windbreakers and gift bags and protected the most vulnerable amongst us. We could have walked as a group to the parking lot illuminating the way by whatever lights we had to make sure everyone got there safely and singing all the while to make light of a difficult situation.

Why not your vision for the world, and why not now?

But instead, we just stood there together, miserable, getting soaked.

Eventually after another long couple minutes, the very late train came around the corner and finally all was happy and well. We, the stuck masses, were suddenly unstuck. We breathed a collective deep sigh of relief and cheered, and our blissful Disney-inspired happiness returned once again. We joked and laughed about the rain when we were on the train, and any memories of those helpless moments were seemingly whisked away.

But I didn't forget.

What if the issue at hand wasn't just some rain, but how to live the only life we get in a way that actually matters to us? What if we had to speak out to change something for the better and instead chose to be silent? What if our lives were on the line?

What if we decided to just waste time waiting for someone to tell us what to do? I certainly hope we wouldn't do that. We could be waiting a very long time indeed. Too long, in fact. After all, our lives really are on the line. Tick tock, tick tock, tick tock – and I don't mean the app.

I had to ask myself why I didn't do any of the things that were needed in the moment to help the situation.

That moment was lost. It was lost not just *to* me but *by* me. I let it slip away, and we all stood there drowning not just in rain but in futility.

Silence inhibits progress. When it matters most, it might be up to you to break it.

If we want something more, we have to take action. We need to reclaim the moment when it might otherwise slip away, and at our own peril. We need to be willing to use our voice when it is needed, and not after the fact. We need to give form to our ideas and motivations and make our words matter.

We could dive deeply here into how we pace what we say, what filler words we use without realizing it, how to use nonverbal communication effectively, but all of that (valid and valuable) technical speaking information aside, what matters most is speaking up in the first place and having those words land effectively.

On that train platform, I experienced a loss of power, and I'm the one who gave it away. I experienced the loss of my voice, and I'm the one who silenced it. I experienced the loss of free will, and I'm the one who chose to not choose. I chose not to feel vulnerable. I chose to feel disempowered instead of sharing my vision for what could be better for us. We could have planned a way to get off that platform, or even just to see our situation differently and have a laugh about it rather than being miserable.

The experience made me focus on prioritizing what I am doing, feeling, thinking, and saying, and to do so far less on the future and far more on what I can do now.

> **We can't let life unlived simply pass us by.**

The thing is, we all just had our own train station moment.

The pandemic was the rain, and answers (whether that was guidance, a vaccine, a cure, confidence from up high, or thoughts simply about what to do) were the train. We waited. We hoped. We anticipated. Eventually, we all found our way through.

We all learned that we had to take the initiative and do something even if that something wasn't what we had planned, and even if we didn't yet have an absolutely clear path ahead of us. The future we envisioned and the world which we imagined living in for it turned out to be completely unpredictable. We were brought up to think that if we did this, *then* we would get that. One thing happening eventually was largely contingent on another happening today. It was the promise that if we work hard for the future that we want, then this or that will happen.

But that's not how it all unfolded. The pandemic had different plans. And we were all immobilized for a bit – or a few years – as a result.

It turns out that if you don't do what you typically do out of routine, for a few *years*, that the world doesn't end. In fact, if every single human on the planet doesn't leave their house for a month or two or three, the world doesn't stop. Interestingly, the world – read that as animals and *nature* – actually thrived when we all stayed home! The pandemic taught people that they wanted something other than to go into the office five days a week. And people are hanging onto that experience. It actually, interestingly, puts people in an adversarial position with employers who are holding onto a traditional mindset and not coming up with clever solutions for how to adapt. This is a constantly changing landscape. Literally as I was typing this chapter, a headline story came out about a major aircraft manufacturer saying that they have shifted policy and that the new worker policy is demanding all the workers to come back to the office full time. That's a moment of potentially being on the train platform too for those workers.

Needing everything mapped out suddenly didn't apply anymore when the pandemic started, and yet for the most part, society managed to make it through. What happens when we suddenly have more time than expected to do what we want? What about times when what we want to do is limited, but time itself isn't? And what about when we have our parameters shifted for us overall?

We had to figure out how to get unstuck when it felt like everything was out of our control. Because *everything*, much like that train platform, wasn't out of our control after all. Some things were. But not everything. Certainly, within our reach, was the potential to want something more and to get it.

That potential is maximized through shifts in perspective offered by the strategies we'll explore. I most definitely could have used this book when I was standing on that train platform in the pouring rain.

- Believe in the possibility of kindness.
- Keep your eyes on the knife.
- Cultivate a revolutionary mindset.
- Leap into the dark.
- Engage with laughter.
- Build relationships that matter.
- Start a reverberation effect.

I believe that leading with kindness even when we feel broken, sharpening our focus on what matters most, living with a revolutionary ideology in a world where rules are available to be bent or be broken, taking creative risks to keep ourselves feeling alive and expanding, opening up to laughter so as not to be silent, and keeping a deep-breath mindset with others amidst the heaviness of the world, will carry us through every moment we face far more fluidly and effectively than if we just remained stuck. These strategies make us better leaders and teammates, better creators, and better innovators. In fact, following this course of strategy will not only help us get unstuck but it will let us describe through an empowered voice how to help others get through their own train platform nights too.

> **Don't be the leader who wants to drive but forgot the keys to the car.**

I am like you. I'm a turning of opposites. I am caught between what I'm supposed to do, what I have to do, what I need to do, and what I want to do. There is less of a way to feel satisfied, happy, content, directed, or focused when you are living on the terms someone else lays out for you. This is especially true when you are trying to manage and manifest something meaningful for anyone else, whether an individual or a team.

We put too much power in metaphorical gods and masters and not enough in ourselves. The trickle-down effect from the proverbial top to the bottom, when the person at the top is like Sisyphus, has an obvious effect all the way down the chain, more often than not, toward the negative.

I have worked with countless groups who have been "led" by directors and managers who have been pushing the same stone again and again up the same hill. They have not been happy, clear, and directed themselves. They are world changers without a sense of the change they want to bring and without clarity about how to share that vision with others as they navigate through the world. They are the ones standing on the train platform asking who will come save them. They are pushing the stone up the hill. They just don't admit that because, of course, admitting that we need help is a sign of weakness.

This is a recipe for disaster. Asking for help is essential, given that we have not been cursed by gods to a solitary, terrible, and futile existence. Strengthening a network based on sharing power at any level of an organization, rather than enforcing authority, is without a doubt a nontraditional model and one whose time has more than come. (We could actually be rethinking the primary effects on team dynamics of outdated hierarchical models too, but that can be for yet another book, another time.)

The solutions revealed to us about finding our voice, becoming decidedly non-Sisyphysian, and finding inspiration for empowering others create a trickle-down to so-called mid-level people, workers, and associates in the organizational world, and it offers a massively enhancing experience in our personal lives.

Without that approach, people absorb the worst of you. We are all seeking connection and guidance, and when your inner frustration and lack of clarity lead, that's what people ingest, for lack of a better word. The entire group suffers as a result as everyone drives forward without fuel, following a roadmap without direction, and following words and a vision without substance to enhance and support it.

When you're a leader and haven't yet figured out what you want to say to empower others and why, essentially you are just standing there in the rain waiting for a train, which will hopefully arrive. When you're on a team and yet you have no sense of why relationships matter, you are essentially amidst a crowd on a platform with no direction or cohesion. When you are an individual with an idea, and you are inclined toward silencing yourself instead of thinking in revolutionary terms about actually giving an idea a try to see if it so much as has merit at all, you are just standing there and getting soaked.

With new ideas around impulse and action, you will have more clarity about what to do when you're standing there in the rain. And in doing so, if future forward thinking is your jam, you'll be able to step into that with clarity and direction.

When I am feeling cursed by the gods and fighting that stone, one of the first things I do is question why I am fighting its weight in the first place. We resist wildly because sidestepping an issue feels like giving in or ignoring it. But sometimes it's a great choice, and the sigh of relief we will breathe when the stone rolls by is the first breath toward the rest of our lives.

Ultimately, and we will get to this so much more later on, the thing that you'll be able to experience most is that this growth is for the benefit not only of yourself, but for other people. It is for the benefit of the people you work with, the people you serve, and even people you have not yet met. Think about that for a moment if you want to feel as though you matter. You can profoundly impact people outside your sphere of immediate influence. These might be people you never even meet or know exist. Your influence will be the grounds for their empowerment. That's cool.

> **Be the person and make the choices you will be excited to remember years from now.**

Feeling stuck, like we are pushing a stone, or simply not knowing what direction to take, feels helpless. And when we feel that way, we certainly don't make the right choices for ourselves or for others. After I was in my car and driving away from Disney, I did what we all do after pressure situations. I thought of a hundred ways I *could* have responded. None of them was so far out of the realm of reality that they couldn't have *been* reality. But the thing is that I had just chosen, from a sea of choices as vast as raindrops themselves, to do absolutely nothing.

There's an immense difference between *feeling* stuck and being stuck. The problem is that often when we feel stuck, we have an inclination to make awful choices or no choice whatsoever. We throw ourselves down the wrong path. We declare ourselves to be failures. But often, the compounding nature of worry and trying to keep up means that we reinforce the barriers we face and exponentially maximize issues until all we are doing is reacting to illusions. The threat is often not nearly as big as we thought it to be. Yes, we each have hurdles to face. But when you look at a hurdle in front of you from six inches away from your eyes, it seems like it's a massive barricade, when maybe it is only the height of a curb on which you can easily step.

We can easily extract ourselves from those situations or with new perspective, leap over those hurdles, or speak up and come up with a plan when the rain starts to fall.

We can admit to ourselves when we've created the problem in the first place. We lash out at others in order to extract ourselves from blame that deservedly should be on *us* for the predicament that we're in. It's the exact opposite of what we need to do. How does it make sense to diminish others in order to make ourselves look or "feel" better? Who are we blaming: the rain, the train, or ourselves?

Lashing out at others and placing blame is simultaneously the easiest and worst way out, but the path of least resistance destroys us in time. We have alternatives to being terrible to one another or blaming others for our own misgivings. There are other paths to take. The question is if we have the emotional intelligence and self-awareness to consider them.

Autonomy is ironic to mention in a book that explores relationships and teamwork. But we will never be good team members unless we understand the potential impact of our own agency. We don't have to wait for another to pull us from safety if we can do it ourselves. We don't have to diminish others to get what we want. We don't need to blame someone else for the behavior that led to the curse of rolling the stone up the hill or for us being on the train platform in the rain.

Let's do what we can to look inwards and to not be outwardly painful to others, even though we inevitably will be at times. That's life. It is because we are fragile creatures and we cause harm and make mistakes. That said, let's continually do our best to reverse that course.

We can move through a point of being stuck and at the same time not let cruelty drive us. When we strive to fill the gap between what we hope for and what we have, or what we aspire to and what we achieve, we can do that work without throwing someone else into the gap along the way. When we are on a train platform in the rain, what could make the difference isn't building an entirely new train system or anything equally immense in scope.

If we want to build a better now for ourselves and the people around us, we can start with something simple.

We can believe in the possibility of kindness.

4

BELIEVE IN THE POSSIBILITY OF KINDNESS to Escape the Trap of Pessimism

"To protect innocence from arrogance we carve this skin of stone and as the weights of caste and character layer with the years ... we drown"[1]
— Trial, "An Awakening"

PESSIMISM STARTS YOUNG.

I was five years old. I was living just outside of Chicago in Highland Park, Illinois, in a neighborhood that seeped with Midwest charm. Parallel streets with two-story houses and shade trees were the norm, each with a yard filled with kids, and often an occasional lemonade stand somewhere along the way to keep you cool.

It was summertime and I was outside on a sunny afternoon, walking up and down the sidewalk watching my brother play. I wasn't wearing shoes, because why not? The worst thing that could happen might be that I could accidentally step on a bee that was basking in the sun on a dandelion.

Life definitely wasn't terrible. Yet.

---

[1] Trial, "An Awakening," written by Greg Bennick and Timm McIntosh, Track 10 on *Are These Our Lives?* (Equal Vision Records, 1999), 12" vinyl.

My younger brother, Darryl, age almost four, was riding up and down the sidewalk on his Big Wheel. For those of you who have heard of the Big Wheel, you might recall seeing that it was a plastic tricycle for kids. But it was more than that. It represented absolute total freedom. The Big Wheel was a product of the 1960s, made wildly popular in the 1970s when parents realized that a plastic tricycle with a low center of gravity would probably injure their kids less frequently than having them ride a metal tricycle that was higher off the ground. Parents bought millions of the things. Everyone had one.

The Big Wheel had two small wheels in back with a seat in between. It had a large wheel in front of the seat, thus the name, and this larger wheel had pedals attached to it for one's feet. You can imagine, if you were three or four or five years old, and you had a Big Wheel, that it was the greatest thing that could ever happen to you. It was basically like having a Lamborghini. And that, obviously, was unbelievably awesome.

So, Darryl had a Big Wheel, and he was riding up and down the sidewalk on it. He would ride halfway down the block, to what probably felt as far away to him as if he had made it to China, he then would skid, turn, and ride back toward me. Always excitedly, and always with a giant smile on his face. This was a truly happy kid.

I decided to play a game with my brother. As he made his skidding turn far off in the distance and started back toward me, I decided to put my foot in front of where he would eventually be riding on the sidewalk. He started to head my way, and was pedaling faster and faster as every second went by.

I knew he had two choices. He was going to have to stop, or, as I expected he might do, maneuver around me. I figured he would have to swerve around me at the last possible moment. This was a great game. It was like the trust exercise when you fall into the arms of someone to strengthen your morale and trust in a teammate, only this was more exciting because it was with my brother. It was also better because a Big Wheel was involved.

As my brother got closer, his little legs were pedaling faster, and his smile was getting bigger and bigger. I was so happy because it was summertime and here we were – brothers – in the sun and playing a game together. What could be better? I loved my brother so much.

Twenty yards turned to ten turned to five, and Darryl's legs were a blur of frantic pedaling. His smile stretched ear to ear. What route was he going to take, and how could I possibly have come up with a better game?

I looked down at my foot and back up at Darryl, smiling along with him. But as five yards turned to three and quickly to one, I realized that the widest smile in the world wasn't a blissful summertime smile. I realized the truth too late.

Darryl's smile was a determined grin of pure evil.

He was playing his own game, the little psychopath. He didn't ride around my foot, or stop in front of it. With a triumphant squeal that matched my horrified scream, Darryl, this three-year-old monster, drove right over my foot. He intentionally rode right over it. And not just with the front tire, but by aiming accurately, with one of the back ones. This was a precision strike because it required some abstract aiming.

The pain was so intense that I was convinced in a moment that he had achieved a geometric impossibility and had managed to run over my toe with all *three* wheels of the tricycle. Realistically he might have actually done it because it hurt that badly.

I stood there screaming. The neighborhood watched in horror. I looked down and my toe was bleeding. The bumblebees napping on the dandelions, jolted from sleep, turned in shock without a buzz.

Amidst all of this, my brother was laughing. He skidded to a stop, and if he had been old enough to wear shades, I am sure he would have pulled them off and let the wind take his hair for a ride as he turned quickly and gave me a look of "How'd you like *that* game?"

That my friends, was the moment that pessimism started for me.

In that moment, I realized that things don't always go the way that I expect them to. I could be a victim of the world. And my sweet, little, innocent brother with his dumb face could actually secretly be a potential killer in disguise.

Thankfully, in the last half of a lifetime, my brother has fully redeemed himself. He has never repeated this terrible crime, and seems to be a well-adjusted father and a business owner. As far as I can tell, he has shed any inclinations to be the bloodthirsty demon he was when he was three. I like him again.

But as for me at the time, I was left to pick up the pieces of a life torn asunder by an act of savage cruelty, the likes of which the world had never known and which it has hardly seen since. Of course, I am being ridiculous. But you get the point.

Hope yields possibility.

I have often wondered where our earliest days of disappointment or betrayal are, and how that experience of them for the first time affects our mindset moving forward. Otto Rank, whom I introduced in Chapter 2, would have had something to say about this. Rank took the ideas of Sigmund Freud and tossed them out the window. Remember that Freud suggested that we start off as children and lust for our mother and are enraged at our dad for taking our love for our mother from us and that *this* disrupts our lives. Right. Freud obviously had issues.

Rank's more levelheaded approach of suggesting that trauma began existentially with the very act of being born resonates even today.

We didn't even have to lust after our moms or want to kill our dads for our lives to be psychologically challenging. What a relief. The circumstances of our lives make the trauma of birth and anything else beyond it worse for us. We are already traumatized enough by being born. It's challenging to find our way. Then you add to that the events that take place that make things more painful and complicated? It's no wonder we are a mess.

I blame Darryl.

The point is, it is no surprise that we are pessimistic. In whatever way it might be that the cruelties of the world made themselves known to you, at whatever age, you have choices to make. Whether you've been through such catastrophic hardships as I have been in the bee-napping-on-a-flower-disrupting, brother – betraying, Big Wheel – inspired, summer-destroying days of my youth, or something genuinely more difficult to manage, the fact is that the world is harsh. Once we find that out, we have a choice to make in terms of how we respond.

This choice is the turning point in our approach to the world and others in it. We can choose to believe that people are evil and that they will destroy and upend us. Or we can believe otherwise.

Thinking "this is not my day" while what you really mean is "this LIFE is not my day" is an example of that trap. All the while carrying a brooding sense that the worst is yet to come, we lock ourselves into a way of thinking where we lost the ability to have authority over our lives because we have given our power away to pessimism. None of that sounds fun for anyone.

This first strategy – believing in the possibility of kindness – works for me when I am most unsure about the cruelties of the world, and when it feels like everyone is Darryl running over my foot again and again and all I am doing is standing there. Sure, I could just move my foot. But the point is more to believe that the Darryls of the world won't run over it in the first place, and that if they do, we can move on without absorbing or passing along that trauma to others. That *new kind of human*, to whom I alluded earlier, is one who believes in kindness as a possibility. This takes practice, but I believe we are in a better place if we devote ourselves to that process.

The possibility of kindness helps us to escape the Trap of Pessimism. And that's really what it is. It's a trap for our hearts and minds, locking us into an existence that is reactive rather than proactive. We are often in defense of, rather than in support of.

When you could use this strategy:

- **Whenever you're overwhelmed by the chaos shown on the news and the relentless clickbait of social media**
- **When you feel as though the world is unnecessarily cruel and you need a reminder that humans are actually not always terrible**
- **When your team or friends are experiencing low morale and need to be uplifted to find their way through a difficult time**

(continued)

> (*continued*)
> - **When your outlook is negative and you need to lift yourself up so you can lift up others as well**
> - **When you need to get centered so you can move forward again**

I honestly think that this experience with my brother put the idea in my mind that "bad things happen to me" or that "I can't trust," and while I don't think it ruined my life, I definitely think it influenced it. The key is not that my brother did that. All he did was ride his Big Wheel over my foot. Anything that I equate between a child on a Big Wheel and the potential cruelty of the world is a story that I created myself. By creating that story in my mind that people are going to do hurtful things and that I need to be ready for that, I took that Big Wheel incident and magnified it a hundredfold. We need to be careful about the stories we create.

Pessimism is a strategically terrible place from which to live. It instills the idea that every client might screw us over, that every relationship is inevitably going to fail, or that everything we try to do is futile. I realized that I had to make a different choice and believe in the possibility that people are kind, that we screw up often, and that we can't condemn people by their worst action, or anything close to it.

I am going to say that again, because it's an absolutely essential component to being a nurturing contributor to the world. When we judge people on their worst action and condemn them for it, it's a statement about our own issues around futility and pessimism.

If we choose to believe in the possibility of kindness, we can start to see others, their actions, and their potential to do better in newly positive and proactive ways.

I started speaking about an idea called The Possibility of Kindness™ in the fall of 2020, after referring to the importance of it for decades as a team strengthening and leadership approach. People pay a lot of lip service to strengthening their teams and don't do the requisite work to ensure that we treat one another with grace. Leaders wonder how they can inspire and motivate and often miss that a powerful tactic to both is right in front of their eyes. When we believe the best about people, they start to believe it too, and their performance amplifies.

In the fall of 2020, the world felt like it was falling apart at the seams. The pandemic was in full swing, politics felt like a quagmire, and tensions on multiple fronts across the country were as high as they have been in years. Optimism wasn't part of our day-to-day conversations, and teamwork seemed like a lost cause. We had an incredible opportunity to come together and we squandered it.

To counteract the pessimism, I pushed forward with a couple of proactive initiatives, one rooted in taking action and one rooted in public speaking. In terms of action, my friends and I had made some energetic moves that summer in our community that have had reverberations for years.

Within a couple days of George Floyd's death in the late spring of 2020, I happened to move for a few months to Portland, Oregon. I was there right in time for the city to explode with political fury. As protests raged through downtown every night, my friends and I realized that we could do more for people in need than simply be amidst the protests. The protests were an incredible moment in history and truly were an immense historical response to longstanding collective trauma. The effect of that protest summer will be felt for a generation.

Late one evening in May of that year, while quickly escorting ourselves away from teargas as police and protestors clashed in Portland, we happened upon two men who were living in a small tent at the periphery of downtown. We asked them how they were doing. They said ironically that they were doing better than we were. They alluded to activists having their "butts kicked" downtown by the police. We asked if they had been affected by the protests. They said that tear gas and police munitions were disruptive but overall that they were OK. We asked if they needed anything, and they asked for food and water. I gave them a banana and a bottle of water, as that's all we had with us, and we continued our walk home.

My friend Andy joked that the most revolutionary act of the evening was the giving of the banana and the bottle of water, and what he meant was that feeding people and taking care of them is revolutionary in and of itself. The protests were historic, directed, and inspiring. They will be felt as reverberations for decades. The banana and the bottle of water don't come anywhere close to superseding them. Andy's point was, rather, that we can't forget the simplicity of taking care of people in direct ways amidst everything else we have happening.

> **Pessimism destroys everything in its path and things that aren't even yet in its path.**

We decided to keep that going. The next night we brought dozens of bananas and dozens of bottles of water. Then shortly after that, we brought sandwiches. Then we asked people, unhoused and unsheltered, who were being affected by the police and the protestors (through having their tents walked by every night and having street fighting disrupt their sleep) what they needed. We responded. Within a week, we had a dozen volunteers. Within two weeks, were in motion helping the community with food and survival supplies, and were conducting anonymous audio interviews with anyone who wanted to share their stories.

The Portland Mutual Aid Network, as we became known, has been active every week since then and has distributed tens of thousands of meals, and literal truckloads of survival supplies to people living on the streets. We have given out endless tents, sleeping bags, personal care products, snacks, drinks, portable heaters, and links to legal advice. It has even helped unhoused people in need of tattoo coverups get those tattoos covered so they could get jobs and get off the streets. And that's literally just the beginning.

The project was all about expanding our level of kindness and caring for people living beyond our typical field of vision. When we expand our horizons, and when we think in terms of kindness and beyond what we might normally consider, worlds of possibility open up.

I mentioned this story earlier in the book, but it's important to explore further because it was in this context, with the world falling apart, that we decided to make a different choice. We decided to focus on kindness instead of on rage. Rather than fight one another in the streets, rather than do nothing, and rather than engage in policy discussions, and most importantly rather than stay absorbed in pessimism, we decided to take action and do something positive and proactive, now. It was the epitome of believing in the possibility of kindness, in action.

Believing in the possibility of kindness opens up possibilities for connection, teamwork, and growth.

As is true when you build a better now, a reverberation effect starts with you that impacts and inspires others and leads to additional good things happening. That's what happens when we choose to focus on kindness and listen to the voices of others rather than fall into a state of only listening to our own voices. We realized that it was simultaneously possible to go in a different direction and also be effective.

But that reverberation is rooted in believing in the power of kindness. When you listen to people. When you *engage, listen, and respond.* That is key. We will be exploring it later in Chapter 10. That's when you have shifted from hearing your own voice to listening to that of others. When you believe in the power of kindness and care, that's when your customers and coworkers, teammates, family, and friends are going to feel seen and heard just like the people we served and continue to serve in Portland.

This perspective shift always feels so much more uplifting and makes me feel centered in this moment as I work to reclaim it. Rather than feeling suspected and apprehensive of people, we can move toward creating a culture of kindness. A first step toward that is believing that it is a possibility.

If you want enhanced customer care and client relationships, and if you want people on board with your vision for the future, don't consider the person at the other end of the conversation or transaction to be suspect, or as if they are a threat. Instead, believe in the possibility of kindness and the potential for people to be action partners with you, and see where that leads you. I expect it will be transformative. I think we have all had quite enough of feeling that the world is against us, or that people can't be trusted, or that everyone has something to hide until proven otherwise. We can create different energy and outcomes.

Be driven by kindness and consider people to be action partners and allies instead of adversaries.

In Portland, we saw the effects of that reverberation right away. We started to get messages from people in other parts of the country who were starting mutual aid initiatives like ours, inspired by what we were doing and serving all kinds of people in need. A burrito group in one city for hungry youth. Another with free menstrual products being distributed to women who didn't have access to resources. This isn't to even mention the hundreds of messages we received from other people, groups, organizations, students, and colleagues who wanted to share ideas and thoughts and help the project grow far beyond the ideas of those who founded or who were originally involved in it. You can find out more about the Portland Mutual Aid Network at portlandmutualaidnetwork.com and on Instagram at @portland mutualaid.

I think you're seeing the point. Amidst the backdrop of the pandemic, the protests, and the politics of 2020, amidst increasing tension and extreme anger, we took a different approach than to be swept up in rage or pessimism. Massive, nationwide, lasting changes weren't being seen immediately. We sidestepped the proverbial stone of infighting and resistance that was welling up around us. The effect on our local community by serving people with generosity has been substantial and literally thousands of people have been positively impacted. We chose to be driven by kindness. We were all transformed by that process.

Everything felt *tense*. And worse. The moment, and indeed the world, felt completely out of control. Things were getting aggressive. Aggression in time only breeds more of the same. It is a never-ending, always losing, spiral down in which no one ultimately wins. Being aggressive or intense toward others will slowly destroy you from within.

Take that, age-three Darryl.

When we believe in the possibility of kindness, it gives us hope. It lets us reclaim the moment in a way that embraces and reflects how we want to be treated ourselves.

Now let's go deeper … to figure out ways to escape the trap.

Believe in the Possibility of Kindness to Escape the Trap of Pessimism.

One of the main positive effects from the choice to move in a different direction that summer was that in the fall of 2020, I decided, as I mentioned, to speak regularly on The Possibility of Kindness™. What I didn't mention is that I started presenting this topic to very specific and unique audiences. The core concept, again, is that in the midst of aggression and intensity, we can build a better now by making different, healthier, more positive choices around kindness toward others.

The possibility of kindness, as I shared in these particular presentations, rests on three core concepts:

- *Be kind.* What a concept! That this even needs to be said, for someone who wants to believe in the inherent goodness of other people, seems unreal. But there it is, and here we are. Lead with hope rather than cynicism. Let kindness drive you. Have that be the baseline for your words and actions. It is clear to me that simple acts of being kind build up over time. When you offer kindness my way, it inspires me to offer the same to others. And vice versa. That in turn spreads and returns to you. It comes back around like a boomerang. Think about what you can do for others from the perspective of being a catalyst for kindness. To silence pessimism, believe in others' potential the same way you (hopefully) believe in yourself. Actively look for ways to enhance the lives of others through encouraging words and positive actions. It takes less energy than being mean-spirited, it costs you nothing, and you'll feel good about yourself at the end of the day. This can be intentional even in the midst of someone else's apparent *lack* of kindness. We can still make enthusiastic choices toward being good to one another, even when we ourselves feel slighted by them. There is no reason not to approach the world first and foremost with kindness. This should be true in terms of how we treat animals, and the world around us as well.

- *Say Yes!* Say yes to the possibility of kindness and to inclusion before you say *no*. Even if turning down a thought or suggestion is your initial impulse to an idea, a request for more information, or a move toward participation in a shared action, could make a huge difference in outcomes. Consider making a different choice. We are intelligent creatures who have the ability to reason and make choices accordingly. That's an incredible trait. We don't have to be rooted in instinct but can instead chart our own course through decision-making. We can focus on possibility rather than the alternative. Saying *yes* means that we open the door for new people, new concepts, and new experiences rather than condemn before they've even had a chance to manifest. Consider embracing new ideas, new connections, and new ideas as possibilities before we consciously deny them. Again, it costs nothing to consider alternatives and we might be introduced to someone new, a new idea, or a path we hadn't considered before.

- *It's up to you!* No one is going to make the choice for you to be kind or to work on yourself. No one else is going to make the choice to build a better now. You have to make it happen yourself. It's like going to the gym or starting that process. The best-laid plans, as the saying goes, often go completely off the rails, and the catalyst for that happening is often a lack of devotion in the form of a decision to not even try before one even gets started. We can make other choices. Through believing in kindness first and foremost, and then putting plans into motion through determined action around that concept, we will see results. But it's up to you to make that happen. It's the "dance like there's no one watching" analogy. How would you be in the world if no one told you to be kind and you still wanted to put something exciting into practice? Be that person.

The results of these presentations? People start working together more effectively, responding with incredible positivity, and supporting one another. They demonstrate the reverberation effect of compassion, and act differently in pressure situations. To do these speaking engagements has felt like a kindness revolution. I think back to Kevin

Costner in the movie *Field of Dreams* from years ago. *"If you build it, they will come."* I built this well-developed system about getting people to think in terms of the possibility of kindness, and people have been responding very enthusiastically. But here is the thing.

Guess who those audiences were? Corporate folks? Associations nationwide? International conventions in dramatic and exciting far-off locations? No. They were students at elementary, junior high, and high schools. Young people, along with the faculty members who support them. That's right. I decided to start a kindness revolution in the youth of America. Yes, when I speak to those audiences the concepts are at times simplified from what I spelled out above to relatable situations and dynamics for the audience, but the messages are still very much the same at the core. The ideas are strong and direct while being entertaining and engaging. I have spoken to tens of thousands of young people because I want to start a reverberation effect and build a kinder world.

When I tell students that the world needs more kindness, they agree across the board. When I ask them to be kind, say yes, and tell them that it is up to you, they totally get it. When I tell them that teamwork is an essential component to success and that they can ensure that through practicing kindness together throughout their days and the year, they respond enthusiastically and are willing to try harder. If students across the United States can respond intelligently and clearly by the thousands to these ideas, I think you can find it in yourself to do the same.

I decided that the one thing a world in crisis needed was a new generation of young people who would cherish kindness and care more than they would embrace antagonism and aggression. I feel like the world is the better for it. I realized that children need role models in one another, to lead them in lessons focused on the kindness that comes very naturally to them, and that the future depends on the building of a generation who moves in opposition to cruelty and selfishness. The Possibility of Kindness is the answer to that. Those presentations are continuous and ongoing.

Interestingly, many administrators at these speaking engagements take me aside to ask if I do the presentation for adults too. That is telling. They describe being unkind to one another just like the students have the potential to do. They describe creating outgroups and enemies from nothingness amidst faculty dynamics. That's real. In the midst of not having an enemy, people have a tendency to create one. Ernest Becker wrote extensively about this. Often that one who is created is the person with the most visibility. In this case read that as the school principal. One school principal told me that going to school board meetings was agonizing because of the cruelty to one another amongst the attendees. In response to my student offerings, I started presenting ideas and talks along these lines to teachers and administrators too. Our education system in future years will hopefully be more effective than ever by all of these people thinking about kindness in a new way.

After seeing the effectiveness of these ideas and how what we wanted for our communities and organizations started manifesting when we switched from pessimism to kindness, I began offering kindness workshops to other groups too, meaning associations and corporate groups too. It is an idea whose time has come. Organizations need it. Your people need this. They want it. We want to believe in the kindness of others and develop being kind as a powerful skill. Workshops and keynotes on kindness and how to benefit from new approaches to it are available.

While sociologists and psychologists will argue about whether human beings are aggressive or compassionate at our core, I think it is clear that our innocence gets lost over time as we delve into and are affected by ruthlessness, competitive adversarial relationships, and also of course by people running over our toes with their Big Wheel.

The thing is, we can return to kindness. And the effect when we do that on the people around us, right here and right now, is substantial. If others have negative intent, we can still be driven by kindness in response so that we don't do layered damage and bring ourselves down further. If they are kind in their intent, we will have reinforced them and helped them to know that we see their efforts as valid. And validating others establishes to them that they matter to us.

When we believe in the possibility of kindness, we:

- Discover that people around us are also inspired, empowered, and essential.
- Remember that without domination, collaboration becomes possible.
- Expand our ability to serve customers, collaborators, and community members effectively.

I have fallen many times into the trap of pessimism and the effect of a culminating series of cascading negative experiences, which then cause me to be pessimistic or negative.

Kindness reverses that. It is essential. Our world is increasingly harsh and unkind at times. We see it in our interactions with others, in our elected officials, in the news, and in our social media comments (don't read them!). We can do better. The effect is immediate. Believing in the possibility of kindness is like turning on a light switch in a dark room.

Importantly, and unfortunately, kindness doesn't mean that we move without cruelty ourselves. Every action having an equal and opposite reaction means that we are inherently cruel, most of the time without intending to be. We tend to take up too much space. We are capitalists in terms of how we manage our surroundings, often using too much physical area, along with too many resources. Our existence can be unfair at times not just to animals and the planet itself, but to one an other.

The nature of individual personality pits us against one another and the world, because part of us is unique. We are therefore inherently individualistic and exclusive to others who are not us. But the good news (yes...more good news!) is that due to being intelligent and rational thinking creatures, we can resist the influences to push away and exclusively individuate. We can move counter to our seemingly natural and socially developed tendencies and instead draw together with others on common ground. This perspective shift works wonders for teams.

What can you do to believe in others more than you suspect or deny them?

To assume that it is possible to live entirely without cruelty is unrealistic. But none of this means that we must embrace and endorse cruelty. Rather, we can work to diminish it rather than just have it run rampant. This is the responsibility that falls on a rational, intelligent, creative, clearly thinking creature. The level at which humans are rational and reflective is unique in the animal kingdom, and with that comes an immense personal responsibility rooted in each of us.

If human potential is about manifesting and maximizing change, development, and expansion, whether that's in business or in our personal lives, we have to lead first with that which creates the potential for us to experience growth. Kindness is that pathway and doorway between creatures who at their core want to connect. Opening that door creates opportunities. Closing it ends them.

Here are some techniques for reclaiming the moment and for seeking the something more that we want. These techniques are rooted in believing in the Possibility of Kindness:

- Take a step back and breathe for a moment when your feelings are heightened. The Possibility of Kindness means that when we are angry, or on the way to being so, or feeling frustrated by someone on our team, we can make a different choice and approach them in another way. Same is true for pessimism. We can make a different choice even if we have to push ourselves into making that choice. Going through the motions at first to explore being kind is far better than succumbing to pessimism and assuming that others have ill-intent and doing nothing, or worse. Remember, I was absolutely convinced that my brother was the devil. He wasn't, as it turns out. I just had to get past my own response, more than his actions. Darryl is actually pretty cool. You'd like him. Just don't let him anywhere near you if he shows up on a Big Wheel. #ptsd

- Reach out to someone. We shouldn't underestimate the power of just making a connection and what that can do to and for us psychologically. In a study published in 2023, researchers in marketing, business, and psychology from four major universities explored how much we appreciate being reached out to, and the effect of reaching out.[2] There will be more on this in Chapter 9 on building relationships. Reach out, send an email or a text, make an invite to go out, ask someone to meet and discuss

[2] Peggy J. Liu, SoYon Rim, Lauren Min, and Kate E. Min, "The Surprise of Reaching Out: Appreciated More Than We Think," *Journal of Personality and Social Psychology: Interpersonal Relations and Group Processes* 124, no. 4 (2023): 754–771, published by the American Psychological Association, https://www.apa.org/pubs/journals/releases/psp-pspi0000402.pdf

an idea. And do these things not just with your typical co-worker base or friend group, but with people outside of it too. The more you expand outward through kindness, the more we deepen inward. It's truly a win-win situation.

- Listen to people empathically, not critically. Give them the benefit of the doubt. Don't shut others down because your inner critic goes berserk and you feel an immediate need to be heard and to be right. Give people a chance. Engage them with in-person conversation. There will be more on this in Chapter 10.

- Remember that people's experiences aren't always conveyed on their face or in their words. I told a friend recently that beyond the bright lights of every major city is a dark alley filled with people wanting to live. My point was that the façade doesn't always convey the full truth of a situation, and that aspiration and hope often reside in places that initially don't seem to offer either. With that in mind, realize that pain points might not reveal themselves at first glance. The conclusions you jump to might mean that you're missing a next important step in getting to know someone on a deeper level.

- Avoid letting yourself make assumptions, especially with electronic communication. Pixels are harder to read than a human face but easier to reply to. If we take the purpose of language as a vehicle to convey meaning, with nuance as an essential element of that conveyance, it is no surprise that when reading pixels our innate insecurities and simultaneous desire lead us to protect our own ego. We jump to conclusions and defenses as we interpret and respond to perceived sarcasm or intensity that wasn't intended but managed unsurprisingly to be conveyed. So, take more time with electronic communication and write more, and descriptively, not less. It's a small bit of extra effort and the development of a habit – which always takes a little training – but the net result is that we will be communicating more clearly in a medium that is constantly developing. Being part of a solution and not a problem can come down at times to simply being more descriptive with our words so that they are more representative of what we are actually thinking and feeling and wanting to express.

- When our insecurities are tested, we feel vulnerable. Remember that humans are most definitely fragile. In a way it is no surprise when we feel weak or confused, or if we have the sense that we are being taken advantage of, that we can lash out. Making a different choice of how to respond in a moment like that means putting our humanity to the test. Our humanity is rooted in our intellect and rational mind. Therefore, tone down emotional response in the moment and return to a place in your mind where there are more intellectual choices to be made. Your team, your organization, your very connections depend on it. I am entirely convinced that we can do just that. To believe otherwise leaves us with no hope for a future, and without any bedrock upon which to stand for hopes of building a better now.

Having kicked off this chapter with lessons eventually learned about believing in the possibility of kindness, now we're going to fast forward to the moment where I learned about the next essential component of building a better now: focus. In addition to the ideas, I am going to teach you something that you can put into action that can help you get clear about your focus, and we will have fun doing it.

The moment that shifted things for me was a powerful one that led to the name of our next strategy. I like to call this strategy: *Keep your eyes on the knife.*

The idea behind this strategy and the realization that inspired it came early for me. I was twelve years old.

5

KEEP YOUR EYES ON THE KNIFE
to Resist the Allure of Distraction

"I feel like a juggler running out of hands."[1]
— Elvis Costello, "Welcome to the Working Week"

KEEPING OUR EYES on the knife is about directing our energy to what matters most and cutting through distraction. This is a perspective shift that is essential to personal and organizational productivity. It redirects energy that otherwise could have been lost, and more likely *would* have been lost, to minor concerns instead of having it remain with what is most important. I showcase this idea constantly for groups, and we will explore the how and why of that in this chapter.

Teams and individuals both function best when they have a sense of purpose. This strategy is about focus, finding it, reclaiming it, and keeping it on what matters to us even while threats to that focus are alluring all around. It is about how not doing this is a choice we make at our own psychological peril.

---

[1] Elvis Costello, "Welcome to the Working Week," Track 1 on *My Aim is True* (Stiff Records, 1977), 12" vinyl.

Distraction is alluring. The call of anything other than a task which we really don't want to be doing can't be denied. Research conclusively shows that distraction negatively impacts the quality of our work, our productivity, and our creative output.[2] But we don't need the research to tell us that. We know it is true.

Unless we are fully invested in the task before us, the allure of anything else can be inviting. We are always scrolling to the next desirable or entertaining thing rather than being situated and focused on whatever is in front of us. All this is in addition to the fact that what is potentially distracting us is algorithmically positioned based on our specific likes and dislikes. The average person checks their phone up to 144 times per day according to a study by reviews.org.[3] It is an itch we can never seem to scratch, and it is one that cleverly changes moment by moment, always enticing us. The Allure of Distraction is very real.

But before we get underway, let's start this conversation by taking a quick detour, ironic as that might be when talking about focus. I promise that this slight detour will give us context, and bring us back around soon enough.

When I was twelve years old, I had one goal, and one goal only: I wanted to be the greatest coin collector who had ever lived. I had been fascinated by coins for six years already, an experienced expert, at least in my own mind. I had made my first major coin purchase with money that took me an entire summer to earn. (It's a coin I still have). I was a subscriber to coin magazines. I was passionately obsessed, and on a mission.

In sixth grade, my middle school offered mini-courses after school on Wednesday afternoons for two hours a week. You could take classes in baseball, gymnastics, painting, Dungeons and Dragons, and

---

[2] Cyrus K Foroughi, Nicole E Werner, Erik T Nelson, and Deborah A Boehm-Davis, "Do Interruptions Affect Quality of Work?" *Human Factors: The Journal of the Human Factors and Ergonomics Society* 56, no. 7 (2014): 1262–1271, doi: 10.1177/0018720814531786.

[3] Alex Kerai, "Cell Phone Usage Statistics: Mornings Are for Notifications," July 21, 2023, https://www.reviews.org/mobile/cell-phone-addiction/ (accessed April 10, 2024).

a whole host of other things. The only class missing from the list of potential after-school offerings, in my opinion, was a class about coin collecting. Since this omission didn't fit with my life goals, and being an ambitious kid, I decided that I wanted a coin collecting course to exist. I petitioned the school for one.

The school principal told me that if I were to go and find somebody who was willing to teach it, they would add the coin collecting class to the roster of classes. He was likely suggesting this as a deterrent, thinking that I would never do it. But to my ears, this was as good as a resounding approval. Step one: accomplished.

I had my parents drive me to the next tiny town over. Southbury, Connecticut, was a side of the highway, neither-here-nor-there kind of town. That said, it was definitely more cosmopolitan than Woodbury, my quintessential New England town known for having more antique stores per capita than any other town in the world, and more cows than people. We didn't even have a highway nearby.

There was a small coin store in Southbury called Pony Express Stamp & Coin. As I walked into the store that day, I was ready for intensive negotiations. I had a $5 bill in my pocket. I walked up to the counter, eyes locked on the coin store owner. I pulled out the bill and held it in front of me with both hands, one on either end of the bill. I placed it flat on the counter and said, "My name is Greg Bennick. I go to the Woodbury Middle School and I will pay you…," I paused for impact, "… five dollars a week if you come in and teach my friends and me about coins."

Strive to say yes to possibility before convincing yourself of the alternative to it.

The coin store man looked at me and smiled. I remember it being much like the climactic scene of the classic early Western film *The Good, The Bad, and the Ugly* where the title characters are seen only by their eyes as they glance back and forth dramatically at one another over a series of minutes and no one knows what the next step in the battle will be. Mr. Coin Store reached out and picked up the $5 bill.

Folding it and putting it into his pocket, assumedly as a down payment, he said, "You've got yourself a deal."

Yes! I told him I would get back to him with details. Step two: victory.

I went back to the school the next day, ran into the office, and exclaimed, "I found the guy!" The school added *Coin Collecting* to the roster of classes. This was going to be the greatest experience in history.

The next week in homeroom, we each got a slip of paper with three lines at the top and one line at the bottom. The lines at the top were for you to write in order your first choice for the mini-course you wanted to take, then your second choice if that wasn't available, and then again, if that one wasn't available either, your third. The line at the bottom was for the school secretary to write on with the class you were officially signed up for. I put for choice one: *Coin Collecting*. If that wasn't available, I put for choice two: *Coin Collecting*. And then to make it a sure bet, and since I figured I was paying for the class, for choice three I put: *Coin Collecting*. I folded up the paper and confidently handed it in.

The next week in homeroom, with courses assigned and written in on that last line on the sheet, kids began excitedly opening up their folded and completed slips. They began to read those bottom lines that told them to which of the mini-courses they'd been assigned. From around the room, I heard "Oh, cool. I got Gymnastics!" and, "Oh, awesome! Ultimate Frisbee!" I smiled at all of them and their nice little hobbies. My destiny was to be greater. I opened up my slip with my life already spelled out before me. I truly, finally, was going to be able to be the greatest coin collector who had ever lived.

Roadblocks can yield possibilities. Be open to them.

But as I opened up that slip of paper, the words at the bottom didn't say *Coin Collecting*. It wasn't even two words. There had to have been a mistake?

At the bottom of my slip it said, *Juggling*.

Juggling?! What the heck were they talking about! Juggling?!? This was ridiculous. Inexcusable. This was a crime against humanity. I was destroyed. The school had annihilated my future. I sat and stared at that slip of paper for what seemed like hours. I ran home and told my parents what had happened. They started in with this whole song and dance about how you've got to turn a no into a yes and that someday they would tell me the story about how they met and that it would all make sense, and honestly, I couldn't care less.

My life was over. Step three: fail.

Finally, my didn't-know-anything parents won the argument, because they were evidently wise and smart and experienced, and I just was a kid. They suggested I go back and try the juggling. I said, "Fine," which as everyone knows is the international word for "Whatever," and "I hate this," and "Leave me alone," all rolled into one.

The next day I went back to school and dreaded the juggling class all day long. As the school bell signaled the end of the day, I dropped into the coin collecting class to let them know that I would be back when I could but that I had evidently been signed up to be a clown, mime, jester, and have my life ruined. I told them I would be back as soon as I could. I walked sadly to the room where "Juggling," the bane of my existence, was to be held.

I stood outside the door for a good long moment, either building up the courage or diminishing my frustration. Eventually, with a shrug signaling that life couldn't get any worse, I opened the door. As I walked into the class, I entered a room full of kids in various states of practice. Some were throwing scarves into the air. Or trying. Some were tossing beanbags and having them rain down and hit them in the face and were screaming in a combination of delight and terror. Some were standing with the objects stuck in their hands, afraid to even try and start.

On what do you need to be focused most?

But my eyes were immediately transfixed on one boy. He was standing about ten feet in front of me and with a look of immense concentration on his face, was juggling three brand new baseballs. His skills weren't perfect, with each throw lofting four or five feet into the air and his entire body repositioning under each falling ball before he tossed the next aloft. But he was keeping it going, and unlike his screaming friends, nothing he was tossing was hitting the ground.

I watched him juggle. It was like a light went on in a dark room. It didn't take more than five seconds before I very calmly said to myself, "That's what I want to do for the rest of my life."

Decision made. I was going to be a juggler. I excitedly ran home. My parents, both of whom had advanced degrees, one from an Ivy League school, heard my exclamation, "Guess what! I'm not going to be the greatest coin collector who's ever lived. I'm going to be the greatest juggler who's ever lived!!!" Their faces looked like the wide-eyed emoji mixed with the sobbing emoji all at once.

The thing is, when I said to myself while watching the boy juggle three baseballs, "That's what I want to do for the rest of my life," I couldn't have known that what I was really talking about in that moment wasn't just the juggling. I couldn't have known that throughout the course of my life, focus would often be nearly impossible for me and that any little thing would instantly throw me off course. I couldn't have known that I would someday, much later on, be diagnosed with ADHD. I thought I wanted to just juggle. But it was more than that. What I was seeing in the boy's juggling was something related, but at the same time quite different. I didn't want to just juggle.

I wanted to focus like him.

I had never been clearer about anything, and I had yet to fully understand why. In fact, it would be decades before I retraced the steps of that moment and what it signified to completely understand the full extent of what I had experienced that day. It would take a journey that started with learning to juggle, saw me perform on stages worldwide, had me practice endlessly, teach thousands of people to juggle, talk and listen to ideas about it, and to explore the art and history of juggling to finally understand why it was that I was attracted to it. The thing is, I haven't just juggled.

Increasing focus helps you reclaim the moment by being directed, intentional, and grounded.

I've used juggling as a tool for interaction. As a means of entertainment. As a technique for teaching and talking about focus. For confidence building. For exploring creativity. I have used it as a metaphor for communication and as a way of determining qualities of leadership. I have used it for corporate clients for decades and we've had amazing results. I've used it for associations and brought people together. I have offered it as a means of sharing ideas in universities and amazed students with ideas around it. The thing is, on a personal level it has been more about focus than it has anything else. Performing onstage – working with people and during my keynote presentations – is one of the times I am absolutely clear and laser focused. When it's "go" time, I am razor-sharp. Juggling has brought me to that place.

I have thought more about juggling and what it signifies than anyone you've ever met. I know, that doesn't sound like much to many people. That's like someone saying, "Be impressed. I am the world's greatest earthworm researcher." But you understand what I am saying. And no offense intended, to my legions of fans and readers who are earthworm researchers.

In terms of what juggling does, what it seems, and what it is, I have many angles of it dialed in. We'll get into that soon enough and I'll apply it to helpful tools that you can use.

But back to age twelve, because *that* brings us to the knife.

A few months after learning to juggle, I had spent what felt like hundreds of hours practicing. Every day, all day, it's all I wanted to do. I performed my first professional show at a birthday party across the street from where I lived. I was paid $5 for fifteen minutes, which meant I was making about five times minimum wage at the time. I also did my first speaking engagement with juggling, at an elementary school across from my own middle school, to kids not much younger than me. I spoke about the merits of juggling and how it can improve concentration, confidence, and physical fitness. I deemed myself ready. It was time to step into the big leagues and perform a public show.

> **If you want to build a better now, keep your eyes on the knife.**

There was an annual celebration in town and I was asked to march in a parade and then perform at a park in the center of town where people would gather around me to watch the juggling. Rumor had spread that I'd been developing my new skills. The town was small enough that anyone doing anything was news, and the fact that the Bennick boy was rumored to juggle and might showcase some dangerous items in his routine was enough to pull people out of the antique woodwork and surround the basketball court where my show was to take place. I had grand plans.

I'd secretly raided my mom's knife drawer in the kitchen and selected the biggest kitchen knife I possibly could, and two smaller ones to go along with it. No, my mom was not aware of this. The plan was simple but awesome. I was going to juggle beanbags or other basic items. Then in a quick switch, I was going to announce that I would be juggling knives. I would take a carrot and the biggest kitchen knife, slice the carrot exactly once with the knife to prove that it was sharp, and then juggle it along with the other smaller knives I'd selected and go down in the history of the town forever.

On the day of the show, things didn't quite go as planned.

I got excited. I got distracted. I lost my focus. I was paying so much attention to the reactions of the people around me and what they thought of me that I literally forgot to keep my eyes on the knife. I remember shouting to the audience as I held the carrot in one hand and the knife in the other that, "These knives are SHARP!" I remember them all responding with awe and dread exactly as I'd hoped. I remember holding the carrot in my outstretched right hand and bringing the knife blade down with my left hand to chop through the carrot. At the time I didn't think that to slice through a carrot once is more than enough to convince an audience that the knife you're about to juggle isn't a toy. But in the moment, I got lost in all the people around me and instead of one swipe with the blade, I was thinking about everything but the knife as I brought the blade down theatrically, dramatically, and unnecessarily, *four* times, once on each word of, "These…knives…are…SHARP!"

And I proved it. The carrot got shorter and shorter as I kept my eyes on the responses of the people around me. Their reactions were building. My intensity was too. In a performing mistake for the ages, I bypassed *the rule of three*, which says that audiences react well to things in sets of three. Perhaps I should have stopped on "are" instead of moving on to the fourth word?

I brought the knife dramatically down and without my focus intact, I chopped into my right index finger on "SHARP." This simultaneously proved my point, and also gave the locals something to talk about for the next few decades. I immediately grabbed the side of my finger with my right thumb and compressed it, hoping that the cut was minimal. It wasn't. The audience oooh'ed and ahh'ed even louder than before, at first because of my dramatic flair on "sharp," and then because they realized that I had chopped myself.

Their wonder grew as I juggled the three knives and even more so just afterward as I juggled three white rings because there was no hiding what had happened. The props soon became white with little red spots of blood from my gushing finger. The wound was substantial enough that even decades later, well into adulthood when I would go back to that tiny town and see friends who were there that day, instead of asking how my career was going and how keynote speeches and workshops and trainings were going, or for that matter how my life was going, my friends' first question was always to ask, "Do you remember the time when you almost cut your finger off down at the park during your juggling show? That was AWESOME!" Thanks, everyone.

> **Keeping your eyes on the knife is about keeping your highest priorities clear.**

OK, let's unpack this juggling experience because it's a big one. Like I mentioned earlier, I've spent my entire life exploring focus, what it means, how it can apply to each of us. I've taken juggling around the world. I've presented to the widest variety of people. From the most rural communities, literally performing in remote villages in Haiti to bring joy to incredible local people immediately after the 2010 earthquake, to professionally elite clients at fancy events in posh hotels in Singapore, I've turned juggling and focus into way of life, a lifetime of adventure, and have impressed some cool people along the way.

"The world's greatest juggler!"[4]

—Ray Bradbury

Yes! Ray Bradbury, the legendary science fiction writer and author of *The Martian Chronicles* said that about me, during a time when we would often write letters to one another years ago. We really did. For those who don't know, science fiction, in my humble opinion, got to where it is today because of a handful of brilliantly visionary people. Isaac Asimov, Robert Heinlein, Ursula Le Guin, and amongst those greats, Ray Bradbury. I was honored to be in touch with him. I once asked him, "It says on the backs of all your books that you are 'the world's greatest living science fiction writer.' Do you believe that, or are you simply someone doing and pursuing what he loves most in life?" Ray replied about his focus and dedication and said, "You are absolutely right! Doing what you love with all your heart is the answer to life! I have loved writing, every day, every hour. You do the same, dear juggler!"[5] What a guy.

But back to my ego-destroying, injury-filled, and ill-fated juggling performance in front of my town. Ray's opinion wouldn't have held much weight that day. The problem in front of my town is that the wrong thing took my focus. I was focused on what people were thinking of me and not on what I was actually doing. Distractions can be so alluring. After all, what if everyone liked and loved me? What an ego boost that would have been, right? Sound familiar? Likes and comments serve the same purpose.

But how does all of this apply to you especially since you don't juggle ... yet? What are the key concepts that we can take from my juggling performance that day? Here's another quote from Ray in one of his books that speaks to that experience in front of the town that day.

"Your mind's always juggling, isn't it?"[6] Most definitely relatable.

---

[4] Ray Bradbury, Personal letter to author, February 8, 1990.
[5] Ray Bradbury, Personal letter to author, February 8, 1990.
[6] Ray Bradbury, "The Fire Balloons," in *The Illustrated Man* (New York: Doubleday and Company, 1951).

Where is your focus? Is it on the action or the response? Is it on what you have to offer or how people might react? Is your focus on the task in front of you or on what the response to it might be? I made the wrong choice that day in front of the town. Instead of focusing on the knife in front of me, I had my mind on the reactions of the people and how cool they must have thought I was. And now I have the tiny scar to prove it.

We can do better than that for ourselves and the people around us. When we focus specifically and completely on the task, idea, and the intention of what we have to offer, we can keep the offering directed. We don't need to have what we do corrupted by expectation of a particular response or what people might think. This is a tremendous distraction that we can easily avoid. I get the allure. What if they cheer, what if people "like" you, what if what you do leads to accolades. Distractions. All of it. Do what you do because it's important to you to do. Not because of the cheering. Sure, think of the cheering, but don't have it be your primary goal.

For example, I don't speak for the applause I *might* receive. I perform and speak for the audience, for potential impact, and most importantly for the message to be communicated clearly. If I can reach *impact* from the ignition point of *intention*, great. I also speak, of course, to create fun in the moment. If the audience has a good time and responds with laughter and awe, then that is a solid measure of the focus I've brought to the delivery itself. Applause at the end of the presentation is simply a show of gratitude for the impact and power of the experience they have received. I always think that if I increase happiness in listeners, I will increase their potential for focus and connection. Subsequently, if we increase connection to one another, we will find ourselves empowered. But overall, the response is secondary to the quality of the delivery.

But let's take a big step back in terms of theorizing. I want you to have a visceral experience that sets you up for really experiencing prioritization, focus, and confidence. I am going to teach what I have taught countless groups at conferences around the world. I am going to teach you how to juggle. Don't skip over this section!

Juggling gives us perspective about ...

- Building a better now through focusing on what's most important
- Saying YES before we say no to open the door for possibility
- Being afraid to try and how it feels to free ourselves from that
- Experiencing steps toward success and the power of incremental learning
- Finding confidence from succeeding and the confidence to move through mistakes
- Learning from others and gaining a stronger team dynamic
- Creating immediacy in the moment and paying attention to what's in front of us

This is going to be fun. It will give you an experience of trying something challenging and new. Most importantly, think of this as an additional, measurable tool in your toolbox as you work toward improving your focus. That's one thing I love about juggling. It is a *measurable* skill. If you count the number of throws (or catches) you make, your ability to focus is directly tied into that ever-increasing number. Keep that in mind as you go along.

Ultimately, the lesson isn't as much about what you gain when you learn to focus as it is about what you potentially miss if you don't. Sometimes, what's at stake is a knife. Profit, whether personal in terms of accomplishment or financial, is often tied to one's ability to focus and a team's ability to move through distractions. So, the more tools we each have, and the more time we put in to practicing, the better.

Juggling isn't a distraction from the goal. Juggling is a powerful lesson on the way to the goal.

Juggling lets us discover little victories in the midst of a challenge. You will learn how you react to making mistakes, and how they impact your workflow. I asked a friend who manages hundreds of people about mistakes and what they signify, and he said, "The biggest hurdle I face is trying to get people to just try out a new idea and not be terrified of making a mistake." When we practice this skill, we get the additional benefit of thinking about whether or not a dropped ball ends the process, and then how willing we are to pick it up and try again, or if we turn away from the challenge. This is why this workshop has been so successful. People discover just how relatable juggling is to their day-to-day and work lives.

We'll also find a new relationship with control, because when you practice, you'll find that you won't be maintaining constant control because everything will always feel a little out of control. But as you learn, you'll find that its OK to have variables and then work with them when they arise. The more we refine our abilities to work with the unexpected, the more we maximize our potential as effective leaders.

Focus, confidence, and juggling are intimately connected. I asked another client recently what focus meant to them and their team and they replied, "We lose more time to distraction than I'd like to think about." Our ability to keep our eyes and minds sharp will help us resist the Allure of Distraction.

Step One precedes the actual juggling. Find something to juggle. Three consistent-sized objects would be ideal, no matter what they are. Just make them something reasonably palm-sized. Balled-up socks, tennis balls, beanbags from a kids' game, baseballs, delicate glassware. It is up to you. Just know that I bear no responsibility if you choose hamsters, hand grenades, or expensive heirlooms.

Step Two actually precedes the juggling too. Get warmed up. If you pull a muscle in your arm, leg, face from laughing, or throw out your back, I don't want to get angry emails from my publisher. In fact, while we're on the subject: *Prior to starting this or any other exercise regimen, please ask your healthcare provider for advice on exercise. The juggling lesson and ideas offered here are in no way intended as a substitute for sound medical advice.* I've done a lot of things in life, some better than others, but a doctor, I'm not. So warm up, stretch out, do some yoga, but do it safely.

Now we can get to the juggling.

Are you even willing to throw a first ball aloft?

The first thing you're going to do is center yourself. Mentally always. Physically definitely. Plant your feet about shoulder-width apart. If you're able, stand upright. (Note: Being able to stand is *not* a prerequisite for juggling!) Let your shoulders relax. Bend your arms so that your forearms are parallel with the floor. (Note: Having two arms is also not a prerequisite for juggling! I know of two highly successful one-armed jugglers, and for those taking it a step further still, there is a long-standing tradition of foot juggling in China that is well beyond my skill level.)

Note to left-handers: I am teaching as if every reader is right-handed. Left-handed comrades, you are me and I am you. I am left-handed as well. I feel your pain. It's a right-hander's world. You know what to do: Reverse the hand positions and you will be fine with the lessons.

Take a deep breath in. Let it out slowly. Take another. Let it out slowly too. Like really slowly. Not the kind of slowly where you're just trying to get to the next step. That's not slowly, that's "quickly." They are different. You want slowly. Like a Zen master during meditation. Remember, this is an exercise in focus. And reclaiming the moment is in part about being centered, which goes right along with slow breaths and sharpening our minds. When we are stressed, doubtful, living by way of our conceived notions about how something might go before we even try – we'd be wise to take some slow breaths in and out and then come back to center and calm.

Mistakes, if we approach them with the right frame of mind, are a roadmap to success.

> **What is your single juggling ball – the one thing that would impact you most if it dropped to the ground?**

If you haven't already, pick up exactly one of the juggling objects you've selected. Don't pick up all three, you overachiever. Just one will do fine.

ONE OBJECT: Hold your arms with your elbows bent, each at a 90-degree angle. Scrunch up your shoulders and then completely relax them and let them drop. Hold your hands in front of you, palms up. Start with only one ball! Hold it in your right hand. Keep your left hand empty. Pick an imaginary spot about six inches to a foot higher than each shoulder.

See the first graphic for reference. These drawings are from *your* perspective. Toss the ball across your body, at an angle from right to left, aiming for the imaginary spot six inches above your left shoulder. The ball will peak at that spot. When it falls, catch it in your left hand. Pause. This is a big moment. You're on your way to being a juggler. You've just learned half of the throws you need in order to be able to do this.

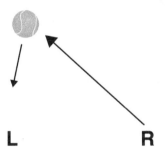

A wise philosopher once said that a thousand-mile journey starts with one first juggling ball. Well, maybe they never said that, but it would have been cool if they did.

Next, toss that ball back from your left hand across to the imaginary spot above your right shoulder. See the graphic for reference. Let it fall into your right hand. Pause. This is also a big moment. You've just learned all of the (read that as "both") throws that you need to be able to juggle. I've put a video of how to do this at gregbennick.com/reclaim so you can see instruction to help you along.

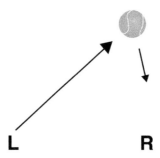

From hand to hand, and back and forth. Nice and easy. Try throwing this time from left to right. Take time to get comfortable with this. Work on throwing this first ball back and forth until you can throw from hand to hand ten times smoothly without dropping. Take time with this. Everyone learns at different rates of speed.

Some thoughts on dropping. A drop is a learning point on your way to achieving success. A drop is also an opportunity to increase your focus the next time you try. Do not, I can't repeat this enough, *do not* (did I say *do not?*) consider any drop a failure. It is a step toward success. That's not cheesy self-help language. That's seriously the best advice I could give you from a motivational and positive outlook. If you think of a single drop as a failure, imagine what that would mean the next time your phone battery dies, your stapler runs out of staples, your product launch is delayed, or the barista forgets a splash of oat milk in your coffee. Career over? Obviously not. There's always space to reframe a setback. Same is true with your juggling.

> **Don't be afraid to drop the ball!**

I actually highly recommend, as you practice, to also occasionally let the objects you're juggling fall to the ground. Get comfortable with making mistakes. Literally let the objects drop during your practice as you try the throws back and forth, and don't try to catch them. This is good practice in setback and making mistakes and remembering that not all mistakes are catastrophic. We are obsessed with perfection and being liked, as I showed clearly with the brutal knife-into-the-finger trick. This is a chance to practice the opposite of that by working on literally feeling the feelings that come up when we make mistakes and our flow gets interrupted.

Now, when I have presented for conventions of surgeons or rocket scientists, I remind them during this juggling lesson that for some people, making mistakes indeed is more significant than others – and you will understand for your own line of work what mistakes might mean for you. I mentioned a product launch earlier. I won't assume that a delayed release date means the same for everyone. But the point is, often we *think* a mistake is a tragedy, when it's really just levels equivalent to an empty stapler or that missing splash of oat milk. That's up to you to determine, but I often make things bigger than they need to be. I think we all have a tendency to do that.

Try something beyond the limits of what you think you can do.

OK, let's move on to the next step in our lesson on increasing focus.

TWO OBJECTS: Hold one ball in each hand. Throw the one in your right hand across your body to that imaginary point above your left shoulder. See the next graphic for details. As the ball starts falling toward your left hand, toss the one *from* your left hand up diagonally across toward the imaginary point above your *right* shoulder. They make an X in the air, but you're not throwing them at the same time. Catch the first ball as it comes down with your left hand. Catch the second ball as it comes down to your right hand. Stop and take a moment to reflect on what you just did.

One solid note. Don't throw these two at the same time. The rhythmic cadence of your hands alternating throws should be aligned with your voice as you say out loud, "Throw, Throw, Catch, Catch." It should be smoothly timed and not rooted in terror of making mistakes.

If you happened to catch one, great. If you caught both, amazing. If you caught neither, that's good too. What an opportunity to try again and learn. I learn so much about myself when I am trying something again and again. Juggling gives us a prime opportunity for that. It is OK if one (or both) fall! An important note is that the goal isn't to have anything be continuous yet. Throw those throws, then stop, reset, reflect. Then try again. Practice until you can do this exchange ten times in a row without dropping. Again, I've put a video of this at gregbennick.com/reclaim so you can have visual instruction to guide you through your practice session.

Don't reach your hand up to catch a ball; instead, let it fall down to your hand.

- **Pause between each attempt to relax and recenter.**
- **Give yourself time to celebrate victories and reset after failures.**
- **If you find yourself throwing too far forward, stand facing a wall or a closed door.**

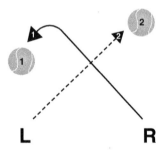

THREE OBJECTS: It is time to stop listening to yourself that you can't do this, and tell yourself instead that you can. Give it a sincere try. I promise there are valuable lessons on focus, persistence, determination, and possibility here even if this doesn't become a new career for you.

You are going to hold two objects in your right hand and one in your left hand. The two in your right hand are #1 and #3. The one in the left hand is #2. Always start with the hand that has two. Ball #1 is thrown right to left just like you did when I was teaching you with only one object. When it reaches its highest point, it starts to fall.

Remember: This is just like step one. You can do this. You've done it already.

As Ball #1 starts to fall from that imaginary point above your shoulder, Ball #2 is thrown across and diagonally left to right. It starts to fall. This is just like step two. You have done this already too! You are further along than you think. People often wait for the proverbial other shoe to drop in terms of there being some complicated secret to juggling that has yet to be revealed. But if you've gotten this far, you literally already know all the throws you need to know in order to be able to do this successfully.

> **Mistakes, if we approach them with the right frame of mind, are a roadmap to success.**

Do not give up! I will assume Ball #2 is defying gravity and in the air above your right shoulder as I make a couple observations for you. This is the point where most people, conditioned to easy fixes, instant gratification, and simple solutions, figure either they will come back to this later (that's generally a fib, and you won't) or they decide already that they can't do it and let negative thinking prevail. Neither is acceptable. Onward to juggling victory! And message me if you're having trouble. I can always post more resources to gregbennick.com/reclaim if you'd like. After all, I said we are in this together, and the only way we will get to a kindness revolution *and* a juggling revolution is if we all succeed.

So, back to Ball #2. When Ball #2 is aloft, Ball #3 is remaining in your right hand. When Ball #2 is at its highest point and starting to fall, throw Ball #3 from right to left just like you did with Ball #1. This is important: It is not a new throw and anything you're not needing anything other than that which you already have learned. Remember that you've already done all of the types of throws you need to learn. You're on your way.

> **Don't listen to an internal voice that says you can't do this. Tell yourself that you can.**

From there, you alternate throws, right then left then right then left, always from the hand where a ball is incoming. There will always be one ball in the air.

Remember, every throw out of your right hand is exactly like the first throw you made. Every throw out of your left hand is just like the second throw you made. For support, check out the videos on my website.

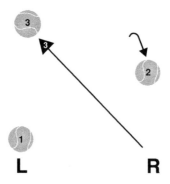

You're almost a juggler! This could be an alternative career path for you. Or for your boss. Remember to alternate your throws, don't rush the process, and above all…focus!

The only juggling ball I want you paying attention to is the one in the air. That's the one that matters most. The ones in your hands are part of the juggle, but you've got them more under control than you think you do. In fact, you've got everything more under control than you think you do. The ball to pay most attention to is the one in the air, not the applause that might come when it lands in your hand.

Would you rather try and fail or never try at all?

Take a moment and think about this from a life perspective. You are juggling your work and the rest of your life and all the elements of that. What is the one juggling ball on which you have to focus because it is the most mission-critical of all the tasks before you? What is absolutely essential that you focus on today? Can you reclaim this moment from the chaos and distraction of the world so that you can make sure that one ball doesn't hit the ground? As you practice your juggling you will see that you will be training yourself in how to focus and pay attention to what matters most.

And what if the stakes were higher? What if one of the objects you were juggling was a knife? I bet you'd be keeping your eyes on it more than the beanbags or tennis balls or whatever else you'd selected that were safely resting in your hands.

Keeping your eyes on the knife means that you're paying attention to what matters most even in the midst of chaos. Juggling can teach us how to do that. Juggling is a natural lesson in focus and concentration and prioritization. If we want something more for our lives, learning to focus is a tremendous step in the right direction.

"When you learn juggling, what you learn is how to feel with your eyes and see with your hands because you're not looking at your hands, you're looking at where the balls are, or you're looking at the audience."

—Michael Moschen, juggling artist and friend of the author

Everyone learns at a different rate of speed. So don't be down on yourself if you don't get this on the first or even the twentieth attempt. It took me a considerable while longer than it takes many people. But I learned how eventually. So will you. Learning to juggle is not as hard as you might think. It is not the same as becoming adept at quantum mechanics, learning fluent Mandarin Chinese, or actually meeting someone cool through a dating app. This, you can actually do.

Remember the benefits. You are learning to prioritize which object to focus on, why it matters, and what it feels like to make a mistake amidst trying something new. You are owning this process.

In a world in which our every move is potentially swayed by our purchasing power combined with a baited hook dangling in front of us, ownership of the self becomes an essential tool for our psychological survival.

Now, let's go deeper to see how we can get clear on your intentions and heighten our focus.

> **Keep your eyes on the knife to resist the allure of distraction.**

When you could use this strategy:

- When you're distracted
- When too much is coming at you too quickly
- When navigating a decision that involves risk and reward
- When you or your team must get back on track together
- When decision-making is a challenge due to having too many choices

I was once asked why I felt I was an expert in focus, and my reply was that between juggling, managing my own brain, and examining societal and business trends over the course of decades, I know what I am talking about. But beyond my own practical applications for understanding focus, there are others who have delved into the topic from really interesting perspectives too. I've studied their ideas at length and from them I draw immense inspiration.

In 1967, a French social critic named Guy Debord wrote a book called *The Society of the Spectacle*. Debord was part of a group called the Situationist International in Paris, who, through their use of language, words, text, slogans, and posters, were trying to disrupt the status quo of society. Theirs was a revolution not by overthrow but by reframing the way that we looked at the world around us. In society, the "spectacle," Debord notes, was the representation of life that we have used to replace actual life.[7]

---

[7] Guy Debord, *The Society of the Spectacle* (Detroit: Black and Red, 1983), 2.

> **We are living in a time where allure is everywhere. It's no won-der that we are confused and distracted.**

According to Debord, we have created a world in which the spectacle reigns supreme and life itself is secondary or nonexistent. The spectacle is the illusion of life that surrounds us. It is the images that surround us. It is the images and the movies and the photos that represent a life we should or could be living. It is the focal points that change our perception of our place in the world. For Debord, a primary concern was not with the fact that these focal points exist, but rather the importance that we have placed on them. His concern was that they have supplemented and replaced actual living with the representation of living. Debord contended that those consumed by the spectacle exist as actual opposition to the individual.[8]

Debord's contention was that we no longer feel, for example, that we have to fall in love, because what we see around us are representations and images of love. We also no longer feel that we have to have adventures, because we see movies filled with courageous heroes who are having those adventures for us. We see images that place us potentially in the status of the elite in terms of our possessions and our desire for them. Yet the desire *for* is not the having *of*. And these things, or rather these perceptions on our part, these shifts of consciousness in our own mind away from who we are and where we are, cause us to be living a non-life to Debord. This is a representation of life, but not life itself. This is a scary thought, given how little time we have!

The life we are living is often a life in response to the spectacle, not a life in pursuit of our own desires and ambitions. As a result, we live as if alive, as if adventuring, as if falling in love, as if wealthy: financially, personally, societally. But in fact, Debord would suggest that we are devoid of those things because our life has been consumed entirely by the spectacle. It is not a very heartening statement on society, or on us.

---

[8] Ibid., 61.

This is heightened by what I described in the juggling metaphor: that when we are distracted by the spectacle of the applause, we forget about the jugging itself. When we are imagining the standing ovation or even the potential boos from an unhappy audience, we are not focused on the knife in our hand or, worse, spinning in front of our face.

What I've always found interesting about Debord's ideas is that we indeed are surrounded by a spectacle and in fact are more so now than he was while he was writing. I like to think of the psychoanalyst Otto Rank, who in 1933 suggested in a letter to a friend, "… for the time being I gave up writing – there is already too much truth in the world – an overproduction which apparently cannot be consumed."[9] Let's think about that for just a minute. The world was suffering from an overabundance of truth, the enormity of which could not be consumed due to the sheer volume of it. The "truth" that Rank saw was evidenced in the cumulative books and papers existing at the time and he felt that no one could ever navigate or wade through all of that.

Can we even imagine what Otto Rank would think of the overabundance of truth that exists today? What would he think about the millions of articles on Wikipedia, the generative nature of new supposed truths by ChatGPT, the posts on TikTok and Instagram, the videos on YouTube, the web pages, texts, DMs, Facetime calls, and so on? If Rank couldn't consume the truth that was available in 1933, he certainly would feel that it was like drinking from a firehose if he attempted to do so today. Generationally, he would be completely lost. But on a level of his humanity and intellectual capacity alone, he would be overwhelmed. But we are too.

If we look at the Situationist International, who were trying to disrupt the way that we perceive ourselves in a world with skewed social perception, we come to realize rather quickly that if in 1933 we were overwhelmed by truth, and if by the time 1967 rolled around, we were overwhelmed by spectacle, then certainly today in the midst of every influence and distraction, we are fully consumed.

---

[9] Excerpt from a letter by Otto Rank, February 8, 1933, to friend Jessie Taft, who later served as his biographer. Published in Jessie Taft, *Otto Rank: A Biographical Study Based on Notebooks, Letters, Collected Writings, Therapeutic Achievements, and Personal Associations* (New York: Julian Press, 1958), 175.

> **We are overwhelmed by truth, opinions, ideas, and images, and all of them seem to matter.**

This doesn't feel like an advantage for us. New generations have come up entirely digitalized, with the barrage of ads from every angle an inherent part of their online world. This onslaught has been normalized, even if it is far more intensified than that experienced by millennials and far more yet again than Gen X, the last generation to have grown up with memories of both an analog and a digital world and who still remember actually calling people on phones. Ah, rotary dial phones, and even weirder, public payphones. Gross. I don't miss them. I'm thankful most people have no idea what they are anymore. The point is, those who grew up digital are not immune to distraction and input. It has just been woven more expertly into their reality.

The issue at hand runs deeper than simply *how* each generation is distracted. The real substance of the problem is about psychology, control, and our agency as we will soon see.

One generation's spectacle, it seems, is another's truth. The rebellious nature of each next generation is reflected in the values it holds in contrast to the generation that preceded it. For example, the generation affected by World War II, the Baby Boomers, seems to have grown up idealistic and hopeful. Gen Xers followed by bucking the trend of idealism and harnessed materialism. Individuality was at the core of their identity. Millennials followed, turning to a global perspective, and while oriented to the self, developed a worldview rooted in environmental concerns and a global perspective shifting away from the individual. Gen Z has embraced a web, in more ways than one. Interconnected, mobile across various digital networks, they have moved the global perspective digital and interact with the fluidity that environment allows.[10] Along with each generation, the potential for distractions has multiplied.

---

[10] Tracy Francis and Fernanda Hoefel, "'True Gen': Generation Z and Its Implications for Companies," McKinsey & Company, November 12, 2018, https://www.mckinsey.com/industries/consumer-packaged-goods/our-insights/true-gen-generation-z-and-its-implications-for-companies.

> **We are creating distractions faster than we can adapt to them.**

Why is it that the spectacle and the Distraction have grown so exponentially? It ultimately is because we *want* it, across generations and increasingly over time. We want there to be an overabundance of truth that we cannot consume. We want there to be a spectacle that we are absorbed into so that we do not have to take as much ownership or responsibility for agency in our lives. We want to be consumed and we want to try to consume all of this material so that we don't have to challenge ourselves to push further.

For while people can indeed adapt, we adjust so inadequately, and have so in the last ninety years as distractions have multiplied, that we could never have grown accustomed to being able to manage everything or absorb all of the input around us completely. No generation has figured out how to do this. We are creating faster than we can adapt. As a result, today we are impossibly consumed by the digital, and for that matter the heightened images of the analog, world, both of which for many have been embodied by the Distraction. Not even distraction from anything necessarily, but overall, as a constant flood of images and ideas.

It is certainly of interest that each of the generations, increasingly as time goes by, are seeing emotional well-being and psychological balance impacted by digital interaction. It is a double-edged sword, as the same mechanism that impacts mental health also makes it possible to more easily find networking and support.[11] Down the rabbit hole we go.

Each generation is increasingly, by their own measure and demand, consumed in the digital age.[12] We can see from a more widespread

[11] Erica Coe, Andrew Doy, Kana Enomoto, and Cheryl Healy, "Gen Z Mental Health: The Impact of Tech and Social Media," McKinsey Health Institute, April 28, 2023, https://www.mckinsey.com/mhi/our-insights/gen-z-mental-health-the-impact-of-tech-and-social-media.

[12] Michael Dimock, "Defining Generations: Where Millennials End and Generation Z Begins," Pew Research Center, January 17, 2019, https://pewrsr.ch/2szqtJz.

intergenerational, and overall human, perspective that the competition for eyeballs and minds is fierce.

The distractions we face on a minute-to-minute basis likely pale versus the distractions we will face ten years from now. They certainly far surpass the distractions faced in years before. But if we go on the assumption that we want it, that we desire it, that we need the distraction, then what is the issue at hand? The issue at hand is us, and our psychic equanimity. The issue at hand is choice.

We don't know what to keep our eyes on or what to choose for our focus.

We are constantly scrolling through social media, supposedly choosing what to watch. This is the illusion of choice. We are constantly on the spinning wheel amidst distractions, choosing what part of it to apply ourselves to in the moment. But we are not spinning, or for that matter stopping, the wheel. We are not stopping distractions. We are not extracting ourselves from them. And we certainly are not living aside from or in spite of them. We are collectively consumed by them.

> **Liking can make us miserable. Oh, the irony.**

The problem amidst all of this is ultimately one of susceptibility. Sound bites, buzzwords, and algorithmic influences are perfect and dangerous bait for influencing us away from goals, dreams, and ambitions. This is the case not just for any one generation but for all of us. In addition, and along with that, when we see imagery disconnected from emotion, or emotional images without context, we react accordingly and viscerally, often without thought. Where having a short attention span leads us, is a path without critical thinking in which we are all too easily influenced and swayed from what matters most to us. If our goals and our *now* truly matter, we need to respond differently than our first impulse might dictate. Focus and clear thinking is essential, lest we be thrown off course.

We would be unwise to fully demonize social media or advertising or marketing because of the interconnectivity it offers and the ways it provides for us to network and seek resources. Many have shared powerful messages and ideas while gathering momentum for causes, or taking another angle and promoting themselves wildly, due to social media. Advertising and marketing have been massively redefined, and this process is ongoing. None of these elements are inherently evil.

But it is important to note for the sake of our conversation about the Allure of Distraction how easy it is to get pulled into the illusion of choice: We feel as though if we watch the funny video, we are truly connecting with our humor, or if we watch the adventure movie, we are connecting with our adventure, or by commenting on the post, we think we are pushing the limits of our connectivity with others. In all of these, we might imagine that we really are living that life. In reality, we are losing ourselves, quite literally.

In researching this book, I asked young people in high school settings what they felt about social media and their involvement in it. While the study wasn't measured, or technically scientific, the anecdotal nature of the responses rang as true to me because they were consistent across different audiences and ages and delivered with sincerity – at least as much as I could read in the room. When asked how they felt about their lives overall, high school students responded with the following:

"We have to be careful because everything is being seen all the time. Everything we do is watched."

"I don't know who to trust because older generations don't understand social media and what we go through, and at the same time everyone our age is immersed in the exact digital world that we are. So, who can we turn to for advice?"

"It's not easy being part of a peer group who are trying to understand the world we are in while it's happening and developing at the same time."[13]

Guy Debord would have nervous fits over this. We attempt to maximize likes and absorb all of the reels, the YouTube videos, the

---

[13] Anonymous classroom responses, received during in-person group interviews conducted by the author in Portland, OR, and Seattle, WA, with age groups in classes ranging from 7th through 12th graders. Fall 2023.

comments, the Instagram stories, all while trying to stay ahead of algorithms that are constantly shifting and which change the rules of the game. The question becomes: Are we simply absorbed into an illusion of choice, or are we being proactive in how we focus? Are we putting energy into vibrantly deciding to definitively live in a way that is nurturing, fulfilling, awesome, inspiring, and powerful? Is our efficacy as creators and activists, action takers and business leaders, family members and world changers as impactful as we believe when we are simply clicking on the representations of those descriptors? Likely not.[14]

It is like thinking of the audience applauding instead of being the performer and actually communicating. I was not an audience-applause-creator that day in front of my town. I wasn't hired to be an applause-creator. I was invited to the event, as I am still to this day, to be a communicator and performer. But amidst the Distraction, I forgot that.

If we want to reclaim the moment and build a better now, meaning if we want our lives back even the slightest bit, then we have to rein ourselves in from the Allure of Distraction. This doesn't look like destroying the digital world, but rather remembering that we are at stake when we give our attention away. We need to remain slightly analog amidst a digital existence. At the very least, we need to be keeping a watch on how we are pulled into distractions of all kinds because the loss of choice is a loss of the self, and not keeping our eyes on what is most important to us can be destructive.

This is hard to do. There are alluring distractions at every turn. We can resist, but distractions seem to come from two main sources: everywhere and all the time. Whom do we follow, literally and figuratively, for guidance? How do we chart our own course somehow amidst all of it? The Canadian rock band Rush had a lyric on their *Hold Your Fire* album in a song called "Second Nature" that captured the feeling for me of being pulled in too many directions at once. This, by the way, was an album that featured a graphic in the center

---

[14] "American Trends Panel Survey Methodology," Pew Research Center, July 2020, https://www.pewresearch.org/wp-content/uploads/2020/09/SMEfficacy-MethodsTopline.pdf.

of the lyric booklet of a man juggling three fireballs, so it fits well in the context of this chapter!

> *Too many rapids*
> *Keep us sweeping along*
> *Too many captains*
> *Keep on steering us wrong*[15]

It is easy to be absorbed by the Allure. Are we choosing or being chosen for by algorithms that learn what we want to see and present that for us?[16] How many of us have gotten lost in a hundred and one different things to do and then realize that we didn't do the *one* thing (the knife!) on which we'd planned to focus?

What's your excuse for being immersed in distractions?

When I'm on stage, I often use juggling as a metaphor. It fully exemplifies chaos in motion. I often take four white juggling balls and one blue juggling ball and put them in motion at the same time. With five objects in flight at once, I ask the audience to simply watch the blue juggling ball. I've put a video of this at gregbennick.com/reclaim to demonstrate the concept.

Now, as juggling is a function of throwing back and forth from hand to hand, we can imagine that each of the juggling balls – and focusing on blue will make this easier to see – follows the same pattern as it flies through the air. But if we only keep our eyes on the blue juggling ball, we see a very simple throw-and-catch repetition between the right and left hands over and over again. That ball simply flies back and forth, but in the midst of four other juggling balls also doing

---

[15] Rush, "Second Nature," written by Geddy Lee, Alex Lifeson, and Neil Peart, Track 4 on *Hold Your Fire* (Mercury Records, a Division of UMG Recordings, Inc., 1987), 12" vinyl.

[16] Maximillian Boeker and Alexandra Urman, "An Empirical Investigation of Personalization Factors on TikTok," presented virtually, ACM *Web Conference,* April 2022, 2298–2309, https://arxiv.org/pdf/2201.12271v1.pdf.

the same thing, it all looks like absolute chaos. This is a perfect metaphor for choice and focus, and specifically for keeping our eyes on what matters most amidst distractions.

This is a lesson in what it means to apply extra focus to one thing amidst chaos rather than be overwhelmed completely by the chaos. We make a hard choice when we focus just a little more on that one blue beanbag. But it is an easier path than trying to maintain focus on the entire swirling pattern flying in front of our eyes.

So then, what do we do when we have a number of priorities moving at once in the workplace, or in our lives? We need to keep our eyes on the highest priority, mission-critical, essential-to-everything task that the moment contains. Think of this as the metaphorical knife spinning in front of us.

What is the single juggling object in your life that has more of *your* focus because it absolutely requires it? Amidst the chaos of payroll and contracts and human resources and sales and marketing and leadership and teamwork and communication and all of the elements that go into a business … or amidst communication and connectedness and navigation of emotion and all the elements that go into a relationship: What in the moment can you do to help resist the Allure of Distraction and push forward and create real progression that matters to you? If we are indeed reclaiming this moment for ourselves, and if we indeed want something more, what allows us to build a better *focused* now is to identify that one blue juggling ball.

What is your most important task? What's your one blue juggling ball? What are you most focused on?

If it was a blade, whether metaphorical or real, upon which you were focused, you should most definitely have more of your attention in that direction. We have to choose to choose, and we often don't have the benefit of a knife edge to know where to look. Sometimes we have to dig a little deeper and wonder which of the things before us needs our attention most.

If everything feels like a priority, we still have to make a choice, and to do this requires accepting some degree of sacrifice. This is going to feel like moving against the grain because we might have to make choices that prioritize something at the expense or sake of something else. There is power in choice, and while the experience places us in a challenging position, in choosing we are claiming agency over our lives. We are reclaiming the ability to define our direction – maybe incrementally, maybe just for a moment. In the moment we are deciding that we are not simply going to be consumed by spectacle. We are not going to be overwhelmed and therefore (mis)guided off course. For an indecisive creature living in a world immersed in spectacle, to choose a solid and meaningful direction in the moment is deeply empowering.

Let's talk about what can help set the stage so that you have the best fighting chance at feeling empowered by the choices you make. What can help us focus when that often feels like a lost cause?

- *Imagining outcomes is an incredibly valuable tool.* What are the outcomes of focusing on a specific task or initiative, versus the outcomes of focusing on a different one? What happens if I don't get that one thing finished that I know is mission-critical? Is the fallout manageable? Really think about that. Sometimes the assumed fallout is more intimidating than the reality of a situation. This brings us back to the idea I brought up earlier about how we create a story in the absence of one, and that it is not always one that serves us well. I apply focus to the one task that would produce the worst outcome if it doesn't get completed. That sort of thinking helps me immensely.
- *Having a single mission can help focus everything.* When I was onstage with Trial, whether playing in front of 3,000 people or 300, I would speak between songs to set up what we were playing next and to give perspective to the lyrical content. I would often have to do this in only a couple minutes at most, amidst distraction from all around (people yelling, feedback from the monitors, equipment going out). All that, and I would have to communicate in a way that was deeply impactful for the audience. The approach I always took was to have a singularity for the speech, for the idea I was working to communicate. One

central idea, with every word aiming toward that goal. Maybe it was to let people know to value connection. Perhaps it was to ask people to take action for a cause. Whatever it was, it was singular. Choose a path and stay in that lane as you go. Let the focus on that mission drive the rest of what you do so that you charge toward that endpoint, regardless of what might influence you or inspire you to veer off course along the way. And now some ideas that might seem basic – but they are essential too.

- *Putting down your phone can reset you.* This goes along with taking a moment for yourself. I have a mode I've created on my phone called "Writing," which, when I have it on, doesn't show me any alerts, notifications, or updates. That way, the desire to just see for a second what the sudden notification is, isn't there. Sure, that's an ADHD preventative measure. But it serves a greater purpose. It frees me from the Allure of Distraction. For as we all know, that desire to see, just for a second, what has come up on our phone means that an hour later we are reading about the next solar eclipse, the history of the vacuum cleaner, or the lives of jade plants and sharing posts about them with our friends, who then share other videos back with us about their pruning and care…and all of a sudden, we've lost two hours. All because we wanted to just check and see who that one text was from in the first place.

- *Diet and exercise make a huge difference.* To start, I've been 100 percent drug, alcohol, caffeine, and tobacco free for decades. A clear mind is a focused mind, and a sober mind is a powerful tool. I find that when my mind is clear, it can stay sharp. Diet and exercise have immediate effects on my ability to focus. They help to support a clear sense of self, which then allows me to choose what I should be focusing on most. Even just getting up and walking around the room a couple of times, if that's all you have time for, is like a reset button for the mind. Do laps around your office. You will look weird and be healthier. That's a good combination. I like weird.

- *Getting outside is essential.* Change your environment and you will change your perspective. The illuminated rectangle in your hand can be replaced by the glowing circle in the sky. If you're struggling with the idea of detaching yourself from screens, just think of going outside as trading one glowing shape for another. Your eyes, your focus, and your Vitamin D levels will thank you. And no, don't stare at that glowing sphere. Just bask in it.

- *Meditation keeps you sharp.* I do ten minutes a morning. I am not a monk or an expert on transcendence, but I know that meditation absolutely helps me get centered to start my day. It lets me concentrate on the proverbial knife, or at the very least puts me in a mental position to be able to identify the thing that most demands my attention that morning. All that, and it is relaxing too. We often get swept up in the idea that doing more, multitasking, will help us be more productive. I find the opposite can be true. Focus is key.

- *Deep breathing centers your mind.* If meditation isn't your jam, try this because it's similar and easy. Throughout the day, take a couple breaths amidst the chaos that are just for you. I take deep breaths in with whatever is on my mind, then slow breaths out to let it all go. To do this methodically, sit in a chair with an upright posture. Relax your shoulders. Position your head so that it is sitting directly on top of your spine. Keep your hands in your lap. Breathe in slowly through your nose while counting silently to five. Wait a moment. Exhale through your mouth on five as well. I work to repeat this for a minute or two. Not long enough that I slip into napping, but long enough that the clutter on my mind gets a bit more organized. Even the most intense person will benefit from the grounding kinesthetic sense one gets from slow breathing and the psychological effects of letting go. I've talked to a number of executives who carve out similar time to do the same. Grounding oneself in the midst of chaos or intensity is a way through to success, not a block against whatever it is you're working on. If you don't have even a single block of ten or fifteen seconds to breathe and reclaim the moment for yourself, then I'd delegate some work elsewhere so that you can be less overwhelmed and more effective through including self-care amidst your work day.

■ *Knowing when you work best can help you work better.* Knowing *when* you focus best throughout the day can make an immense difference in your ability to stay on track and to keep your eyes on the knife. When are you most sharp? During the day I tend to be a jumbled mess of distraction, likely because that's when everyone else is awake and in motion. I tend to be on fire with creativity and action later at night.

So, what *is* the knife? What does that mean to you?

The knife is the idea, person, concept, task, goal, or mission that would be irreplaceable if it were to fail or fall apart. It is the game changer. It's the focal point of your passion in the moment. It's the one thing that you can't live without. That's where your focus needs to be. If that knife comes your way and you've got your focus intact, you'll handle it without catching the business end due to distraction.

The knife is what truly demands your attention. Its outcomes matter most. It is what holds the greatest impact if you find yourself accidentally distracted, whether by allure, out of desperation, or for the sake of applause.

The threat of somehow messing up with the knife has filled this chapter, but I want to make sure that we don't put too much weight on the potential that a mistake will *completely* derail us. Often, we can correct what we've done wrong. Part of building a better now is working through self-doubt. Another part is having the confidence, even in the midst of challenges or momentary failures, that ultimately, we will make it through, even if we have to take a step back and reassess. Keeping our eyes on the knife certainly diminishes how many major mistakes we will make, but it will never negate their existence completely.

Let's not let ourselves get immobilized by the prospect of a mistake. Rather than imagine a setback as an endpoint, let's perceive the chance that we might experience defeat as a basis for inspiration, pushing us to reach toward greater possibilities.

6

CULTIVATE A REVOLUTIONARY MINDSET to Break Free from the Deception of Defeat

"The place in which I'll fit will not exist until I make it."[1]

– James Baldwin

"TELL ME THE story again, Mom," I asked.

The simplicity of the question makes me sound like I was a child, but it was only a few years ago. I was at my parents' place, sitting up toward the end of the night before bed. My mom was sitting across the room poking around on her iPad. She looked up and smiled. She knew exactly what story I meant.

I've been raised by revolutionary thinkers. My mom changed careers every ten years, regardless of how things were going. She did this so that she always stayed fresh, never still. She was an aerobics instructor back when people wore leotards and leg warmers and had no idea what they were doing physiologically. They just jumped around until they were really sweaty and then kept going. She was an

---

[1] James Baldwin, from a 1957 letter to his friend Sol Stein, reprinted in *Native Sons* (New York: One World Books, 2004), 72–73, Kindle.

amazing aerobics teacher too. My brother and I could never keep up with her workouts. I grew up watching her destroy rooms full of people, mostly men, who thought they were showing up for an easy hour of movement and instead got a lesson in pain. After she taught aerobics, my mom became a hypnotherapist, and even though I didn't believe in it any more than I believed in the Easter Bunny or Santa, she eventually won me over, proving both me and all other naysayers wrong by helping countless people lose weight, stop smoking, and feel better about themselves. I would watch it happen week after week. She wouldn't allow people to keep their stories intact about being defeated. Revolutionary thinkers can't handle that sort of thing. While she didn't put it in these words, she saw defeat as a deception. She continually told people to shift their perspective and to keep going.

> **"If they give you ruled paper, write the other way."[2]**

After being a hypnotherapist, she ran an educational center for kids with learning disabilities and convinced them constantly that they weren't defeated. Her message was that learning was a road, not a destination, and that they should keep trying. After a decade of that, she worked as a personal therapy assistant and chair class instructor for elderly people, letting them know to never give up. At the same time, she was a speaker, connecting with audiences on the topic of "Exercising as We Age," sharing ideas on challenging ourselves to keep moving even when it got hard to do. My mom, in a word, was a total badass. Revolutionary thinker, level eleven.

My dad, at face value, could have been seen as a corporate guy, but he was way more than that. He was a suit-and-tie executive who was a disruptor decades before the term became cool. He worked for major

---

[2] Ray Bradbury, *Fahrenheit 451* (New York: Simon and Schuster, 1967). Mistranslated when used by Bradbury. Originally: Juan Ramón Jiménez as "Si te dan papel rayado, escribe de través; si atravesado, del derecho," *España* magazine, November 20, 1920.

multinationals and for banking firms, as a decision-maker and consultant. What made him a renegade was the approach he took to every day of his career as he challenged authority, worked his own angles on situations, and thought around corners to create possibilities. He ultimately was truly the most revolutionary-minded on the day he started his own business working for himself doing exactly what he had done for others all those years. He figured, why wear a suit and commute into the city when he could wear shorts and work at home? I like to think that he was the first remote worker. Live your life on terms you most believe in and have values supporting that path. This is the way of the world changer displayed on a personal level.

I've learned an immense amount from both of them about the Deception of Defeat and how to manage it, and I continue to. They've inspired me to change my perspective on feeling defeated when I have doubted myself and have taught me how to think with a revolutionary's mindset when defeat appears before me as a deception trying to convince me that all is lost. It often – or more accurately most always – is not a point at which all is lost. The Deception of Defeat would have you believe otherwise, though. During times when I have felt bound by the deception that things were over, they constantly reminded me to believe in myself first and foremost as a foundational steppingstone for moving forward.

Believing in yourself is a revolutionary act.

My mom, ready to tell the story I'd asked to hear, put her iPad to the side.

My dad was lying on the couch, and he perked up with my question. Mom gets animated when it comes to stories. A natural storyteller (the apple, it seems, has not fallen far from that tree), she brings her full self to center stage when it comes to relaying a story. My dad chimes in from time to time with comedic bits to spice things up. They are sort of like Penn & Teller, but a bit more senior, and they don't do magic, or shoot each other in the face with guns onstage, or live in Las Vegas, or have a TV show, or have bank accounts packed with millions of dollars, and my dad actually speaks. But you get the idea.

Mom went into performance mode.

I had heard this story many times before. In fact, I'd not only heard it, I'd been opening my keynotes with it for the better part of a decade. But recreating the story in my mind and hearing from the source were two totally different experiences.

My mom said, "Well…," and the story started once again.

The year was 1958 and summer had turned to fall in Wilkes-Barre, Pennsylvania. On this particularly rainy night, there was a dance getting underway at the community center on South River Street. The dances were regular, and they always gave the youth of Wilkes-Barre a chance to listen to a DJ spin records and socialize. On this night the youth had a chance to be inside and have fun while having a reprieve from the weather. Eight hundred teens were converging on the community center.

As the Pennsylvania youth started to file in, separated between young women in one line and young men in the other, all of the women could be seen wearing long dresses. That is, with the exception of one young woman.

It was unheard of for women to be in anything other than long dresses at the time for a social event like this. But this young woman didn't care. She decided to make a bit of a fashion statement on this particular night and to be a bit of a fashion revolutionary. She was wearing slacks and a blouse – unheard of for young women at the time.

As she got closer to the front of the line, she sensed resistance, and by the time she was next in line to get in she could tell that there was going to be an issue. As the woman in front of her walked inside, the dance officials took one look at this young woman's outfit and, with a protest on moral grounds, barred her from the dance.

She walked dejectedly outside. She had been dropped off half an hour before by her brother, who was now long gone on his way to some other adventure. There was no way to reach him, or for that matter to call for a ride home: We were decades before cell phones and texting. The rain continued to fall.

Back at the door, the lines were getting shorter as more and more people filtered into the dance. The guys' side of the entrance was having a problem of its own. There was a young man who had approached the door. He was looking good. He had a new haircut, a flat top, and he was wearing a long overcoat.

What he didn't realize is that at the last dance, a young man with a flat top and a long overcoat had started a fight and was kicked out and banned from all future dances. As this next young man on this rainy night walked up to the door, he was mistaken for the guy at the *last* dance with this new coat and crew cut. Since that last kid was told that he could never come to another dance again, *this* young man, mistaken for him, was kicked out of the dance, by mistake.

There were 798 people inside the dance hall. Outside, in the rain but thankfully under an awning, there were two: a young man with his crew cut and a young woman with her pants. Neither was sure what to do. They couldn't call home. They couldn't walk home. They couldn't go inside.

The young woman – who many years later would be my mom – and this young man – who many years later would be my dad – were standing under this awning and they shared an awkward glance. It was still raining. It was still 1958. They'd been presented with the greatest "no" that they could imagine in the moment. This is what defeat looks like.

But then the guy looked over at this young woman and thought, "She's dressed pretty cool." She thought the same thing about him. He smiled at her. She smiled back.

He decided to make his move. And here I am.

Boom! What a story. Two people facing defeat turn it into a solid *yes* amidst a situation that had clearly tried to shut them down. That's the key to that story for me. They turned a no and the seeming end of their process into a yes and thus into new possibilities.

When you could use this strategy:

- **Whenever you have not gotten what you wanted**
- **In case you need a blast of personal empowerment**
- **If you want to feel that the world is possible to transform**
- **While you're in a moment of feeling hopeless and defeated**
- **Anytime your team needs to step into their creativity**
- **When you could use a reminder that possibility starts with you**

I love this story mostly because of how my mom and dad look at one another after they tell it, even after more than half a century. But it also gives us a reminder of what we can do when a situation that seems like defeat is handed to us. Is that defeat absolute? In this case it could have seemed so, but it definitely wasn't. That's the lesson. If we default first to not thinking "this is the end," then we create (and it's revolutionary to create) the possibility that the situation is a beginning. That's not ridiculous positivity. It's a match for the fire that is within us in the midst of it potentially being extinguished.

My parents could have ignored the moment and missed out on a lifetime together (married sixty years as of this writing!). They might have thought their night was over, but their life together had just begun. They could have focused on what *didn't* happen. They could have focused on what they *hoped* to happen. They could have focused on what other people *wanted* to happen to them.

Instead, they reclaimed that moment from what could have been a disastrous evening, and made it their own. They imagined a different outcome from defeat and created possibility from it. They wanted something more.

How many times have I shut myself down because I assumed defeat was absolute instead of even considering the chance of success developing? I do it all the time. Defeat is a deceptive and challenging adversary because we quickly convince ourselves that no forward movement is possible and that we've done everything we can do. In doing so, we shoot ourselves in the foot. Having a revolutionary mindset and shifting perspectives is the ignition point for possibility.

My parents didn't have to create a new series of teen dances, change social conditions, or transform the planet. They just needed to reclaim their moment. They didn't build their future, they built their *now* and did it on their own terms. The future – *their* future – flowed from there.

> **When we build a better now, we set ourselves up to be able to do that for others as well.**

As my mom got to the end of the story, I was as enthralled as always. I'm a romantic at heart. And even though I'm not married and have never had kids, I still really appreciate the idea that a moment between the two of them turned into such a brilliant and amazing life together, plus marriage, plus kids. They started dating that night and never looked back.

But wait! There's more! On that particular night, this wasn't the end of the story. Mom kept going. I always figured there was more between Dad making his move and "here I am." But now I got to hear about what happened next.

My parents got married and were living in Philadelphia, where my mom became a teacher at an inner-city school, one that didn't provide many opportunities for students. So, my mom did. She held the school's first field trips. She put on school assemblies (where she read classic literature to the student body, who had never heard anything like that before). She was a point person for student trust. This was a double-edged sword, as students started to confide in her about potential violence between rival factions at the school and she decided that it was time to get out before her conscience took a hit. For her own safety, she had to leave.

My parents ended up in a suburb where she got a job at a safer, more sterile school. Early in the school year, a faculty meeting was called where introductions were made amongst new staff. Mom sat in the back and happened to be chewing a piece of gum. As she awaited her turn to be introduced to the other faculty, the principal turned to her from the front of the room and said, "Mrs. Bennick, I'm not sure what school *you've* come from. But here at *our school*, we do *not* chew gum during faculty meetings." There was an icy-cold staredown between them. My mom thought to herself that her last school had issues of actual violence. This school evidently had such a beautifully safe learning environment that their biggest concern was gum. She defiantly took the gum out of her mouth, walked to the front of the room, dramatically opened her fingers to let the gum fall into the wastepaper basket, and then walked the walk of shame back to her seat and sat down.

During the next available break that day, she went to the school office and asked to use the telephone. She called my father at work, and told him, "When you're done at work, I want you to come home. I don't need this job. I don't want this job. They reprimanded me for chewing gum. I'm done here. Come home after work. I want to get pregnant."

Mind. Blown. I know. This is the concept we all fear, the idea of our parents hooking up. But the effect on me was the exact opposite of what you'd expect, because for the first time, like a lightning bolt going through me, I knew who I was, and where I'd come from.

I basically jumped out of my chair, unphased that I'd just been told about my conception. "Wait, what!?" I shouted. "You mean to tell me that I was conceived in an act of rebellion?!?" My parents laughed. I was an act of defiance. I'd made my living as an artist and sung in punk rock bands and traveled the world speaking about believing in possibility and building a better now because this was my genetic makeup.

My mom went on to say that I was born at a teaching hospital, where fifty students-in-training watched from levels above the delivery table as she gave birth. She laughed and said, "You were born in what was a theatrical performance for medical students, and the first sound you heard was their applause."

Mind. Blown. Again. An entire life on stage in front of people inspiring them, laughing with them, creating wonder, and building a better now, and I was born into performance? How perfect could that be! First standing ovation at age five seconds. Well done, Baby Greg. He bows, and as the doctor slaps his butt, Greg begins crying. *Curtain.*

Unphased by roadblocks, side-stepping issues that arose, my parents were the first in my life to show me that Defeat is a Deception. It's a mindset, and as hard as it might be to shift that mindset, there's no denying that the same experience seen from different perspectives can have remarkable outcomes. If we take a step back and do some intellectual work, we might literally change how we see an experience. Research shows that two people can evaluate the same experience differently even in terms of our internal landscapes and how we perceive the experience.[3] That internal landscape is key.

---

[3] Anil Seth, "The Big Idea: Do We All Experience the World in the Same Way?" *The Guardian*, October 3, 2022.

To have a revolutionary mindset doesn't mean you burn the city down. In fact, it's the opposite. It means you are building up. When a seeming defeat is in front of us, we are at our worst when we define ourselves by it without questioning it. This goes back to us listening to ourselves rather than talking to ourselves about who and what we are and what we want. We have to disrupt the sense of being defined by things not going as we hoped. Studies show that teamwork strengthens when we have a positive mindset.[4] Imagine a team trained in the idea of positive reinforcement, self-esteem boosting, and encouragement. It would reap a dual benefit: people being more positive and engaged, as well as a stronger team dynamic overall. Teams who want to be effective, and individuals who want to remain engaged and inspired, have to learn to overcome The Deception of Defeat.

The Deception has a single trajectory: to impact our sense of self-worth and to undermine our self-esteem. It wants only to have you stop believing in possibility. It instills the feeling that you are ruined when something doesn't go as you hoped. You feel more of the deeply embodied frustration and resulting cynicism that has slowly seeped into our psyche from a generation of being overpromised and underdelivered to. The world changer who wants something more strives to sidestep this trajectory like you would a truck barreling toward you off the highway when you're in a bookstore.

Self-conscious individuals are empowered individuals in a world that tends toward absorption into the negative. We can do better than to be consumed by that mindset. When defeat surrounds and encroaches upon us, we indeed want something more.

Now let's go deeper … and imagine the power of seeing the world from new perspectives.

---

[4] Jack Green, Carl T Berdahl, Xin Ye, and Jeffrey C Wertheimer, "The Impact of Positive Reinforcement on Teamwork Climate, Resiliency, and Burnout during the COVID-19 Pandemic: The TEAM-ICU (Transforming Employee Attitudes via Messaging strengthens Interconnection, Communication, and Unity) Pilot Study," *Journal of Health Psychology* 28, no. 3 (2023): 267–278. https://doi.org/10.1177/13591053221103640.

Cultivate a Revolutionary Mindset to Counteract the Deception of Defeat

---

It was summer, around 7:30 p.m. I had come to that point in my comedy show where I always did something unique, even to me. I'd realized a year before, while on tour across the American West, that my shows had become standardized. I used the same routines every time and decided that I needed to mix it up from now on by adding a routine that would always be different. The show, a comedy juggling show at the time, was themed to community and coming together, and this particular event was no exception. The stage was outside in Montana, and the audience consisted of about four hundred people ranging in age from teens through adults.

The routine was simple in its concept.

I would juggle a machete, an apple, and then a random third object from the audience, suggested from and by the audience. The audience would actually offer three different objects as possibilities, and from the stage, I would let the audience choose which of those three was the one that I would juggle with the blade and the apple. It was fun, and based on a routine I'd seen the famous juggling troupe The Flying Karamazov Brothers do when I was thirteen. I never forgot it, and though their version was wild and involved a challenge, incredible theatrics, and ultimately the threat of a pie in the face, I figured my stripped-down version was fun for audiences regardless and solved a problem for me: It created a situation where I never had any idea what was coming, and it meant that every single show had a break from the sameness of the last. I could therefore keep things fresh.

On this particular day, I looked to the audience and said I needed an object. People always raise their hands with different things. Someone in front raised a shoe into the air. I pulled it onto the stage. There was a huge commotion from the right side of the audience. I looked over and someone had a pinwheel, the type of toy that you blow into or hold into the wind and it spins. Undoubtedly hard to juggle. The audience was intrigued. I asked for it to be brought to the stage.

While it was on its way, there was a commotion to my left about a hundred feet from the stage, on a level of joy that has never happened before in the history of human beings. There were people cheering, laughing, and screaming jubilantly. A massive amount of people. I put the pinwheel down at center stage next to the shoe and turned to my left to see what the commotion was about. What I saw was astounding.

There was a young man, maybe 16 or 17 years old, and he was entirely surrounded by his friends who were cheering him on. This young man had the biggest smile on his face that I've ever seen on a human being. It was almost as if the smile extended past his face, into the air around his head. He had one hand up in the air and was leaning on his friend with his other hand. But what was in his raised hand was most astounding. It was the object that he was asking me to bring to the stage to juggle.

This young man had removed his own prosthetic leg and was holding it up in the air as an invitation for me to consider juggling it. Yes, you read that correctly. He was laughing wildly. His friends were cheering him on and everyone around him, including him most of all, were jubilant. There was no possible way for me to unsee it. I wasn't sure if I should say yes to it, but by now the entire audience had seen it too and *everyone* was cheering. I asked that the leg be brought up on the stage. His friend brought it to the stage as the seas of the audience parted for him to easily make his way to me.

I had the audience cheer loudest for which object they wanted me to juggle (sorry, kid with the pinwheel). Obviously, they enthusiastically picked the leg. At the time, cell phones weren't as developed as they are now, and I told the audience I would pay $50 cash to the first person who could capture and present to me a video of the moment if I could successfully juggle the leg.

I picked up the leg, said very few people in the history of the world. I juggled it with a machete and the blade, said fewer. I steadied myself before I started. I thought a million thoughts about what I might say if I dropped the leg. I thought about what I might feel like if I succeeded. Then I paused, focused on the task at hand, and with a deep hopeful breath, tossed the leg into the air.

I juggled it back and forth for a few rotations and then I stopped with the leg held high and the audience went absolutely wild. The ovation was tremendous. I loved that we were collectively cheering for the young man who offered his leg as much if not more than we were cheering for the performer who had juggled it.

After the show was done, a little boy came up to me with a cell phone in his hand and said, "Mister. I think I have the video you wanted." He had a postage-stamp-sized video on his mother's flip phone. I had him transfer it to my laptop, and I paid him $50 cash – which he walked away clutching in awe as if it was a million dollars. I have that video, and I'd be happy to show it to you sometime when you get in touch with me.

What I like to think about is how powerful it was that this young man broke free from the Deception of Defeat. It wasn't at all about how he lost his leg, but the way he brought hundreds of people into laughter and awe as a result. His perception and approach to the world had shifted. He side-stepped the Deception. Where is the rulebook that says if you lose a limb you use that fact to bring overwhelming joy to hundreds of people? It doesn't exist. This revolutionarily thinking kid wrote that book that day.

Talk about wanting something more and getting it.

He definitely reclaimed the moment and he built a better now for hundreds of people through a self-conscious decision to be willing to enter into an unknown space for which there was no precedent whatsoever. I like to think about what he'll be like when he's eighty years old and his grandkids ask, "Grandpa, tell us the story about how you lost your leg?" I hope he replies, "Now, why would I do that? Let me tell you about the time this guy *juggled* my leg!" A lifetime of joy created because this revolutionary thinker, in the moment, was willing to put himself in an unusual and creative position for the benefit of others.

We can learn so much from that young man. What are the limitations that we each put on ourselves? What are the limitations that are *actually* on ourselves? We can think beyond the scope of what's in front of us, beyond the scope of our reality. That day, it was almost as if that young man created a new reality of which none of us were yet a part. And once he was there, he invited us all in to experience it with him. Talk about a *new kind of human.* He had entirely vibrant perspectives from which we'd all be wise to learn.

I will never forget that young man or the lessons we can learn from him about defeat and success, engagement and inspiration, and making sure that even if it's unconventional, we can approach situations with an entirely new mindset. In terms of our potential to innovate and create, with that young man as a guide, our potential is limitless. Defeat is only a mindset.

> **We need to rethink defeat so that it doesn't immobilize us.**

We walk a fine line between being afraid to succeed and at the same time afraid to fail. I've often done a keynote called "Don't Be Afraid to Drop the Ball" about stepping into the unknown and taking risks along those lines. It is about peak performance from the perspective of overcoming worry, fear, apprehension, and The Deception of Defeat.

How many of the following statements from workshop participants sound like your experience or your cohorts', day to day in the life that you lead?

"I have to work really hard to keep my focus."

"I have so many things going at once that it always feels like something is going to crash."

"There's always something out of control that suddenly demands my focus more than anything else."

"I can hardly keep up. But I do my very best, and I manage to keep things moving."

"There sometimes seems to be no way to have everything not collapse."

"It feels like I have to somehow stay on top of every situation at all times."

Do any of these statements sound familiar? How about:

"Everyone has their eyes on me? I can't possibly make a mistake."

Or, "If I let one thing slip up, everything will fall apart like a house of cards."

Think like a juggler for a moment. The potential for mistakes isn't going anywhere. We have to sidestep that mindset if we want to succeed.

Mistakes: the bane of our existence in a world where perfection is in front of us all the time. In what we watch. What we see. What we hear. What we experience. We live in *like* culture. Perfection is a tall order to keep up with. How can a juggler even *try* to succeed if we think about mistakes as being the end of the road?

The perception of defeat is often nothing more than a deception.

If you're a business leader or people manager, what you do is not easy work. People have good days and bad. They are unpredictable. They have certain needs and ongoing issues. You might have someone balancing budgets and timing, or arranging schedules and examining regulations, or leading research and development. The team has a thousand moving parts. Alternatively, if you're a solopreneur, you're doing it all yourself.

None of that is easy, but none of that has to be constantly perfect. It's OK to learn as we go and to develop as we grow, and if we encounter a defeat, to sidestep the narrative that we have failed overall.

Setbacks don't have to be catastrophic. Setbacks of whatever kind can be momentary resets. They can even be victories if we think in revolutionary terms. What seems like a day-ending loss could be a leg-juggling victory or a marriage that lasts for sixty years. I often find that when I drop something, the audience actually loves it. They bring me along for a ride because my first impulse is "Ugh. I dropped." But it is the experience of two different people seeing the same thing from different perspectives. The audience doesn't say, "This show is over. He dropped something!" The audience thinks, "I can relate to him more now because he is imperfect and human." Some of my greatest moments and performances have come when people see something they didn't expect that humanizes me to them. These are immense opportunities, not defeats.

I often default to feeling defeated during times when I need an excuse to justify not wanting to try again. Let us please leave lazy for another day other than this one. There is always another chance to try again to get what you want. That is, unless of course you're dead, which would be bad. Dead defines the number of chances you get to try again. Let's please not be dead. Instead, consider each new moment to be a potential ignition point, whether for sharing an idea that inspires a room or asking someone to juggle your leg, which then inspires hundreds.

Beyond the parameters that you've created in your daily work and life so that you feel safe, there is another world waiting. It is a world in which you make different choices when presented with the deception that defeat is absolute. This is a world within this one and separate from it. It's a world that doesn't appear before us immediately unless we make a choice to create it, just like James Baldwin's powerful epigram that started this chapter.

It's no wonder that sometimes we can't see beyond defeat. We embrace it for a reason. It keeps us safe from challenging ourselves. We create the path of least resistance in our response to the world, and we end up adrift amidst what happened, rather than steering our way with a sense of possibility through what is happening now or what could happen next. It's the difference between being defeated and done, and inspired and hopeful. Success might be intimidating, but that fear beats the regret that would come along with not ever trying at all.

Let's take a look at why success is intimidating. We don't want to watch the world go by as we hesitate. Let's dive into all of that and explore what is possible.

7

LEAP INTO THE DARK to Embrace the Possibility of Success

"What we want we must create; what we risk will be regained."[1]
— Trial, "Unrestrained"

YES, I QUOTED my own band for a second time. It is my book. Shush.

Creativity is terrifying. Connection is terrifying. And oddly enough, success is terrifying. Leaping into the dark is about taking a *courageous step* forward, not even toward a specific goal necessarily, but instead to deny stagnation when we otherwise have the impulse or the inspiration to get somewhere. If there *is* a goal, then this chapter puts us in motion.

Success can be intimidating. Sometimes we have impostor syndrome and think that others will see through our façade if we succeed. In this instance we question our intellect, our skill set, or our accomplishments.[2] Apprehension to engage with something that might put us in the limelight would be worrisome to anyone feeling

---

[1] Trial, "Unrestrained," written by Greg Bennick and Timm McIntosh, Track 8 on *Are These Our Lives?* (Equal Vision Records 1999), 12" vinyl.
[2] Martin R. Huecker, Jacob Shreffler, Patrick T. McKeny, and David Davis, "Imposter Phenomenon," *National Library of Medicine* (StatPearls Publishing, January 2024), https://www.ncbi.nlm.nih.gov/books/NBK585058/#.

like they might be seen as an impostor. But even that aside, it is often intimidating to imagine being looked at or critiqued at all. As a result, it is easy to make the choice to not stand out.

At other times, we simply fear change. What if we have to work harder as a result of advancement or success? What if our friends, colleagues, or family judge us for that advancement? This has been researched as a cultural phenomenon as well: What if the achievement or promotion we seek leads us to be ostracized or alienated by our community?[3]

If we want something more, we need to take steps toward that *something more* or forever live with the regret of inaction. What we risk will be regained. Steps we can take in the right direction include reassessing what our emotions are around the fear and getting to the core of why we'd rather sit uncomfortably than make a move forward. Why is it that we would rather sit amidst an idea rather than take action on changing the situation or propelling the idea into the world? It makes sense in a way. Innovation and risk are inextricably intertwined. Pushing ourselves forward, or putting ideas into motion, requires taking risks in order to reap rewards. That can be scary. But without that first step, nothing happens.

I find that when I am immobile, it is due to fear of failure. I consider so many potential outcomes in which an idea might not work that I forget that it actually could work if I try. Funny, right? It makes no sense if you think about it. It is like we are willing to sit in the gap between what we want and what we can have, wondering what that other side looks like, instead of making an effort to bridge it.

With that in mind, I have a method I use to get started when I am feeling stuck.

If I am stuck, I force myself into action. I start doing something, anything, toward the goal. I pick a direction and make a move, even if it seems like a small or insignificant one. That at least gets me active rather than passive, and I can correct whatever has gone wrong after

---

[3] Jo-Hanna Ivers and P. Downes, "A Phenomenological Reinterpretation of Horner's Fear of Success in Terms of Social Class," *European Journal of Psychology of Education* 27, no. 3 (2012): 369–388, http://www.jstor.org/stable/43551117.

the fact. Having the impulse and not taking a chance at all out of fear of either failure or success feels like defeat from the start because I know it won't lead to any progression. Small steps beat no steps, every time.

In terms of writing, for example, instead of staring at a blank page, I write something. Again, anything. I put words in motion. It gets me underway in *a* direction, even if that pathway needs to be reworked in time. The chances that a first step will include such an immense mistake that it can't be corrected are very small.

I sometimes do this when I write: I start with my fingers on the keyboard for ten minutes on a timer without stopping and I start typing. If I make it through ten, I push to fifteen. I know that I can always SELECT ALL > DELETE later, or worst case EDIT > LIFE > QUIT WRITING, but as yet it hasn't come to that. Putting yourself in motion through action is essential if you feel stuck, confused, or uninspired. What is the worst that can happen? You will write something you don't like, paint something that needs to be covered up later, or go running when you should have gone swimming. None of these is terrible, and all of these are better than feeling stuck or immobile.

When I was working on this book, for example, I had initial days where the blank page was not just intimidating but rather overwhelming. I couldn't get started with writing no matter how hard I tried, and the harder I tried, the more impossible the task seemed. I decided to put something into motion, and that something was me.

I got in my car and drove to eastern Washington, which, for the geographically uninclined, is a few hours away from my home in Seattle. I spent my time contemplating the book and what I wanted to say. On the drive back I started a voice recording, and started talking to myself. I spoke out loud for two-and-a-half hours nonstop. That recording, when professionally transcribed, became the basis for the first twenty thousand words of this book, laid out chapter by chapter. This book wouldn't have existed without that leap into the dark.

This doesn't mean that you have to talk to yourself for hours. It works for me. You just need to get into motion. I had to put myself and the ideas literally in motion and out into the world to get them underway. It made a massive difference. Something, rather than nothing.

In the theater we have a saying, when it is time to go from reading from scripts to actually rehearsing. We say that it is time to get the text "off the page and onto the stage." This means to put it in motion so that we can experience what it is like to actually *feel* the words rather than just read them. The same was true for my book. A thousand thoughts were all jumbled in my mind, but I can speak out loud about only one at a time. That is what I put into motion with the voice recording and hours of talking to myself.

> **In terms of creative development, moving in any direction is far better than having no movement at all.**

Direction matters less than action. Our creative exploration, development of a new idea, trajectory for finishing a project or having a relationship come to fruition with a friend or client...none of them is linear. They are occasionally one step forward, two steps back. Or one step forward, pause. Or three steps forward, one to the side, one back, two forward. You get the idea. It is not as simple as one foot in front of the other and eventually in a straight line you get to where you're wanting to go. Sometimes it takes just getting started, failing a little, then setting back on course to show you that you will eventually get to where you need to be.

This is all aside from the fact that the *what if* of success is intimidating, too, because succeeding at something implies growth, movement, and change...three things at which we aren't intellectually always the best.

And of course, a culture of comparison doesn't help either. Why should I try when I am clueless about where to start, when so-and-so has a million likes on a similar thing that she seems to have mastered? Will my attempts even matter? Will anyone notice?

The attempts do matter. It's all about that leap into the dark and the confidence boost that comes after it. The leap starts a shockwave from which we feel the effects for long after the leap takes place. And the leap doesn't have to be a scientific breakthrough that changes the world and saves lives all over the planet. If you can make that happen, good for you. But a leap can be simple. It can reclaim the moment so that you can propel yourself further, later.

I'd like to share a story about the results of stepping into the unknown and trying something, anything, to kickstart a new reality and to change a situation for the better. It was a "leap into the dark" moment under the most bizarre of circumstances, but it had an incredible outcome that tells us that taking the leap to try something when in doubt can yield results we couldn't have imagined possible.

When I was 24, I thought that I was never going to experience joy again. I had gone through a terrible breakup and was at a really low point. The irony of that was that I had made my living my entire life as a juggler, performer, and entertainer making people happy. At the time, I was doing a lot of street performance, so I would juggle fire and knives on the streets of Seattle and then balance out the excitement of that by making animal balloons for kids. Amidst all those smiles, I was still a wreck.

Joy is something I had been waiting for. As if it would bump into me on the street or fall out of a tree. I didn't seem to have that luck. Part of it was attitude. I figured I was just very lucky at having unlucky things happen to me. In my mind, my life was as if I had broken a mirror while walking under a ladder on the thirteenth day of the month while a black cat strolled back and forth in front of me. It was either that, or my life had been doomed by Darryl and his Big Wheel.

A good friend of mine suggested I take a break from life and fly to India to join her there and travel around a bit. Being an impulsive, adventurous sort, I not only said yes but I bought a plane ticket to India. After a couple weeks of wandering and exploring, my friend suggested that we travel up north to try and meet the Dalai Lama, and I thought that sounded like a good idea. Maybe I'd get a chance to meet the guy who is the embodiment of the opposite of being without joy. Sounded like a friend I needed to make.

As we were planning our trip to the north to find the Dalai Lama, my friend got incredibly sick with dysentery and had to fly back to the USA, leaving me on my own for the quest to see the human embodiment of joy. It was the last thing I wanted to do. I thought about quitting and flying home, too. I wasn't sure how to proceed. I decided to go for it anyway. I bought a ticket for a train the next day.

> When we step into the unknown, it can have powerful and even positive consequences.

Trains in India, in case you've not been on one, range from super-comfortable to not the least bit, and the train class I bought was the latter. It was more like a boxcar with benches. I climbed into this boxcar in New Delhi, and I sat down on my bench. I was by myself in the car.

The train started lumbering along. After four hours of me staring contemplatively through the thin-barred windows into mental oblivion across the landscape, the train stopped in this little village and a family got on. They had a choice of all the benches in the entire boxcar, but they chose the bench right across from me so that we were all sitting and looking right at one another.

The family consisted of two little kids, a boy and a girl, with their mom and dad. They sat, and as is the case throughout India (it's a cultural thing), they started staring at me. There was no expression on their faces. The stare isn't rude. It's more inquisitive. But it is unsettling to someone who doesn't have that behavior as a cultural norm. To each their own, I guess, but it was challenging to sit there in silence as they stared.

I was an anomaly on this train as a westerner in this part of India. They were just staring. And they each had a different stare on their face. Little boy, little girl, mom, dad. Each checking me out in their own way. Inquisitive, disinterested, unnerved, skeptical. I felt very uncomfortable, so I just tried to smile as if to communicate, "Hi. I'm actually secretly very unhappy." But I got no reaction at all, and that made it ten times worse.

The train lumbered on to the next stop, far out in the country, and all the while the family was staring. My mind started racing. Am I being judged? Do they like me? What did I do wrong? Should I get off here in the middle of India? Do they hate me? What do I do?

The family kept staring.

> Our brains can be minefields of worry, impacting our ability to get anything accomplished. We can change that reality.

We pulled up to the train station. I was relieved to see people on the platform about to get on, too, but that relief turned quickly to confusion.

There was an entire company of Indian Army men standing on the platform. Almost a hundred of them, all dressed in full regalia. They were all heavily armed with every possible type of rifle and shotgun slung over their shoulders, carrying boxes of grenades heavy enough that two soldiers needed to work on the lifting together. They had rocket launchers and machine guns and Rambo-like strips of bullets across their chests. The weaponry never ended. Over a few minutes, they all piled onto the train, one by one at times but also two by two, like they were boarding a Noah's ark of violence. They packed into the boxcar, situating themselves all around me on the bench, as well as next to the family.

The soldiers immediately started staring at me, too.

So now every single person on this train, ages five through sixty-five, was staring at me. Most of them had guns and bullets and hand grenades and rocket launchers, and this might have been the worst moment of my entire life. Seconds turned to minutes turned to hours, all in the first moments they were on the train. I had no idea what I was going to do. As the train started to roll along, no words were spoken. There was only staring. This was the ultimate moment of social awkwardness. Olympic gold medal-level, unfathomable social awkwardness.

About twenty minutes went by of me crumbling inside. Then suddenly, like a lightning bolt in my mind, I had a thought. It didn't make sense, nor was it relevant to the situation, but it was at least something. I was about to take a leap into the dark. I'd suddenly remembered, "Wait! I have some balloons in my pocket for making balloon animals from my last gig before I came to India!" And for whatever reason, it made sense to reach for them. I reached quickly into my pocket, which in retrospect was perhaps not the smartest move while being stared down by a hundred heavily armed men. I pulled out a deflated royal-blue balloon and, without fanfare or introduction, I filled it with air.

The instant I blew up the balloon, there was a shift in the train, from curiosity to wonder. I was suddenly holding what looked like a four-foot-long blue snake, where before I was holding only a foot-long blue worm. The two little kids' eyes went wide and they made a sound like "Whaaaaaaat?" The mom was looking at the balloon, not her kids, and her face registered total surprise. She too made a sound like "Whaaaaaaat?" The dad suddenly looked like he was five years old again, and he as well, you guessed it, sounded like "Whaaaaaaat?" Their reactions were amazing.

But what truly caught me by surprise is that, without exception, amidst the rattling of gun barrels hitting one another and bayonets being pushed aside and ammo rustling around, every single one of the military guys suddenly leaned in and around corners and over shoulders to get a better look. Every last one had a look on their face registering wonder. Simultaneously in an army chorus, they all vocalized a unified sound like "Whaaaaaaaaaaaaat?"

I had a captive audience. I started twisting the balloon into a dog. The entire train watched like I was inventing fire for the first time. These were sophisticated professional adults, but they were caught off guard by something they hadn't seen before. They lost their collective mind.

I gave the first balloon to the little girl. She stared at it in awe, and although I don't speak Hindi, I could tell what she was saying, "No way!" Her brother was instantly jealous, which I interpreted via the international language of siblinghood. I blew up another one. I twisted that into a dog, too, and I handed it to her brother. They both looked down at the balloons, then at one another, then at me, and both in a state of awe, said the equivalent of "No way!" The mom and the dad looked at one other and then looked at me and together they started smiling.

I turned and looked to the soldier next to me. He had a shotgun accidentally leaning towards my face. He simultaneously looked like a little kid and an assassin all rolled into one. I did what anyone in my position would have done: I made him a dog balloon.

I blew up the balloon, twisted it, and handed it to him. He lost his mind. "No way!!!!" Instantly all of his friends were dropping their weapons, or adjusting them to hang from their bandoliers so they could be clamoring for balloons. I was blowing up balloons and twisting them as fast as I could. Guns were rattling all over the place, and the soldiers were actually putting down their rifles to play with their dog balloons. Laughter started to fill the train. All the while, the kids were playing together with their balloons, and their parents were beaming.

Never before has any heavily armed audience been so filled with joy. I kept twisting. As you can imagine I didn't want to disappoint a guy with a bazooka.

I dug into my pack and found more balloons there. Over the next hour, I blew them up and handed them to everyone I could. The soldiers were giddy (said no one ever). That leap into the dark had created total brilliance.

A few stops later, the train arrived at the army destination, and the soldiers started rounding up their bullets and grabbing their grenades and slinging their machine guns. They now had the extra challenge of needing to juggle dog balloons as well as weapons in order to depart. But they made it happen. They filed off the train. From the platform they all started waving to me and holding up their dog balloons so I could see them through the train windows as we started to lumber off.

At this point it was me who had the blank stare like, "Whaaaaat?" I waved goodbye to the army men, and at the next stop the family all got up to collect their things to get off the train. As they left, they were smiling and happy and waving, too.

I realized that I had been waiting in Seattle for joy to happen to me. And this time on the train was a reclaiming of the moment and remembering that the experience of joy is one that is *given* first and foremost rather than one that we should be waiting to receive. I wanted something more than being uncomfortable, so I took the initiative and took a step into the dark, by twisting that first balloon.

After that train ride, I ended up meeting the Dalai Lama. See gregbennick.com/reclaim for a video of the story!

When I think about that moment, I remember the leap getting me past intimidation, fear, anxiety, and nervousness. I remember all of the feelings that keep us from sharing our brilliance with those around us. How many opportunities have been lost in moments like that? For me, perhaps those feelings were justified, because everyone around me had guns and they all were staring at the side of my head.

In the moment, I could have responded differently to my anxiety:

- I could have fallen into bravado and likely literally died.
- I could have done nothing and figuratively died.
- I could have started crying.

Instead, I tried *something* proactive and positive. Remember before I said that when in a total jam with writing, I try something, anything. I would most definitely define blowing up an animal balloon in that moment on a train as a random something.

Whenever I think that it is impossible to reclaim a moment and get myself back on center, or if I need a reminder to step into the unknown and leap into the dark, or even if I have a sense that the resources at my disposal aren't enough to make a change, I remember that time on the train. Whenever I feel that forward motion isn't worth the effort because I can't imagine where it will lead, I remember that moment on the train. And whenever I think there's nothing at all to be done, I remember that experience on the train. The tools I put into play to make a difference and to leap into the dark were literally worth about a dollar. The effort needed to make them into something incredible was about a hundred or so breaths of air. But the net result, total gain, and profit in terms of life experience were unreal in proportion.

Imagine your team or friend group energized in a way that they would leap into the dark like that and try something, anything, in order to put themselves into motion and leave stagnation behind.

When we leap, we don't know where it could lead, but we definitely know where it will lead if we don't.

It is important to note that creativity, along with our relationship to it, is at a critical turning point. With the rise of ChatGPT in the last few years, we are having to ask challenging questions about what original work and creativity mean. As a result of the way that artificial intelligence draws its source content from previously existing material, and as a result of how it synthesizes that material within seconds into seemingly new creative output, we are having to grapple with questions that we haven't before. What is the role of artists in a world where their work is immediately appropriated, with no credit or renumeration given? How can we move into that space and use that technology ethically, one in which writers and creators on many fronts are feeling invisible and as if they no longer matter? Should we apply regulations to a technology that has been forecast famously in Hollywood and science fiction to have the potential to destroy the human race? Evidently, no one else has seen *The Terminator*.

Let us hope that science fiction doesn't become science fact. That said, we have to maintain our own role as creators amidst changing times and integrate ethical use of technology when we can. Our choice to make is primarily a psychological one first and foremost, while the technology, which will only advance from here, continues on its forward-facing trajectory.

What might it look like for you to move forward with psychologically positive and encouraging steps and take a leap for your own creative mind and actions to thrive?

- Take a risk with an idea you've been playing with. Share it. Get it out. Make it real with words or actions. Tell someone. Show someone. Do something. Even if it's dead wrong or not where you eventually plan to end up. You don't have to present this grand idea to your boss. Try it out first with your friend. It doesn't have to be an idea that you put in motion in a critical situation. Take a test run with it somewhere with someone first. Just don't keep it inside you.
- Write, and use that writing to generate creative flow. Get a pen and paper, or a drawing app for your phone or tablet. Make whatever it is that you are feeling real. Draw scribbles if you have to. (This technique worked for Jackson Pollock.) Draw lines. Draw shapes. Draw Abraham Lincoln lounging on a beach. Draw a squirrel attacking your grandmother. Write a limerick celebrating parakeets. Write a haiku about your breakfast. It doesn't matter what you draw, write, or where you start, as long as you create something. You are trying to kickstart your creative mind rather than remain immobilized in your static mind. You will end up mentally, after you're done, somewhere

other than where you started – and that's exactly what you want. You've bridged a gap like we've been talking about throughout the book.

- Listen to someone else's hopeful and creative idea. It will help get your mindset in the mode of creation. This is a new language, especially for teams, and needs to be treated as such. By listening, you open the opportunity for someone else to make that breakthrough first step. The basics of this kind of process start with communicating an impulse, which can absolutely be abstract. If you can be a listener for that for someone else to help them define their idea, you also will gain through their advancement, which is a win.

- If you don't know where to start with any of this, let me know and I can share (or post to gregbennick.com/reclaim) ideas for how to kickstart your creativity.

Creativity can look like effective teamwork. My friend Drew Wilkinson, while at Microsoft, started asking colleagues about sustainability. What started as just a couple of people discussing possibility turned into ten *thousand* people, all meeting online in groups and breakout groups. They began networking around ideas on sustainability and how to bring it more regularly into the workplace and then took action on those ideas. Talk about a world changer. This was done without a roadmap. Drew thought it up and did it. This was creativity in action.

While defeat or fear of failure is a barrier to creative development, it's essential for us also to not be intimidated by the Possibility of Success. Both are open to us when we try, and that is part of the deal. Failure or success might be waiting in the wings. The point is, it's too easy to allow ourselves to be defeated before we even start. When we take a risk, it allows us to feel that we are contributors that matter to a meaningful world, and again, this is primary for self-esteem development.

How can you offer this strategy to your team, to the people around you, and to your friends?

- Encourage people to take risks and promote a culture of *risk-taking* as valuable over *result-making*.

- Explore process as a necessary part of development, human resources, and of being a good person overall. Your friends and coworkers will appreciate feeling like they can contribute.
- Recognize people for the attempts they make and the sincere contributions they offer. Don't underestimate the impact of recognition on the personal development and self-esteem of the people around you. This is a human resources goldmine.
- Eliminate the idea that critique is a measure of engagement. Allow people to explore first until they want critique. And only accept critique that has positive or encouraging suggestions for change that are unique to you and your experience. Our culture is addicted to that kind of critique as it is the language of the lowest common denominator. It engages in a way that requires no creativity and no emotional buy-in whatsoever. Side-step it. Focus on process.
- Imagine and act as if the world is waiting for our contribution. That can allow us to feel worthy enough to share or valued enough to take a first creative stride. If we can't even let ourselves imagine it as a possibility, then we aren't going to be able to actualize it or make first steps to that goal.

When could you use this strategy:

- **When you need a reminder of your valuable, unique *mattering* in the universe**
- **When your team needs to be inspired and motivated to take big risks**
- **When you want to connect with clients or people by whom you feel intimidated**
- **When you hope to make a mark in the world and aren't sure where to start**
- **When you feel bogged down and just want to push forward**

Why does all of this matter?

Well, I expect that when most people hear "tick tock," they don't think of my incredible, hard-to-wrap-your-mind-around TikTok account that as I write this has a cumulative total of exactly one video on it with about that many likes. (Check it out at @xjugglerx) They likely hear "TikTok" and think of the platform overall.

What do I personally think when I hear that onomatopoeic (there's your word of the day) sound? I hear seconds counting down. Like a timer counting down to zero in this, my only life. I hear a match strike and ignite against the hardened surface of my excuses.

This is why all of this matters. "Tick tock" and the clock overall is a reminder to light the fuel in my heart and get moving. We have very little time, so let's make the most of it.

Tick tock, tick tock, tick tock...

- Think of each moment as chunk of rock and you as a sculptor. A block of marble is challenging to an artist because it represents pure possibility. As time slips by, are you going to let that rock stay just as it is, a rock? Or are you going to start carving? Could you imagine doing nothing as your legacy and having the rock just remain exactly as you first saw it?

- Strive for meaning, yet have it be entirely OK that we have to constantly be reinventing what matters to us in the moment as each new moment presents itself. We don't ever get to be complete. Well, maybe the Buddha did. But for the nontranscendent among us, we need to cultivate a sense that being in process is exactly where we need to be.

- Be present in how all of this feels, but never let yourself get overwhelmed to the point of being immobilized. When you stop, it all stops. Be present, feel overwhelmed or confused, but always try to remain in creative action, even if that's just being actively reflective or planning your next step so that you can make a move soon.

When we leap into the dark, it opens us up to the power of process and riding a wave toward what we want.

Now let's go deeper to explore how to engage with process in the best way possible.

Leap into the Dark to Embrace the Possibility of Success

Creating ideas and going after what we want isn't easy. In addition to process just being hard (though worth it), it is too easy is to compare ourselves to others and be driven out of our minds by it. Clear connections have been cited between social comparisons and depression.[4] We see others having success and we want that, but sometimes we don't believe that it's possible, or if we do, we can think of half a dozen reasons why we can't have that same success.

At face value, especially in the digital world, success often seems to start at one level and steadily increase until someone is miraculously and triumphantly at a high point, and then that's what they post and everyone likes them. The end. But this seemingly straight line upward is an illusion. Creativity isn't like that. Life isn't like that.

Success isn't like that.

It doesn't just follow one simple trajectory. There are ups and downs – often in rapid succession. We don't get to always simply blow up a balloon and an entire army is thrilled. Process is always more like a sine wave. The setbacks and the problems we face are integrated into my vision of this wave, shown in Figure 7.1.

I call it the Sine Wave of Creativity.

You'll notice that the wave has two axes: one for *time* and one for *achievement*. It also has two lines: one for *process* and one for *trajectory*.

---

[4] Adele Samra, Wayne A. Warburton, and Andrew M. Collins, "Social Comparisons: A Potential Mechanism Linking Problematic Social Media Use with Depression," *Journal of Behavioral Addictions* 11, no. 2 (June 2022): 607–614.

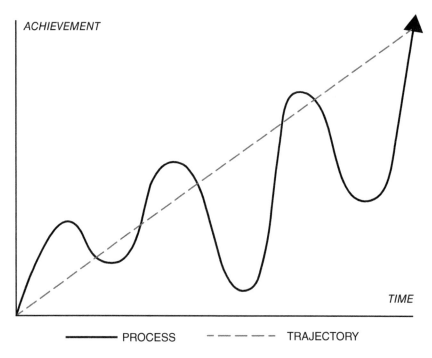

Figure 7.1   The Sine Wave of Creativity

The *time* axis is the length of time you put into a project, and that, of course, will be variable. It could represent five minutes or five years. There are no rules and no judgment about that. Something you think is going to take minutes might take months. And something you thought should have taken a year suddenly got finished yesterday. There's sometimes no rhyme or reason to how long it takes for a project to develop creatively. At work you might be on a schedule. But even then, there's a time consideration against which achievement is charted.

Achievement, as you can see, is all over the graph. Think about the low points in the graph as downtimes, uncreative moments, little advancement, feeling stuck, or not believing in yourself. The high points are moments of inspiration or flow, where you feel like you're really close to completion.

At times when we're at the top of one of the waves in the Sine Wave of Creativity, we feel successful. We feel open to ideas. We feel creative. We feel successful. This is the high point of *Process*.

At other times, we're at the bottom of one of those waves in the sine wave. We feel defeated. Lost. Maybe we feel an interpersonal block or an impediment to our process. We feel the overwhelming sense perhaps of a deadline rapidly approaching or the convergence of too many people's needs at once.

Or maybe we just feel simply that things aren't going smoothly. Over time, the *Trajectory* of the sine wave elevates toward the outcome we want. The key is to stay in the process and along that sine wave, regardless of if we are in a peak or a valley. The overall trajectory, the dashed line, is what we need to remember.

Check out that dashed line. That's the overall trajectory even as the sine itself wavers between "I rule" and "I am a clueless disaster." The through line from concept to completion requires that we stay the course regardless of whether we're at a high point or amidst a low point.

If we are in the process, we will get to where we want to go. If we drop out, it's over. A low point isn't a losing moment. It's just a single point along the sine wave that will eventually lead us to where we want to go.

What is our motivation for staying in the process or jumping out? Fear of failure makes sense, but what about the alternative to it? What about fear of success? That's a little more ominous, because if being restricted by fear of failure can be counteracted by trying harder and succeeding, does it make sense with fearing success that the alternative is that we try less hard and fail?!

Embracing courage is the key to overcoming intimidation by The Possibility of Success

---

"Keep going." This has been my mantra during times when I've literally dropped objects on the ground that I needed to keep in the air. Or when I've had challenges, disappointments, issues in business, challenges in life. Or when I am not sure where I am going and the process seems overwhelming.

Keep going. Literally keep going, keep breathing, keep moving, keep being. Keep thinking, keep doing, and keep creating. Ernest

Becker, whom I mentioned in Chapter 2, ends his Pulitzer Prize–winning book *The Denial of Death* with this line (spoiler alert!).

> The most that any one of us can seem to do is to fashion something – an object or ourselves – and to drop it into the confusion, make an offering of it, so to speak, to the life force.[5]

What Becker meant is that creating something, whether in a more traditional physical sense like a piece of art or a more metaphorical sense in terms of developing ourselves, might just be the highest that we can hope for. His words are curious and a bit ominous. Are we to drop that thing (that art or whatever it is that we create, whether a business, a child, a painting, a career, or, for that matter, our own life), into the "confusion" of existence with no guarantees or promises? What does that even mean? Do we just put it out there and hope for the best? That's terrifying! We are just going to initiate a new idea at work, or build something in life, and then put it out into the business, the community, the family, the world and not have a guarantee that anything will come of it?

Yes.

That's the key. That yes, with no guarantees or promises. That's what "the confusion" offers. His addition of it being an offering to the "life force," as he calls it, isn't meant to imply that we are putting a sacrifice on an altar or donating our business to charity. What he meant, is that we are tossing what we develop into the universe with hope, but without expectation of anything coming to pass to us from that. This is an act of empowerment, confidence, hope, a deep breath in, and generosity – all combined at once. We create for the sake of creation and for the benefit of others. If it does lead to brilliance for us, great. If it doesn't, it doesn't. We can't control that. But we can control the quality of the creation and the integrity of the process and push forward in support of all of it.

"To live is to play at the meaning of life."[6]

Ernest Becker, *The Denial of Death*

---

[5] Ernest Becker, *The Denial of Death* (New York: Free Press, 1973), 285.
[6] Becker, 201.

Perhaps in the midst of being a complex animal, an absolutely complicated creature, one that continually talks itself in circles, maybe instead of hearing we need sure bets or absolute confirmation before something happens to us, we can find the courage instead to explore and step into the unknown without knowing what comes next? We can let go of needing to hold on. If we can do that while in service to others, we might just make some great strides.

We can step into courage in a similar way that an artist steps into process. We can embrace the possibility of success.

An artist puts pen to paper, paint to canvas, chisel to stone without knowing every exact detail about what is going to be created at the end of the process. As a juggler, if I throw an object, I have a pretty good sense that it might come down again and generally *where* it will as well. But what angle, what spin, what velocity is anyone's exacting guess.

Does that mean that I don't throw? It means the exact opposite: I throw with experience and courage. If something is to hit the ground, it likely won't be my dead body from trying to juggle. The number of people killed by tennis balls annually might just be zero. Don't quote me on that. The point is: Trying isn't going to kill me. We aren't talking about someone's first attempt at base jumping here. We are talking about taking the risk to generate new ideas and turn them into active projects. Whether for something physical like a statue, or more realistically something like better communication, a new innovation, enhanced leadership, more powerful relationships, or increased and effective team dynamics, the motivation behind your process can be the same.

Keep going.

When stepping into the unknown, I remember something my friend Michael Moschen told me. Michael is a profoundly brilliant, literal genius, as noted by him receiving a MacArthur Genius grant. When I met Michael, we talked at length about approaches to creativity and artistic process. I told him about long hours spent practicing, and he took it a step further by explaining he often doesn't know if a technique is even possible when he starts practice on it.

I asked him about how he goes so many steps beyond that and develops something from nothing with his exploration of techniques. What Michael does is so much more than juggling. He manipulates objects in ways no one has done before. He literally steps into the unknown. This is essential artistry at its best.

Michael told me, and it has resonated for thirty years, that for him, the creative process wasn't one of knowing what was coming next. I even asked him, "How do you move forward, not knowing anything of what the process or the results hold?" For me, I like to at least have an idea.

He said we all know the concept of stepping into a tunnel and seeing light at the end of the tunnel and pushing forward and aiming for the light. He said it is different for him. In his process, when creating a technique that has never been created before, there's often no light at the end of the tunnel. Michael steps into that tunnel, into the pitch-black darkness, and places one foot forward and then another foot forward and then another, even though he sees no light as a beacon. Hearing this decades ago, for me, was the dawn of *keep going*.

Step into the tunnel, even if you don't see light at the end.

So how do we find that courage? Here are some approaches you can take. I recommend thinking this list through, and if you find them to be challenging, get in touch with me through gregbennick.com and let's talk about how to integrate them into your life and your team for maximum impact.

- Admit what scares you about process and developing new ideas.
- Talk to yourself like a best friend and be sincere, genuine, and honest.
- Establish a better relationship with what you perceive to be failure, recognizing it is often a step toward success.
- Get real about the fear in your mind and imagine the inevitability of it: Can you imagine a possibility where a setback doesn't actually kill or destroy you but instead helps you along the way?
- Believe in something, and start the first steps toward going after it by stepping into the dark.
- Go with peers, not against them. The more we work as a team, the better – even if that means sincere and open feedback.

Humans are the only creatures who can imagine something that doesn't yet exist and then through will and creativity, imagine it, develop it, create it, and infuse it with meaning. Whether we choose to do that is entirely up to us. But creators who have gone before advise us to say yes.

I like learning from artists. In a letter from Impressionist painter Vincent Van Gogh to his brother Theo, Vincent said, "If you hear a voice within you saying, 'You are not a painter,' then by all means paint ... and that voice will be silenced."[7] It's up to you to make the move.

Movement and courage combined *is* the leap. This is the mental currency of the world changer and of someone who wants something more. It's what gets people doing things like jumping out of airplanes (with parachutes, thanks). It is what transforms collections of people into transformational teams of inspired collaborators. The leap into the unknown and into action is the vehicle that can drive the team through a difficult time, amidst upheaval, past self-doubt, and beyond inevitable challenges. The leap sees us solidly in the midst of building a better now.

Now let's take a look at the drive within you that is going to propel that leap forward and start the process by which you can share your vision with others.

---

[7] "Letter from Vincent van Gogh to Theo van Gogh, *Drenthe*, October 28, 1883," https://www.webexhibits.org/vangogh/letter/13/336.htm (accessed March 2024).

8

ENGAGE WITH LAUGHTER
to Connect Amidst the Weight
of the World

*"It is well known that humor, more than anything else in the human
make-up, can afford an aloofness and an ability to rise above any
situation, even if only for a few seconds."*
– Viktor Frankl, *Man's Search for Meaning*[1]

THE WORLD CAN be a heavy place. Thankfully, some extremely funny
people have created brilliant things to balance out the weight.

*Ferris Bueller's Day Off. Napoleon Dynamite. Elf. Office Space. The
Big Lebowski. Monty Python and the Holy Grail. Anchorman. The Grand
Budapest Hotel.* If you don't think any of those movies are the least bit
funny, we have work to do. Message me for a humor consultation.
It could either be a workshop or a movie-watching night. I'll make
the popcorn.

This chapter is about connection – with our colleagues and
customers, with our friends and with ourselves. It is about embracing
your inner weird. It is about what we can do when we want something

---

[1] Viktor E. Frankl, *Man's Search for Meaning* (Boston: Washington Square
Press, Pocket Books, Simon & Schuster, 1985), 63.

more than the weight with which the world burdens us every day. I hear from clients regularly about their need to delve deeper into communication. I hear from friends regularly about the weight of the world and how it burdens them. The ideas in this chapter will help us connect with other people and lessen that weight so we have more space for other ideas. It will help to bridge the gaps between us.

We need to laugh more, and we need to laugh more together. The chapter's title is a play on words, though you probably picked that up. Engage with laughter, meaning *you* laugh more in the face of the world. And it also means that you connect with *others* through laughter. I know. I am a genius.

We will take a look at both of those angles.

The world is challenging, to say the least, and the news isn't great. We have wars and violent conflict. We have disease. We have people who still put too many words on their PowerPoint slides. It doesn't take a nuclear physicist (or for that matter, a bald author/keynote speaker) to tell you that the world feels tense on the good days and *really* challenging on the bad days. Sure, there are amazing days and hopeful times all around us if we choose to look for them, but if you watch any online news or TV broadcasts for too long, you're likely going to end up hopeful that a giant meteor collides with our planet sooner than later. Or if you don't, you'll be carrying and feeling the burden of the news and all that comes with it.

Regardless of which side of the aisle you pound your ideological flag into, science speaks truth. Studies looking into the psychological effects of watching news programming for even fifteen minutes showed negative impacts substantial enough to require "a directed psychological intervention" to counterbalance the effects of doing so.[2] These studies were done with television news, which leads one to wonder the profound effect of the constant barrage of news via assorted digital channels that is in our faces every single second and

---

[2] Attila Szabo and Katey L. Hopkinson, "Negative Psychological Effects of Watching the News in the Television: Relaxation and Another Intervention May Be Needed to Buffer Them!" *International Journal of Behavioral Medicine* 14, no. 2 (2007): 57–62.

the effect it all has on us and on those around us. Work stress, news stress, life stress. There's enough of it to go around for all of us.

However, there is hope. As leaders, world changers, friends, supporters, good collaborators, teammates, or just nice people, we need to put in effort to counterbalance the effects of just *living* in the world and the impact it has on the people we care about and work with. We can be proactive in this. We have to be. The world isn't going to get kinder or more fun without us putting in the work to make that happen around us. Remember the reference to *think global, act local.* The forces of not-goodness (yes, a technical term) continually default to the lowest common denominator of verbal and physical violence and aggression. We can work toward balancing that out and create conditions in which to thrive.

> **We can initiate powerful change if we choose, both in ourselves and in the world around us.**

One of the reasons I have always included interactive comedy in my keynote speeches, whether it's me balancing a chair on my face (yes, you read that correctly), engaging with people creatively, having audience members spontaneously decide which ridiculous object I should juggle next, or doing some impossible magic trick that instills awe and wonder, is because it brings people together. It's a binding agent. Laughter raises morale and maximizes engagement. I have seen it happen again and again all over the world. One doesn't need to be a rocket scientist or a bald keynote speaker ... never mind, because actually being a bald keynote speaker does indeed help with this one.

Point is, don't just take my word for it. Research has shown that humor and group effectiveness, even though these seem unrelated, have a combined positive influence on communication and connection, goal-setting and achievement, and productivity overall.[3] We want to

---

[3] Eric Romero and Anthony Pescosolido, "Humor and Group Effectiveness," *Human Relations* 61, no. 3 (2008): 395–418, https://doi.org/10.1177/0018726708088999.

be laughing. We would be smart to remember this, whether we are in an office and sharing a new bold idea, in a workshop creating a brilliant new product, at a university exploring theory and learning practice, or in an organization working as a group with focused intent.

It is about having a throughline in your mind of lightheartedness: an undercurrent to uplift and help counterbalance the weight. When the world gets to be too much, we can balance out that weight ourselves without waiting for someone to do it for us. Laughing is certainly one mechanism for that. Waiting for salvation from someone else harkens back to our power-versus-authority discussion from earlier. We have the power to positively shift our mental and group dynamic from one in which individuals bear burdens toward one where shared experience elevates all. I see this happen in my keynotes all the time.

Be willing to laugh, connect, and take joyous risks.

Laughter and connection are brilliant engagement tools, and you don't have to be a comic genius to think in these terms. You just need to be willing to step out from the weight of the world and interact with a different mindset. Think in terms of lightheartedness and a desire for connection. When the weight gets piled on and the difficulties we face feel increasingly insurmountable, or when we are in conflict with ourselves, finding the courage within to engage with a sense of how truly weird the world is rather than allowing ourselves to bear the weight of all of it can lead to that weight diminishing or hopefully disappearing. I've said it before, and I will say it again: I like weird. I like new perspectives and alternative angles on traditional ideas.

Thinking in terms of weird means seeing the world differently and being able to bring new perspectives to a situation. It doesn't mean you have to be a standup comedian. It just means you have to be willing to think in ways that are unconventional and share them with others. You already do this. You do it when you're on your own. You just need now to do it more often.

I recognize introverts and extroverts have different approaches to this. I am sort of an introverted extrovert myself. I love being around people, but every so often I wish I lived in the middle of Iceland in a hut and communicated only via smoke signals with nearby towns. That said, even introverts could work toward thinking weirdly as a technique for engaging others and being relatable with them.

One of the things I hear when talking about laughter to groups is that people fear all eyes being on them if they were to bring their real selves to social situations. We all walk through life wearing different personas for our social interactions, whether work or otherwise. We don't need to have a single consistent identity throughout every aspect of existence. We can be serious at home and funny at work, or vice versa. But what matters most for our conversation here is to bring more of ourselves to the process of connection with others and to be willing to laugh with them. Realistically, I have met very few people, like hardly any ever, who aren't funny at all, or who hate laughter, or who aren't good at connecting. You don't want to be around those people anyway.

Laughter is cross-cultural within groups. It bonds people together across levels, so to speak. Learning this firsthand through professionally speaking is when I realized that presenting and performing to managers, thought leaders, and C-level executives at the same time as the people who work for them was not only necessary but essential to bring people together in an organization. It isn't just a corporate thing, either. I've found this true through personal experience in the mountains in rural Haiti all the way to corporate boardrooms in the Netherlands. Laughter is so deeply social. We are thirty times more likely to laugh together than we are alone.[4]

Presenting to audiences at global conferences and making people laugh from all different strata of organizations has shown me that laughing enhances our relationships and strengthens teamwork and

---

[4] Robert R. Provine and Kenneth R. Fischer, "Laughing, Smiling, and Talking: Relation to Sleeping and Social Context in Humans," *Ethology* 83 (Berlin: Paul Parey Scientific Publishers, 1989): 295–305

connection. And it is not just me saying this. A study published by Princeton showed this binding effect to be measurable across twenty-four different societies.[5] Laughing together strengthens the idea that our relationships are valuable. I have been talking about this all throughout the book. When we feel as though we matter amidst a world of meaningful activity, our self-esteem grows and our commitment to the cause, idea, mission, or brand to which we are attached deepens.

I got my first lesson about this very early on in my career, and it was a total game changer for me in terms of how I looked at ways to connect with people across different hierarchical or horizontal levels in an organization. We can never discount our own potential to make positive, team building, and relationship enhancing contributions to a situation.

I did my first corporate events when I was fifteen years old. I was hired to perform stage shows and strolling entertainment as a comedy juggler at an amusement park in Connecticut, where companies would reserve picnic areas and host summertime outings for employees or other guests.

One weekend, I was told that Remington was renting the park. Remington was a personal care and electric shaving product company that was owned at the time by a man named Victor Kiam. Kiam, later the owner of the New England Patriots, was a celebrity because of Remington television commercials in which he starred. These commercials talked about the merits of the Remington razor, how his wife had bought him one, and at some point, in each commercial, Kiam would hold the razor in his right hand, smile at the camera, and say a variation of "I liked this razor so much, I bought the company." It was a testament to his sincerity and his devotion. *Everyone* at the time knew that line.

There I was, on a hot summer's day, walking through the Remington picnic juggling three colorful juggling balls – red, yellow, and blue – for

[5] Gregory A. Bryant, Daniel M. T. Fessler, Riccardo Fusaroli, and Yi Zhou, "Detecting Affiliation in Colaughter across 24 Societies," ed. Susan T. Fiske, *Proceedings of the National Academy of Sciences* (April 2016), https://doi .org/10.1073/pnas.1524993113.

hundreds of guests. People liked the tricks but suddenly there was a bit more energy. I knew I hadn't done anything *that* impressive. I turned toward the entrance, and there he was – the reason why people were in awe: Victor Kiam, walking into the party along with a suit-wearing entourage, all of whom looked very serious. They looked like bodyguards. Kiam himself was wearing a light-colored, button-down dress shirt, with the sleeves rolled up. He saw me and walked in my general direction.

I made my way closer through the crowd, and as the Remington seas parted, I was face to face with Victor Kiam himself, still juggling the colorful balls. He smiled and asked, "Can I see those juggling balls?" I was taken by surprise that he was actually talking to me.

I obliged and handed him the juggling balls. He took them and, much to the delight of his handlers, prepared to juggle. He steadied himself for a moment and then started juggling in a haphazard, unpracticed, but experienced enough way that he could actually keep it going for a few moments. His sharply dressed men, his bodyguard/handlers, erupted into polite golf-clap applause and the insincere laughter that typically accompanies it. Victor Kiam stopped his juggling. He handed the juggling balls back to me and said, "Those are pretty nice juggling balls."

I put all three into my right hand, held them up like Kiam held up his razor in the TV commercials, and smiled. I looked Victor Kiam right in the eye and I said, "Thank you. I liked these juggling balls so much, I bought the company."

There was an eternity of silence. In reality, it was probably only a couple of seconds. But no one laughed. Not one. And in those seconds, I thought I might just be the first person to be killed by Victor Kiam.

But what broke the silence wasn't Victor Kiam's rage but his own laughter. Victor burst into laughter first. And then upon this cue, in unison, so too did his handler/bodyguards. Along with them, all of the employees around us laughed, too. Kiam smiled sincerely at me and nodded with approval at this young kid who had just turned reality on its side for a moment. This was a career-changing moment for me.

> **Laughter is a powerful thread that binds us together.**

Fifteen years old, and I just made not only one of the most powerful businessmen in New England laugh but also the people who protected him, and also the people who worked for him – from middle-level managers all the way across the organization to the shipping people, secretaries, janitors, and clerks. The entire strata of the company laughed at one, simple, customized joke. Game changer. That was a moment where I realized customized comedy and being willing to be weird goes miles in terms of engaging and bringing an audience together. But to the point from the study I cited just a little while ago, I also realized laughter can bring everyone together from across every level of an organization, and really create some common bonds.

The moments of no one laughing held a lesson, too. I realized there was a level of restraint in the strata of the corporate world which in turn can restrain the potential in a team. How much elevation are we weighing down with our unspoken agreements about how things should be? I was *very* relieved that Victor eventually, after what seemed like an eternity, laughed at my joke!

These were important realizations. They made me think about laughter and connection in an entirely new way. There are so many levels to laughter that are worth exploring, all for the benefit of the people with whom we work and create.

Now let's go deeper … to explore how and why we can and should invite laughter.

> **Engage with laughter to connect amidst the weight of the world.**

You don't need to be a comedian. Leave that to the professionals. You can set the stage, though, for better engagement and for building stronger teams. So you don't have to wonder how you can make this happen, I will share some ideas to help. You can boost connection and manage the weight of the world in a variety of ways.

Ramp up your positivity. Not just laughter, but also even optimism, confidence, and hope increase people's effectiveness. When we laugh together, or even when we are under the influence of positivity, our ability to solve problems improves.[6] What we can learn from this is not that we have to be comedians but that we can ramp up the positivity and encourage people rather than commanding them. (I hope we remember the distinction between "power" and "authority" from Chapter 2.) We will inspire them, not necessarily to work more, but definitely to solve problems better. When I have problems, I want solutions, not more process. The way to get there is through positive influence. Laughter is simply a bonus, so you don't need to feel stressed about whether you are funny. Engagement goes so beyond just a laugh. Anyone has room to ramp up their positivity and bring out their inner weird.

Try to not be Michael Scott from *The Office*. Making everyone feel uncomfortable is not the best way to success, even if that show truly is a riot.

Set the stage for connectedness. That's the prerequisite to laughter: a background of connection. This is a simple concept. Imagine putting on a play this bizarre way: You sell tickets, the audience comes in, the actors walk out on stage, then they try to figure out what the play is all about. It sounds like *Whose Line Is It Anyway?* or an improv show. It could work, if that's what the audience was expecting. But what if they thought they were coming to see a non-improvised, traditional stage production of *Hamlet*? The stage would need to be set before the play is underway, not only to give the audience a solid experience but also to give the actors a shared world in which they can relate to one another and follow the script. That shared world helps create an understanding of what is happening. So that's what we are talking about here: creating a shared world of experiences for people before we can expect them to connect and create.

---

[6] AM Isen, AS Rosenzweig, and MJ Young, "The Influence of Positive Affect on Clinical Problem Solving," *Medical Decision Making* 11, no. 3 (Jul–Sep 1991): 221–227. doi: 10.1177/0272989X9101100313.

All too often, we jump to trying to be funny, or trying to make people laugh, and the net result is that from trying, without any basis of a shared experience, we end up feeling or looking like Michael Scott in the American version of *The Office*. That is exactly what makes those moments in *The Office* so (deliciously) awkward: Jokes are told without a shared background of relatedness for the setup or the punchline with the people on the receiving end of the joke. The jokes backfire because the background of connection isn't there first. We need a background of connection. Also, P.S., if for some reason in the world you've not yet seen *The Office* (the USA version), please set aside a week and binge watch the entire series. You're welcome.

You've experienced the type of connection we are describing in moments where you meet someone and find something in common. What lets the conversation develop from there is the shared experience that provides the foundation. Think of this in the same way as establishing emotional buy-in for a vision, or increased engagement for a team.

If you just hit people over the head with a vision, it will never land the same way as if you get them onboard with the reason *for* the vision first. That's the connection point for the team, as well, as it lets people relate to one another and how they are involved. They see and define themselves through the lens of the vision overall. People have been found to open up to one another more when they laugh together. *That* is science.[7] When you have an idea and need to bring people together to support and develop it, find *fun* ways to build connection with them, first and foremost. The dynamics of the team will strengthen.

I see this happen all the time when I speak from the stage or teach juggling to corporate groups as a team-building exercise. People love laughing at one another and at themselves. They love seeing their friends succeed. A breakout session of juggling instruction at a conference works wonders for teamwork and solidifying group dynamics.

---

[7] Alan W. Gray, Brian Parkinson, and Robin Dunbar, "Laughter's Influence on the Intimacy of Self-Disclosure," *Human Nature* 26 (2015): 28–43, https://doi.org/10.1007/s12110-015-9225-8.

Get weird. I know I keep bringing up weird. Did I mention I like weird? I think I did. The point isn't to be bizarre. It is to continually remember the value of your own unique perspective and to bring a little of that, or a lot, to your interactions with others. You will feel more authentic if you do. They will sense that, too. And this can provide the foundation for a shared background that can strengthen connection.

Shake things up, and think of laughter as a tool for positive disruption. Who wants their life, work, love, or creativity to be boring? I hope no one. Laughter disrupts the status quo. It turns something that was seen one way on its ear and makes us suddenly able to look at the same situation in a different way. Perspective shifts are extremely valuable for innovation and for team development, as well. We fall into habits and patterns and in doing so find the routines we have fallen into are limiters to progress. New perspectives bring potential for rapid growth.

In addition, new angles on subjects feel fresh and exciting. This is exactly what I need to do when I am coming up with ideas for a keynote speech for a client: I imagine what has been seen and heard before, or what has been worked on before and how. Then I imagine alternative ways of looking at the situation, working on it, pursuing it.

What makes something interesting or funny in comedy is the twisting of a premise with a surprising punchline. You don't need to know how to do that. You just need to know that it works. So, as we laugh together, we are seeing the world differently because of a perspective shift. We can take that lesson and apply it to development and innovation. New angles on old ideas can turn those ideas into brilliancies where they might have just been dead ends before.

This leads us to one of the most important things laughter does. This is going to sound heavy, but I will unwrap it. Laughter helps us navigate the double bind of human existence: We are temporary creatures who imagine ourselves to be limitless. That is a situation of opposites existing at the same time. It is a tricky psychological situation, to say the least. Heavy-sounding topic, but we touched on it earlier. The double bind is any situation in which we are caught between irreconcilable opposites. Success/failure. Life/death. Win/lose. Laughter is one technique that can help us through.

Laughter helps us play with the weight of the world. It helps us ... favorite slogan alert: *play with gravity*. This means like a juggler, sure, but playing with gravity also means anything that helps us navigate the weight of what we feel or the challenges we face. I have loved this idea for over a decade. Go to playwithgravity.com and see what I mean. (Surprise. It's me.)

> **Laughter doesn't have to poke fun. It can honor, engage, elevate, and inspire.**

What do you do in the face of opposites that are impenetrable, unnavigable, impossible to comprehend? What approach can you take when none provides a solution or clarity? One route through those opposites is laughter. It upends the status quo and, like we've been discussing, allows us to begin fashioning a new one through looking at the situation from a totally new perspective. Should you always laugh at tough situations? That's your call. Read the room. Make sure you're not offending anyone or ignoring their needs. But it is one technique that can refashion perspectives and help us build a better now.

I remember having this idea reinforced by two Austrian sociologists, Peter Berger and Thomas Luckmann, who wrote a treatise called *The Social Construction of Reality* in which they offered ideas around each of us constructing our reality through our perspectives.[8] When we laugh amidst a double bind, we create our own version of reality through a perspective shift we bring to a situation that otherwise wouldn't have been easy to navigate.

One of my favorite papers on the effects and meaning of laughter was done by a dear, departed friend. The late Dr. Neil Elgee wrote an often-overlooked piece in 2003 titled "Laughing at Death," in which he talked about the double bind of our existence and how we can get through it with laughter. His discussion surrounds how we can most effectively navigate our lives and our interactions with others amidst conflicting influences. Elgee wrote, "Especially in modern times, we

[8] Peter Berger and Thomas Luckmann, *The Social Construction of Reality: A Treatise in the Sociology of Knowledge* (New York: Anchor Books, 1967), 1–18.

have seen that the fabric of culture is not always so tightly woven; is not impervious."[9] He meant that what we see as absolutes and what we face as obstacles are potentially malleable. Elgee explored the idea that laughter is a way to cut through those obstacles. Overall, we can build and create new perspectives and approaches to reality and shift our experiences for the better. We can do this even if we are in a tough psychological situation – or even if we are in actual conflict with one another.

This ties into our earlier chapter on revolutionary thinking. Perspective shifts aren't just helpful, they are life-enhancing, problem-solving, and team-developing. When we want something more and are feeling stuck, we can find that something more, together. It might have been right in front of our faces all along but we just couldn't see it until we laughed at the double bind – or, at the very least came together in different ways.

> **We can create the something more we are looking for.**

I've seen this happen as far away as Singapore, all across the United States, in Europe, across all of Russia and Ukraine, Mexico, Iceland, the UK, the rest of North America and around South America, Africa, and Japan. Everywhere I've been, when people laugh, they unite. They change the face of their surroundings. They shift the social fabric and the creative boundaries in which they've been bound up until that point, and they expand outward. People see one another differently after positive shared experiences. This is why I love being on stage and in relationship with audiences so much. We start the keynote as one thing and end up as another. It is like we create a new reality together.

Laughter is a catalyst for transformation, and smart leaders, collaborators, managers, and teachers know this. Historically, some very smart people have explored these ideas, as well.

---

[9] Dr. Neil Elgee, "Laughing at Death," *Psychoanalytical Review* 90, no. 4 (August 2003): 475–497, doi: 10.1521/prev.90.4.475.23917.

One smart guy, who eventually went completely bonkers, named Friedrich Nietzsche, challenged us to dance and laugh, saying, "False be every truth which hath not had laughter along with it!"[10] His was a contention that laughter was essential to sanity. Ironic. He should have laughed more. But the point, and his, was that laughter rings with truth and to laugh together with your team and have the truths which you speak be shifted and driven by that new energy.

Let's talk about how to be lighthearted amidst the weight of the world. Here are few ideas that could elevate your approach to creativity with your team and at the same time, enhance dynamics with them for the better:

- **Be willing to laugh at yourself.**

  Being able to laugh at yourself is an incredible skill to culti-vate. Unfortunately, we often fear doing this because we've cre-ated the illusion that everyone is judging us constantly and we don't want to look foolish. Realistically, few actually care. But when we poke fun at ourselves or when we can laugh at our mis-takes, we become relatable to others. This is true especially if we are not overtly harsh in the angle we take. Make a joke at your own expense and people will connect with you. Make too many and people will connect you to a therapist. With that in mind, balancing that out and being able to laugh at ourselves with jokes that are self-*elevating* is uplifting and unifying. The goal is to bring the group together, connecting by way of shared under-standings and experiences.

  A couple of creative approaches I've taken with clients might help demonstrate the effect that laughter has on people. I had a group want a fun activity that lightened the mood in a conference session. I had people bring in anonymous photos of themselves from when they were nerdy teenagers, and we used those to try and guess which person each photo was connected to today. There was a lot of laughter as people tried to justify their hairstyles and lack of fashion sense from years ago.

---

[10] Friedrich Nietzsche, *Thus Spoke Zarathustra* (Ware, Hertfordshire, England: Wordsworth Classics of World Literature, Wordsworth Editions Limited, 1997).

Another strategic connection around laughing at ourselves organizationally originated with a client for whom I worked a few years ago. They had a corporate culture rooted in acronyms. I won't divulge their company name or their specific acronyms, but everywhere you looked there were new acronyms. Their PFR, and TWMD, and DCDM (not their real acronyms), played really well to joke about the need for simplicity amidst complexity. I was able to tie in well-known acronyms, too. CNN, ATT, ESPN, LOL, OMG, and others were instantly relatable. We had fun laughing not at the company but rather about the angle I took, which was that being specific and having a shared language was extremely positive for the group even if it was an alien language to the rest of the world. It was funny to have them see their acronym culture in a new light.

■ **Remember our first strategy: Be kind.**

It might sound basic and obvious, but in the context of laughter or connection, it is important to explore. Laughter often comes at the expense of an out-group. The in-group, meaning the people in the know, is able to laugh because of a joke made at the expense of an out-group. I use this in my presentations when I pit the company I am speaking in front of against a main competitor in the marketplace during a moment of verbal play. I make a joke that directly, and gently, pokes fun at the competitor, and everyone loves it.

That said, our laughter shouldn't come at the expense of those within our own organization or close to home. Simple rule: Don't be a jerk. In fact, we can use our laughter to enhance others' lives. This is going to happen organically with laughter through disrupting or upending mediocrity in a meeting or conference. When people are amused and happy, that disruption of the norm happens automatically.

But like I said, you don't have to do stand-up comedy to make this happen. Shared experiences and acknowledging people also enhance a sense of meaning in those around us. Remember, things as simple as letting people know they are valued, trusting in them, and letting them know you're glad they are on the team and part of the mission are all things that are important for productivity. They boost self-esteem in others and leave them feeling as though they are valuable contributors to something meaningful and bigger than themselves. High-performing teams have been shown to be enhanced by positive feedback and in team interaction.[11] You can be the catalyst for that for your team, family, or your collaborators by just being positive. Engaging people with laughter takes that a step further. What a relief. You don't have to be funny. You just have to be kind and a good person who appreciates those with whom you work and create.

This is a reason why when a conference, meeting, or event really matters, and they all do, having outside experts rather than internal hopefuls is always the best choice. Go with what is best and what works best. The impact can be rock solid for your group.

- **Create unsolvable problems as a creative exercise.**

This is an actual team-building exercise that is really engaging and fun. I came up with this about fifteen years ago when presenting for a major corporate group training at a tech conference on the East Coast. I love the idea. I had people split up into small groups and then had each group brainstorm and invent impossible-for-the-moment but future-forward ideas based on what the company did and the service it provided. These were ideas for the company that couldn't, or certainly didn't, exist today. Then I had people fantastically imagine ways to make that wild idea a reality. It was fun, interactive, and solid in terms of strengthening skills of listening and teamwork. Ideas truly got weird and ridiculous as people came up with funny and unexpected angles to bringing their wild ideas into reality. My goal at events like this is always to get people laughing as they learn. One enhances the other.

---

[11] Marcial Losada and Emily Heaphy, "The Role of Positivity and Connectivity in the Performance of Business Teams: A Nonlinear Dynamics Model," *American Behavioral Scientist* 47, no. 6 (2004): 740–765, https://doi.org/10.1177/0002764203260208.

The attempt, the mindset of trying to engage with laughter, humor, or light-heartedness amidst a world weighed down, has value in and of itself. We often measure the effectiveness of an action by its outcomes. But being driven now, to build a better now, means we disregard the need for the outcome and recognize that the now we are building and the more we are finding is rooted in our continual attempts to bring it into being. Utopia might not yet have been discovered, but that shouldn't stop us from trying to find better solutions for situations we face and for those we work with, care about, and develop with.

> **We have to dream impossibly and at the same time act from a mindset of possibility.**

Taking joyous risks with engaging with laughter will inspire us to embrace vulnerability and courageously try something new. It will motivate us to do things we haven't done before or in a new way.

I worked with a group just before the pandemic who were being managed by a more authoritarian style. The approach works in theory, and for some I am sure, but for those less inclined to adhere to intensity and demands, the approach can be demotivating. Teams are most effectively supported when approached by individuals who take varied forms of connecting with people.

But don't take my word for it. A research study published in 2021 looked at motivation styles and noted that sticking to only one approach potentially alienates those for whom that model is culturally unfamiliar.[12] What about interdependency and connection? How could it be that we strive for that in our personal lives but leave that for discard when we get to work? My suggestion for this group was to

---

[12] Xingyu Li, Miaozhe Han, Geoffrey L. Cohen, and Hazel Rose Markus, "Passion Matters but Not Equally Everywhere: Predicting Achievement from Interest, Enjoyment, and Efficacy in 59 Societies," *Proceedings of the National Academy of Sciences* 118 (March 2021): 11, https://doi.org/10.1073/pnas .2016964118.

approach with a leadership and managerial angle rooted in laughter but also with connection and support, top to proverbial bottom. The effect was increased sales, which isn't a testament to my brilliance nearly as much as it is the inherent strength of the team.

Ultimately, let's close on this thought: If the world is going to be heavy, then let us face it while laughing because it brings us together in the midst of facing challenges. At least then we can be uplifted together as we focus on making it through difficult times. The operative word is *together*. We reclaim the moment for ourselves and for our team every time we draw people together. Laughter bridges the gap between us.

Let's now explore our togetherness and relationships, because if we can laugh together, we can certainly transform together. Relationship-building is a principal way for those who want something more to build a better now.

9

BUILD RELATIONSHIPS
to Outsmart the Dread of Isolation

"… the individual must rely on others to complete the picture of him of which he himself is allowed to paint only certain parts."[1]
— Erving Goffman, *Interaction Ritual*

I STUDY YOGA and work on staying in shape under the online instruction of an incredible yoga instructor I met pre-pandemic while overseas. Duncan Parviainen taught some powerful in-person classes that aligned my body and mind. He then pivoted brilliantly during the pandemic, creating an online community of devoted practitioners. He said something during an online class a couple years ago while talking about self-care that really resonated with me. He said, "In a society which profits off our self-doubt, one of the most rebellious things we can do is like ourselves."

I agree. It starts with us. But as we will see in this chapter, we take it a step further and expand that feeling of empowerment when we allow the rebellious act we're engaged in to be one of connecting with other people. We end up finding ourselves in the process. Feeling isolated stunts progress. Relationship transforms it.

---

[1] Erving Goffman, *Interaction Ritual: Essays on Face-to-Face Behavior* (New York: Anchor Books, 1967), 84.

When we cultivate a feeling in the person across from us that they matter and that together we are part of something meaningful we discover a game-changing approach to teamwork and leadership. When we see people for who they are, for the qualities within them and not simply the attributes on the surface, we will bring a sense of real value to them. People, and the relationships we form with them, are building blocks of our own foundation.

Instill that sense in the people around you and you'll have set a marker by which you can gauge a very new kind of progress. When people are acknowledged, recognized, and valued, their motivation comes from within. They have a buy-in to ideas and to goals that is authentic and generative, rather than it coming from external sources. Most importantly, they will have space created in which they can develop, which otherwise would have been restricted. Building a better now through this, and any of the other strategies in this book, creates new space for expansion and growth.

Let's start with these simple solutions to strengthen connections:

- **See people for who they are, for the qualities within them, and for what these qualities mean to you and your team. When people are seen, they are going to feel elevated, and chances are good they are going to see you back, which elevates you in turn.**

- **Make this process genuine and essential, not calculated or tactical.**

- **Recognize you are the result of the people around you, just as you are the result of your own self-work. The listening you do to others, and the depth to which you take that, not only strengthens bonds with them but also deepens your sense of self.**

Leaders often ask me how to motivate their teams. I always say to stop looking for quick fixes and start building relationships. If you want to motivate people, work to create a culture of meaning and value.

Make sure the people around you feel they are a part of it. The reason to do this is not just to increase productivity or profit. The reason to do this is because people want and need it, and you'll be honoring them where they are, not forcing them into where you want them to be.

Your focus, along with the resources available to you and a solid plan, will go only so far unless you can incorporate the abilities and congruent personalities of the people with whom you pursue your vision. It's not only that people matter. They are essential to the achievement of your shared goals and of your own fulfillment, as well. In a world that pulls us apart, and in which we often feel tremendously isolated, that connection is psychologically essential.

This is the best approach to leadership I've derived over decades of working with leaders across all social strata and around the world. It is drawn as much from my time in community-organizing as it is from my time working with people in corporations. Taking action isn't about doing good for the sake of doing good. It is about genuinely connecting with other people about ideas and inspirations that really matter.

We need other people. Jean-Paul Sartre famously wrote, "Hell is other people!"[2] But the smart leader and, more specifically, the world changer take a different perspective. The epigram above says it clearly: We need one another to complete *ourselves*. More on that later in the chapter.

Sartre's point, via his character, was that it is challenging to see oneself the way others see us: basically as an object amidst *their* consciousness. I take a more inclusive position and see others as developers of *our* identity. Our own sense of self is as rooted in those around us as it is in our own generative potential. We need others, and they need us. This means the time for a perspective shift on leadership and teamwork, away from authority and control and toward connection and interactivity, is right now.

---

[2] Jean-Paul Sartre, *No Exit* (New York, Samuel French, 1944). Garcin, speaking at the end of the play, "There's no need for red-hot pokers. Hell is other people!"

This makes teamwork more than just a buzzword. Instead, it is a truly valuable and meaningful resource for the development of individuals and groups. It takes more work to see things from this uplifting and encouraging perspective. But the results, in terms of strengthening connections and elevating people, are absolutely worth the work it takes.

While we are on the subject of the work it takes and changing the game, take another look at the epigram starting this chapter. I want to think academically about it for a moment, from the standpoint of imagining social change. The words in that quote are powerful in terms of taking a position on the value of interaction, but I have been intrigued by its gendered language. Having read a considerable amount of work from this era, I have wondered about an entire generation of psychological explorers who left behind a legacy of language that wasn't gender-inclusive. At the time, it wasn't a priority. Today it is, for many people. I mention this as a means of showing how times change, perspectives shift, and culture expands, as long as people make the choice to make it so. Values change, and culture, society, and even language can shift along with it, created as a better now built by people who want more and who work to bridge the gap between the now they have and the future they envision.

We can shift, mold, change, and transform the world around us. That's what world changers do. That's what you can do. Social change is not about cutting people down, or being self-righteous. Both are boring and reveal a sophomoric understanding of people, of social science, and of our potential for change. Transformation starts with a thorough analysis of a situation, then planning and imagining possibilities, then working with others toward that goal. Every step of the process is rooted in human interaction and how effectively we develop relationships.

> How will you be a driver of relationship culture instead of simply being a passenger

Can you make the decision to do the extra work to bring about change around relationship dynamics and values that need to be enhanced? Are you willing to put this at the forefront of your work and creative environment? Relationships and how we develop them, whether in the midst of being strained, fractured, building, or developing, can be transformed. We have the power to do that. We all want to feel like we belong, and I hold it as a truth that people want to be inclusive of others, even if societal trends or historical experiences push us in another direction. We can actively work toward that change.

We didn't have to be patriarchal in our historical language around social issues and psychology, so we have started to transform it over time. The very language we use to describe things – the common currency of our existence in terms of sharing our perspectives on the world with one another – is shifting. We have started to change it. The time has come to look at relationships in a new way. We need a deeper understanding of their significance and an increased push toward developing them and thus initiating that shift.

The need for relational transformation is increasingly evident in our connections to one another today. An issue of increasing importance for organizations is building multigenerational teams. This work is rooted in finding ways for generations to work together, whether they are based in individualism or interactivity.

A new generation is stepping into its own at the time of this writing. This is one inclined toward sustainability, diversity, social responsibility, and relationships influenced by independence. Theirs has been a world built digitally. Their values have developed amidst trends rooted in interaction and experience, yet they interface with the world in continually individualistic ways.[3] That's the key element to keep in mind. There is a duality here between individualism and interactivity, but both of these thrive in a culture where meaning and value are prioritized. Those elements don't change generationally.

Workplaces struggling with, wondering about, and working toward improved interpersonal and intergenerational dynamics would be wise to focus on working to instill meaning in people. The *how* is tricky but not impossible, because our core desires for connection and meaning

---

[3] Alyssa Khan, "The Most Diverse Generation in the Workplace Can Agree on This One Career-Builder," *Fast Company*, December 8, 2023.

are consistent even if our numerical age is not. It just might seem that way at times.

People typically don't do well with uncertainty, new situations, and generally not knowing. We default to defensiveness when something is new or unusual. I would suspect this is due to some genetic encoding that taught us if something wasn't a tree or a rock, and instead was mysteriously hiding behind one or the other, it might eat us. With this in mind, embracing new ideas and inviting others to do the same could take an approach of reframing or redefining the challenge from realistic terms. Have this be inviting. Are your team members focused on individualism? Reframe that for them from the perspective of teamwork since empowered individuals are essential parts of any team. Are they more interactive but you need people to be thinking on their own? Reframe from the perspective of individual thinking being a vital component to interactive success.

This is always going to be a new frontier. Like aims for gender-inclusivity or sustainability, it requires commitment and an onboarding of your team to keep minds open for a vision of a better now that includes the *more* that people are wanting. How will you hear the call for transformation unless you are open to it? Have you ever gone to the gym when you said you would and then felt the massive triumph over the self that comes from getting out the door and not just sitting on the couch? If you have felt the excitement of actually putting yourself into motion, you will understand when I offer this: It is time for us to change how we interact with others and lead with instilling meaning and recognizing value in them. We have to get out the door and into the world, so to speak, so that we can actively connect, creatively inspire, and begin to make that relational shift a reality.

To build a better now, we are going to have to explore connectivity and relationships and how we can strengthen our connections to one another and how can we enhance individuals. We have to do this amidst a world that is increasingly both disconnected and connected at the same time, in ever-changing ways.

We need a new kind of listening.

After the 2010 earthquake in Haiti, I made many trips to the country to establish relationships. On one trip the following year, I received a lesson in deeper listening. I was in a tent city, which were groups of hundreds or sometimes many thousands of tents that had been set up as makeshift survival camps all around Port-au-Prince. Conditions were dire, and people were desperate.

I was walking through a tent city with a Haitian friend, who was introducing me to people so I could hear their stories and help to formulate an action plan. At one point, a little girl, maybe 7 years old, walked up to me and asked for money, motioning that she was hungry. This was an occurrence that happened about 10 to 20 times an hour in Haiti at the time, maybe more, and there was no way, given my resources, to provide money for everyone who asked, regardless of need.

I had to say no, heartbreaking as it was. The girl walked away. A few steps later, my guide casually turned and told me more about her. He'd seen her before, he said. Evidently there was a man on the other side of the tent city who had a bicycle that he would rent out for the equivalent of a few pennies, and he allowed the person who rented the bike to ride it around the tent city a few times. What this girl was doing with the money she acquired was to feed her family first, and then take whatever was left over to rent the bike so she could ride around the tent city three or four times. I was stunned. In the midst of one of the greatest catastrophes in the Western Hemisphere, this little girl was simply trying to hold onto a sense of her little-kid-ness amidst it all.

I called her back over. I asked her, in my rudimentary French, if she was trying to ride the bike. Thankfully, she understood. She was shy at first and reluctant to admit it, but yes, she told me, she hoped to ride the bike after she fed her family. I gave her the money she needed for the bike, and hopefully more. She smiled from ear to ear, and clutching the money in hand, ran off to feed her family.

It was a moment in which I relearned there are levels to listening: the primary, and the deeper listening beyond that. The face-value listening was me hearing only the ask for money. The deeper listening was actually taking the time to learn why and to hear the story beyond the face-value story.

> **Taking the time to really listen changes relationships and helps to build a better now.**

Listen as if we are the other. Listen as if their story is more important than ours. Listen as if who *we* are is dependent on who *they* are. This is the future of connection, and it is one we will need to be growing into together. It is going to be the key to making people feel like they belong and are truly connected.

People don't do incredibly well in isolation or when they start to feel unheard. Isolation might be productive at times. I know, for example, that I have been typing for many weeks without much interruption. I have experienced being an odd hermit, and I know that it can lead to successes. But isolation, when it leads to actual loneliness, wears people down. Feeling lonely versus being alone is just too debilitating. The effects socially and psychologically are deeply impactful.[4]

The problem of loneliness, of disconnection from a team, or, more to the point, of not feeling uplifted by our community, is entirely counterproductive to any team with whom I have ever worked. I generally don't encounter teams who want their people to feel like expendable outcasts. Our apprehension about being ostracized or isolated leads to measurable psychological issues.[5] We can do better with this in our determination to build a better now for ourselves and for those around us, and we are creating that together.

An approach I have seen work in successful teams is to shift our mindset to continually be building relationships through actively working to listen and to instill meaning, rather than being

---

[4] "The Loneliness Epidemic Persists: A Post-Pandemic Look at the State of Loneliness among U.S. Adults," *The Cigna Group: News and Insights*, December 2021, https://newsroom.thecignagroup.com/loneliness-epidemic-persists-post-pandemic-look.

[5] Amy Novotney, "The Risks of Social Isolation," *Monitor on Psychology* 50, no. 5 (May 2019): 32.

hierarchical, undermining people, or breaking them down. When you work to infuse people with a sense that they matter, growth and expansion regularly follow.

> **Building relationships is an art form, a solid approach to how we work and live, and is an essential life skill.**

Chad Rapper is president of True North Payment Solutions, powered by PayCompass. He is a sales expert in the payment-processing industry in Chicago area, managing a team of twenty-five people, and has been in business for almost thirty years. Chad has built his career on listening and on teamwork, both with his actual team and with the people he serves. He approaches every conversation with clients as a *learning* opportunity rather than as a *sales* opportunity. This is true with long-time established clients as it is with potential new clients. I see him as always looking to listen and learn. It is impressive, and puts into practice my ideas around interactivity and what it does to both parties in a conversation. The client feels heard, and this is not a tactic for sales. It means that both parties strengthen a relationship and grow so they actually want to be in touch. After all, we want to do business with people we like. I can't think of anyone who thinks otherwise, along the lines of, "I can't wait to buy a car from that auto dealership I absolutely despise," or "I truly hate my hairdresser, and this is why I keep going back." I asked Chad about how he puts effective teamwork to use and how his workflow is rooted in relationship and listening. He said, "The one saying I use all the time, whether I am with new people or industry veterans, is that if you focus only on price, you're missing the mark." He goes deeper with potential clients to really see them, hear them, and establish relationships with them.

Chad approaches clients not from a sales position but from what he calls *a consultative standpoint* rooted in listening and relationship building. He added, "I like to say that price is only an issue in the absence of value. That goes for literally everything in life. If a restaurant is inexpensive but the food tastes terrible and the service is awful, then the experience is going to be viewed negatively. But if the food is beyond comprehension and the service is top-notch, the price is an afterthought."

This approach represents a new kind of profitability. There's a direct connection between valuing what people have to offer and whatever profit might flow from those relationships. Lead with the first, and if the second follows, then it's a double win. From Chad's example, we see how focusing on people, on service, on relationship-building, and listening definitely help to establish value. His successes with True North are a testament to that.

Making people feel like they matter, matters.

I often open my keynotes with customized comedy that everyone can relate to in the moment. For example, at a recent keynote in Iowa, the client and I miscommunicated in advance of the event about the dress code. She'd told me that "no jeans were allowed" and meant that dress was business casual. I took the "no jeans" comment to mean that everyone would be in suits. I showed up at the event in a perfect suit, ready for a room full of serious professionals. What I found instead was a room of casually dressed people who themselves had missed the memo about the jeans! I was by far the most formally dressed person in the room. They were the furthest thing from serious. I made a joke from the stage at the start of the keynote by saying that these were the friendliest serious people I'd ever encountered, and also the most casually dressed formal people. We all shared a good laugh. Being onstage is all about establishing relationships.

I just took a room of people who had no idea what to expect and gave them what to expect. I invited them into a shared familiarity and added some fun – all in under half a minute. The audience felt I was there with them, not just speaking at them. When I do this from the stage, it makes such a difference.

When we identify someone and make them feel seen and heard, we give them a sense of belonging. This is essential in the quest for making people feel valued. In my keynote, I involve the audience and work with volunteers and let them know I couldn't have done the keynote without them. I tell them they are deeply appreciated. I remind them their contribution matters. By the end of the keynote, those people feel like heroes. As does anyone with whom I have interacted during the hour. They feel like they are a valuable contributor to something meaningful. They feel like they belong.

The first few seconds matter when I'm onstage in the same way that interactions in your work and life matter, too. When you establish connection, really *be* with the person at the other end of the conversation, and start the relationship-building early in sincere ways. Use people's names from time to time. Ask for *their* opinion, and check in to see what they think and how they are doing. Take a Golden Rule approach, and imagine someone actually caring about what you have to say instead of being half into their phone or with one foot out the door. Presence creates potential. Everything will just flow from there.

> **Let's continually work to make our relationships clearer, stronger, and more significant.**

Enhancing a feeling of relationship and belonging in the people around us is a core component in relationship- and team-building.[6] This is true at work just as it is true interpersonally, as we discussed above. Here are some things we can do, even if we are not onstage in front of a thousand or more people, to support this goal:

- Celebrate people's accomplishments so you enhance opportunities for them to feel valued. When people feel valued, they will be encouraged to continue contributing.
- Establish mentoring programs where people can connect with and learn from one another so we can interact in different ways with people who have different experiences. Stay open to possibility. Have the goal be to have experience, educate, and inform intergenerationally. Remember this goes both ways,

---

[6] Kara Dennison, "Why Companies Should Prioritize Employee Health and Happiness in 2024," *Forbes*, October 24, 2023.

with the mentor potentially being the older generation, but also just as valuably with the younger generation taking that role and offering a new kind of wisdom.

- Appreciate ideas by recognizing individuals and letting them know that what they have to say is meaningful and that it matters. And I don't mean to just do this for the sake of doing it. If someone has an idea next year that there should be a thing called "a light bulb" that illuminates the room, you don't have to give them a trophy. But if a good, innovative, or enlightening suggestion comes up, be sure to recognize it and the person who offered it.

- Collaborate as a way of life both at work and in the every day. Instead of just coexisting, when we collaborate, we are enhancing and uplifting others through recognition of one another's contributions.

- Value and support inclusion and diversity by making creative decisions together.

- Actively work to *intergenerationalize* your team (yes, that's a word now … you heard it here first) and work toward that with determination. For as I said above, it is inspiring and enhancing for a team to learn from alternative contributors and experience different approaches to team-building and developmental process. Work to make that happen through including new ideas and diminishing stereotyping based on age.

- Continually revisit the vision for your group or organization, and listen to one another's perspectives on these goals. Do this in open meetings, one on one, or in a forum where people feel able and invited to share.

- Make space, too, for emotional well-being and reflection. This is increasingly important in a generationally diverse workspace, and also in any collaborative team environment. People tend to diminish the effect and importance of soft skills. That's an old-school model. If you want to solidify your team, embrace dynamics that give increased priority to soft skills, such as listening, empathy, and time management, while moving forward with traditionally hard skills that drive progress in different ways.

Those are practical approaches to strengthening connection. While I think it is valuable to look at issues practically, theoretical approaches are important, as well.

When we build and strengthen a team through relationship, the new collective dynamic experienced amidst those involved has never existed before. We create something from an idea – from nothing, essentially. We are human-resource magicians, just without rabbits coming out of hats or sawing anyone in half. As a general rule, just FYI, sawing people in half is a human-resource fail.

> **To build a better now, we need to strengthen relationships with those around us, and prioritize their position.**

Teams and their members are like artists in a way. Artists create something from nothing – through taking colors, brushstrokes, a canvas – and from those seemingly disparate elements actualize a vision. You're involved in the same process. The goal is to create something tangible out of seemingly abstract parts consisting of personality, goals, creativity, passion, intensity, ideas, interactivity, and your communicative dynamic overall.

The team essentially becomes a creator-artist-developer through developing its dynamic. When a team steps into that mode, it takes on a new life as creator and developer of something that has never existed before. In creating something together, the team expands on a background of connectedness with one another. The act of creation gives a shared language during that process of development. The team experiences cohesion as a result. If your team is all over the map, feeling like a mess, or just generally being weird, remember to unify them through reminders of a shared vision.

When we focus on a concept or a brand, on a mission statement or an idea, we feel that cohesion, connectedness, and camaraderie. This is the essence of teamwork. Authors and speakers share about it. Companies worry about it. Audiences request it as a subject. But the essence of teamwork transcends almost everything we always hear about it. The essence of teamwork is in the transformation and development of the relationship between individuals as they create something new that has never existed before.

Isolation might be real, and we may indeed dread it, but we outsmart it when we come together with others and pursue a meaningful goal. Whether that's a product for a company, a new idea for a campaign, an approach to process, a way of connecting with others, a mutual-aid group, a collective, an innovation, a new system for efficiency, or any other team-based initiative, strengthening connection to others is at the core of development.

> **While in relationship, we are continually redefined by the interactions we have, so let's make them count.**

The *more* we want is dependent on this. Psychologically and socially, when we triumph over isolation and its negative effects, we can finally get to work as the world changers we are meant to be.

If we really do want something more, the pathway to that is through one another. It's with one another. When we build connections, we are building a better now for ourselves, but we are also building a better now for the people with whom we are connecting. This *generous* element of teamwork and relationship is one of the greatest elements of relationship. We get to enhance others as we build a better now. It's a bonus, and part of the process, all at the same time.

Now let's go deeper ... to explore how relationships can be analyzed and strengthened.

Build Relationships to Outsmart the Dread of Isolation

I have seen relationships develop most effectively throughout my life from and on the stage. When I am onstage, these are often high-pressure situations where I have to be establishing connection quickly, in front of hundreds or thousands of people, for clients who matter. Often this has to happen with new individuals in the moment with whom I have not worked before. Having volunteers come to the stage puts me in a position where the make-or-break of the keynote can depend on the quality of the relationships amidst it. Without relationships, speakers offer only canned speeches. You can tell them from a mile away, and I don't do canned speeches. In these moments of building a relationship, I have little other choice than to really dial in my focus and connect, relate, communicate, and create a presentation *with* people, my audience and interactive volunteers, whom I've not known previously.

Developing experience onstage with focus, connection, and relationship-building over four decades has taught me about being in the moment with people. I've learned how to build a better now in front of live audiences, and also how to prepare for these events.

In terms of the preparation, I often am creating something from nothing. I prepare material for clients to strengthen the perception of their vision amongst the audience. I plan out the ideas I share from the stage and make the content relevant and meaningful. This is not solitary work. Ultimately, it is interactive. I can imagine it on my own, but I can only put it into real practice with others. The adage I mentioned earlier that rehearsal can only take you so far about getting off the page, and onto the stage, applies here as well.

Otto Rank, the Austrian psychoanalyst I first mentioned in Chapter 2, explored the idea that humans have the capacity to make the unreal real.[7] He meant we can envision something that doesn't yet exist and then make it come into being through our powerful creativity, manifesting it in physical form in order to reflect our inner selves.

Being a world changer by definition can seem like a lonely task. There often is no roadmap. Isolation can indeed be dreadful. When we are creating and developing ideas, it is easy to fall into isolation. We are trying to be immediate and focused on something that does not yet exist in space and time. Humans are unique in this role: as creators of something that doesn't yet exist and the process with which that thing or object comes into being. We can imagine something, create it, and make it real. This process often doesn't start with others, but in our own minds.

---

[7] Otto Rank, *Beyond Psychology* (New York: Dover Publications, Inc., 1958), 64.

Put into practice, though, the work always manifests interactively. We don't get to create and live in a vacuum. The ideas you have and the action you want are going to be best actualized and amplified when you're interacting with others.

When we work in isolation and try to be the originator of a concept, the developer of an idea, and the guide for its advancement, this can be a potential whirlpool that can draw us down into the depths. Wanting something more and figuring out how to share and develop it as an idea can be a lonely reality. Relationship is the way through. All the work we do on our own needs to be shared in some way with others, even if that's getting perspectives at some stage in the process.

Isolation and loneliness are a threat to one's psychological equanimity. We can become absorbed with our own ideas like Narcissus being obsessed with his reflection, and forget – or not realize – that it is through relationship that we are defined. More importantly in that instance, we can avoid missing details or angles on an idea, which others might illuminate for us.

It can be challenging to reach out to others for perspectives and to trust they will align in some way with what we are trying to develop. But the world-changer culture I envision includes this kind of dynamic.

We are creatures desperate for meaning. We desire and demand and crave it. It is the currency with which we trade in identity. Even though we would like to envision ourselves as taking on the world alone, that's simply not how humans work. We don't get to generate ourselves from nothingness.

A father-and-son psychology team, interestingly named Thomas Patrick Malone and Patrick Thomas Malone, wrote a brilliant (though at times slightly cumbersome) book called *The Art of Intimacy* about what relationship is and how we as participants are defined by it. The idea is that we come into being *within* relationship, not outside of it. When we are reflected in the eyes of another, figuratively, we see ourselves through their reactions to us. We create ourselves in response to others. We are *seen* as others see us, rather than as we see ourselves, and we define ourselves accordingly. This is much like the idea I brought up earlier about talking *to* ourselves for definition and clarity, rather than listening to ourselves with voices that are entirely internal. It also relates to the epigram that launched this chapter.

The Malones saw that the person across from us behaves and interacts in ways that affirm what we are bringing to the moment. In this, there is a vision to be experienced, and it is a vision of ourselves. When we offer, they accept or reject, and we are shifted accordingly. Their affirmation enhances our own self-definition. Their denial does, as well. The effect on us is profound. We define ourselves based on how we are reflected. We come into being not individually but relationally.[8]

This is important for a world changer to remember. Through connection is where we grow. The *new kind of human*, whom we've been exploring throughout this book, is one who values connection and explores and pursues it.

This can be challenging because we live in a world where being a solo force is triumphed amidst a historical championing of the same. We love the idea of the rugged individualist.[9] This mindset has existed since the frontier days in the United States as a mythologized, romantic account of what we can be. I believe it falls a bit flat today, however, given global changes valuing interaction beyond the self. This is especially clear given generational shifts in how connections are made and maintained. The rugged American wasn't really thriving. Often, as they ran around trying to find food or taking that of others, they were barely surviving. They just had bigger guns and more bullets. Force is not a force multiplier. *Relationship is a force multiplier*.

Today, individualism remains challenging for those working in teams and immersed in shared goals that affect the lives of others. Individuals can think they are impervious, immense, and undeniable in their myriad abilities. After all, who needs anyone else when we can each become famous, in our own circle or globally, with just the right post on social media?

We rely on the clicks of others for our mental well-being. It is relationship-like, yes. But we can do better by bringing in other

---

[8] Thomas Patrick Malone and Patrick Thomas Malone, *The Art of Intimacy* (New York: Prentice Hall Press, 1987), 29.
[9] Alex Zakaras, *The Roots of American Individualism: Political Myth in the Age of Jackson* (New Jersey: Princeton University Press, 2022), 1–11.

approaches to relationship along with the digital. Because we definitely want something more. Our interactivity needs to be developed along with the technology that provides it. We can't just have expansive technology and not develop ourselves as well.

We come into being not individually but relationally.

There certainly is valuable information in the "like."[10] That can't be denied. Clicking that we *like* something is useful information to connect with others who have shared values. Of course, there is also the side of likes that serve to compile information for anyone who profits from people buying something. The "like" certainly makes people easier to market to, as we've just told sellers what we enjoy.

We are not solitary creatures. When we enter into relationship and work with others, we find immeasurable value psychologically. Interaction and relationship outsmart isolation or loneliness. By thinking interactively, whether in person or through digital connection, we can bypass being dragged down into the depths of loneliness. Having millions of followers is likely overrated as a measure of happiness, if it is indeed a measure of happiness at all. What matters more is connection beyond the superficial.

The act of creation for generative creatures secures confidence and self-awareness.[11] It's almost like we become mini-gods in a way. We typically reserve the right to create something from nothing to magicians or the divine, yet we each can do exactly that all the time. We can engage in developmental process together. Isolation need not be part of our day-to-day existence as world changers. Those working to build a better now through developing and expanding on what currently is and what could be would be wise to remember that.

---

[10] P.W. Singer and Emerson T. Brooking, *LikeWar: The Weaponization of Social Media* (New York: Houghton Mifflin Harcourt, 2018), 139.

[11] Tom Kelley and David Kelley, "Reclaim Your Creative Confidence," *Harvard Business Review*, December 2012.

We have to be *in relationship*, whether as extroverts or introverts. The interactivity doesn't even need to be in person specifically – I just felt a collective sigh of relief from the introverts among you – but if we completely isolate, we can't get to where we want to be.

When we enter into stronger relationship with those with whom we collaborate, we soothe the Dread of Isolation, but we also enter into a space where the creation of magic is literally possible. Creative alchemy develops when we work together as a team. We create something new that has never existed before: a widget, a slogan, a brand, a concept, an idea, an image, an invention. It all derives from nothing, essentially. We gain on a personal level from the alchemical process. The psychological effect of being involved together in something meaningful lets us outsmart isolation and loneliness.

We benefit when we value input, ideas, and alternative points of view other than our own. The world changer pulls back from control when they realize their own identity is dependent on others, regardless of established objective hierarchies. Considering creative impulse from others as valid even if those ideas are originating from someone with "less" perceived experience or a hierarchical level "beneath" yours leads to more potential for empowerment for all involved. Please remember that.

Hierarchies might continue to exist, simply because it is beyond the scope of this book to offer a plan to replace them. But relationships that share a foundation of trust in one another's contributions are going to serve all those involved more thoroughly than interactions built solely on authority. The subjective invitation rather than the objective demand will always strengthen team dynamics and allow our collective *now* to be stronger.

Let your vision be a shared one. Ownership need not look like a name on a deed or contract. It can begin with recognition, reflecting outward, so that others are defined and seen as meaningful. Each member of a team, and even simply the person on the other side of the conversation, needs to feel they are a valuable part of that clearly identified purpose.

A world changer, who has developed trust from their team, will never need to use authority to push the team along. They recognize amidst a shared vision and reason for doing what you do that all contribute not just to the team but also to the identity and meaning of each of the participants.

We, as meaning-hungry creatures, need to feel as though we are valued contributors to something meaningful here and now. We need to be connected to something that is significant to us today and feel as though we are part of something greater than ourselves as valuable, vital, and important participants in this moment. This is true for us and the people with whom we collaborate.

I am entirely convinced that as social creatures, our relationships with others, our effectiveness as a team, our ability and desire to communicate are all rooted in the meaning that is created through the relationship, through the teamwork, through the communication we share, and most importantly, through the power dynamic we embrace and enhance together. When we share power from within, and each person is on a journey that is appreciated and supported and understood as meaningful, then we can truly grow into our potential.

> We would be very wise to open our minds to new approaches that value people as a priority.

Here is a clear to-do item for the near term: Are you an authoritarian communicator or leader? Do you require rigid structure and absolute control of words and situations? Both, while effective approaches when everything is on the line and there is no margin for error, can lower morale and make people feel they have no room to develop personally or professionally. Consider taking a new approach, and reconsider your balance of authority and power. Ramp up how much you empower others. You can do this through encouraging people to collaborate, asking for input, being more transparent in updating people and communication overall so your supporters and colleagues feel that they are part of a shared vision. Shift your approach to be more inclusive and truly team-based. Without that shift, you will be continuing amidst a model that is outdated and less effective and leaves people feeling empty.

Consider the fact that within the next few years, Gen Z will represent 30 percent of the workforce.[12] Ideas around interactivity are essential to implement and consider now. This, in a book about the moment and the now, is a forward-thinking gift. Ideas around teamwork and relationship development will be key in the years ahead. To ignore generational transformation is to be left behind in relationships and in the future of work, let alone in the now we want to create and enhance.

Attaching ourselves to the idea that a dictatorship of ideas has merit establishes hierarchy, but it doesn't mean that we have to build from that. We can build a better now rooted in sustainability on a human resources level to support quickly transforming social and human dynamics. These are changes that are not just coming – they are imminent.

> **Authority disrupts. Relationships define.**

Disconnected, upended, imbalanced relationships create a situation where authority is the only mechanism for control. Any leader holding onto power through the *image* of relationship and not the *development* of relationship knows there is a sneaking feeling in every moment that authority will slip through one's grasp.

Real power isn't illusory in the way that authority is. Genuine power transforms. Authority disrupts. Relationships define. It is indeed a rebellious act to like ourselves, and even further, to like those around us and strive to connect with them.

What we risk when we develop and step into the possibility of relationship is we might just bring more meaning to people and to ourselves. A world changer does not see this as a threat. Or as an undermining of themselves. They instead see it as potential.

---

[12] Vibha Sathesh Kumar, "Gen Z in the Workplace: How Should Companies Adapt?" *Johns Hopkins University*, April 18, 2023, https://imagine.jhu.edu/blog/2023/04/18/gen-z-in-the-workplace-how-should-companies-adapt/.

A world changer devoted to process and real development and advancement realizes through taking the risk to reclaim the moment on the grounds of relationship means they might just find others who feel the same. Together we can outsmart the dread of isolation through building more powerful connections and recognizing, appreciating, and seeing one another. Already, that sounds like the springboard into a new future.

From there we can create a reverberation to impact others, which is how we will close our exploration of how to build a better now.

10

START A REVERBERATION EFFECT
to Build a Better Now

re•ver•ber•ate \ri-'vər-bə-rāt\ vb - to resound in or as if in a series of echoes[1]

Merriam-Webster Dictionary

LET'S TALK ABOUT a technique to enhance collaboration and to strengthen teams even further than we have before. This starts with an approach to ideas. From there, I want us to think about how to build engagement with others. Creating space for all of that starts with two words.

I strive to be about possibility. I work to make it my default mode. I often fall short, and even have a running joke about it with a friend in which I say my mantra is "You win some, you lose…all the rest." But when I am starting to feel discouraged, confused, or even hopeless, I kickstart a feeling of possibility through two simple words. These are two words that I said to my brother (yes, Darryl the lunatic with his Big Wheel) a few years ago. At the time, I said the two words to be funny, but since then they have become a mantra of sorts.

---

[1] *Merriam-Webster Dictionary*, 2016, s.v. "Reverberate."

Darryl was visiting me in Seattle from where he was living in New York. We drove out to eastern Washington so he could see how geographically vast this state really is. We have rainforests, alpine mountains, cities, and miles upon miles of essentially flat sagebrush desert. I wanted to show him those vast expanses, so we took a long drive.

When we got to where we were going, which by all accounts wasn't really a destination as much as it was a somewhere that didn't appear on a map, he wanted to buy a drink. There was a tiny gas station at a crossroads of two perpendicular roads, each of which led all the way to the horizon. Darryl got out, went inside to get his drink, and when he came out and walked back to where I was idling in the car, I waited until his hand was almost at the door handle and I drove off and left him standing there. But I didn't just drive ten feet, stop, and let him in. I drove off and continued all the way to the horizon. Like, all the way to the horizon. I left him standing there at the gas station with his drink in his hand. I knew he could see me driving away for five full minutes before I disappeared into the distance. Once I had crested the horizon and was completely out of sight, I pulled over, waited a moment, then turned around and slowly drove back to him.

As I got closer to the gas station, Darryl was standing with his drink, in tears with laughter. I drove up to him and stopped, rolled the window down, looked at him, and simply asked, "What if?" I was suggesting, "What if ... I had driven away and left you here forever?" But I offered only the first two words. We laughed about this for about a decade, saying, "What if?" to one another all the time remembering how I'd almost stranded him.

I guess in a way it was revenge for the Big Wheel incident. But it also served as a really fun reminder of a very important question. I never would have let my brother stand out in the middle of eastern Washington for the rest of his life. The idea is ridiculous. But asking "What if?" meant that I at least entertained the idea as a possibility. That question, of asking "What if?" as a means of asking myself about possibilities that were ridiculous, became a call to action for times in which I was feeling down or when I needed to kickstart myself. At the same time, some real substance developed around that two-word question.

What if … I try something new? What if … I think about this situation in a new way? What if … I reach beyond my comfort zone? What if … I start a project that is far more immense than I can imagine? You get the idea. Words are powerful in a specifically incredible way. They create the world by giving tangible shape to ideas which otherwise would have remained abstractions.

We can use that as a tool. By asking ourselves "What if?" when we are feeling stuck, we can start to give shape to new ideas, even unfathomable ideas. Ideas that couldn't possibly be possible can at least take shape and form in the question. From there, we can enroll others in the possibility we want to manifest.

That brings us to the main focus of this chapter.

What is a Reverberation Effect? Let's take a look.

We all know the concept of a "ripple effect." The idea has been shared and repeated throughout modern history. We hear it more often as people seek to make an impact in the world. It makes sense why: It is simple, and it inspires people.

To imagine a ripple effect, think of throwing a stone into a still body of water, like a pond. As a result, ripples echo out from that center point. It's a good metaphor for how one single action can produce outward influence, in concentric rings of impact. Taken a step further as a metaphor, people like to talk about thinking of ourselves as being at the center of that ripple.

I like the idea, but a ripple isn't developed enough as a metaphor for the real capability of the intersection of how people interact, share, and expand on communication, teamwork, and idea development. I like to think of people and teams as having the potential to *reverberate*, not just ripple.

I've been talking about the potential impact of groups and individuals for twenty-five years. I first codified my thoughts on motivation when I wrote the song "Unrestrained" with my band Trial, eventually released on our full-length LP *Are These Our Lives?* In case you are unfamiliar, and I expect fully that you are, I will type out the lyrics for you in a bit.

We played that song to full-on audience engagement all over the planet. People were *feeling* it. The live shows with the band were a time I was able to take a closer look globally at what individuals and groups were inspired and motivated by cross-culturally. People connected powerfully to the ideas in this song because we, everywhere, want something more and this song was a roadmap for how to get there when we take action on what we want. When we ask that two-word question of ourselves, we put ideas into motion.

Since then, I have asked thousands of people in interactive settings what they think of the potential for their ideas. People sometimes see themselves as the ripple, or the more ambitious ones, as the stone. That's a good start.

A Ripple Effect

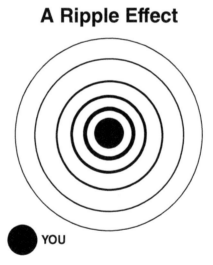

A ripple effect, with the requisite center and waves rippling outward

But we can go a big step further. I ask people to think instead about reverberation.

The Reverberation Effect™ is about both initiating and then amplifying ideas instead of letting them fade. It is teamwork, maximized. When an idea starts with "What if..." and then reverberates, it stays actively in process and can actually amplify over time. This is more effective than a ripple because it actively includes other people and their ideas. Most importantly, it contextualizes those other people as essential.

Note that I use the term *reverberation* a bit differently than it is used by audio engineers. I approach it as you can see in the diagram below.

A reverberation isn't just circles of an impulse rippling outward until they fade away, but an interworking network of energy and ideas. The Reverberation Effect is like a ripple effect on steroids. It is you asking what if this was possible, and putting it into motion, and then having someone else take that idea and run with it and amplify it. This isn't energy that spreads outward in concentric circles that never themselves overlap. This is a dynamic system of ongoing engagement toward the end of maximizing the potential of new ideas and the engagement of all involved.

To make this happen, we need an actively engaged team, all of whom have committed to this idea. Instead of hearing an idea and simply giving it a nod of approval, a team committed to reverberation is on board to amplify, expand on, and develop ideas to see where they can go when taken to a next level. Imagine trainings that inspire your team to think this way. This is the work that needs to be done.

The Reverberation Effect

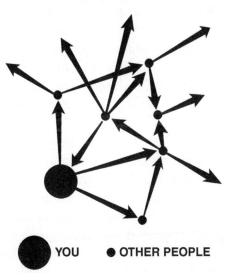

YOU   ● OTHER PEOPLE

The Reverberation Effect™: a network of inspiration and ideas

Ideas and energy impact people, which causes them to engage and react and respond. In turn they *amplify* the original idea, adding to it and offering input, and then they share from there to adapt and transform it. Sometimes they share back to the originator of the idea and cause the idea to develop and grow. Sometimes they share with others and inspire new growth to the idea, which then gets sent out from there. Each point in the process is a relay that amplifies. There aren't ripples that fade. It is a series of people keeping a vision in mind and continually asking, "What if…?"

Unlike a ripple effect, where the ripples quiet to a murmur by the time they reach the edge of the pond, a reverberation effect is one of amplification, multiplication, and scalable growth for an idea, a product, a mission statement, or a movement.

This is a teamwork model. Imagine training your team to hear an idea, run with it, add to it, and share it back. When ideas bounce off of other people who work as what I call a *relay*, the original idea can transform and spread further than it ever could have otherwise, especially if people are inspired to feel a sense of ownership for the idea creatively. It doesn't have to be their idea. They just would benefit from being acknowledged and seen for their contribution to it.

The essential component is to be committed to action. If we truly listen to the idea and to the person sharing, if we have the confidence to offer our input, and if we are in an environment that has been set up for that level of creative engagement, possibilities expand wildly. We become, instead of a single mind, a group mind. If we stay limited in our engagement, the energy might just bounce off the walls. Imagine people just repeating the same things over and over again to one another having not really listened to one another or feeling their contributions matter.

To listen is active. To hear is potentially passive. When we listen to one another, we stay engaged. Listening to embrace and magnify ideas is how we avoid limiting the potential for their growth. Rather than be restricted, if impulse and creative intent are augmented by energy from others and are shared in an environment that allows for enhancement and development, the reverberations won't become repetitive. The initial two-word question magnifies with possible solutions. People add their own perspective on "What if…?"

The world, as we've explored, is packed beyond full with ideas. There's no shortage of them. But this chapter is about having clarity and contributing amidst constant input, and expanding our ability to listen. We reclaim the moment through refining the input we receive and filtering it based on what is most important to us. We learned that in the chapter on focus. From there we can enhance our role as part of a team that reverberates, magnifies, and spreads ideas that are worth listening to.

The lyrics to that original Trial song bear repeating here, even if only for the sake of inspiration. The idea behind the song lyrics was to inspire with its epigram, and then to deliver impact with the lyrics to remind people who want something more that the limits of the room in which we find ourselves are illusory. If we imagine people we haven't yet met, beyond the walls of the room we're in, then we can imagine being in direct service to them, engaging with them, and impacting them as well. We can then work toward amplification and actualization of ideas. Through action, change doesn't just happen. It manifests and magnifies.

Now, remember this was a punk band, so the mention of "screams" means excitement, energy, enthusiasm … not pain and torment! I will include the original epigram that preceded the song as well.

Unrestrained

"He only earns his freedom and his life who takes them every day by storm."[2]

– Johann Wolfgang von Goethe, *Faust*

> take what you feel inside of this room and
> break away
> I'll bring the feeling of this moment
> when I leave

---

[2] Johann Wolfgang von **Goethe,** *Faust: An Abridged Version,* translated by Louis MacNeice and EL Stahl (London: Faber and Faber Limited, 1965), 287.

envision what life could be
if we move beyond our comfort and ability
we'll rot in this tomb until we start to move
no one is handing "change" our way
facing each day with so much to say
and in the absence of action even our screams
    are worth something
what we want, we must create
what we risk, will be regained
what we'd assume, we must forsake
what's been destroyed…
what have we done?
what do I know?
how far are you willing to go?
never restricted by who I am supposed to be
looking beyond all that I can see
to make this a movement again instead of
    only a scene
do you realize what that means?
what we make of this energy is everything
but in the absence of passion our screams are
    worth nothing
what we want, we must create
what we risk, will be regained
what we'd assume, we must forsake
what's been destroyed…can be replaced
too many years spent "screaming for change"
and I see now that what remains
is the time I give
and the chances I take
in the way I live
and the choices I make[3]

---

[3] Trial, "Unrestrained," written by Greg Bennick and Timm McIntosh, Track 8 on *Are These Our Lives?* (Equal Vision Records 1999), 12" vinyl.

Imagine rooms full of energized people singing along with those words. Then picture hours of discussion afterwards in countless languages and different social circumstances worldwide about what we want, how we can create it, what the roadblocks are to it, and what steps we can take to turn those ideas into reality. The best part of those conversations was the *we* element. I wrote the words, yes, but it was the reverberations of others and the amplification of their ideas that turned the experience from one of just a song into one of observable and initiated action steps. *What we want…we must create.*

Through music and connection as we played this song worldwide, I was essentially doing global research in venues night after night all over the world on teamwork and peak performance. I was looking into choices and motivation, pessimism and the inspiration to bring about actual change. I was taking that two-word question and seeing what happened when people put it into motion. *What if…?*

We can use what I call *reverberation multipliers* to amplify and intensify ideas as they extend outward into the world. Think of this like relay towers for electronic transmissions. A radio or TV station that needs to reach people in distant areas unserved by the original transmission point uses relay towers to amplify signals and extend range.[4] You're likely the original station, and you can think of the people around you as relay towers, or *relays*. You might find yourself serving as a relay yourself for someone else's idea or for their development of yours. The *multiplier* element is what makes you a better relay.

Ultimately, we have to include and consider others as important for *The Reverberation Effect* to work effectively. We could do work for and by ourselves, but to what end? Do we really want to be an echo chamber? If we want to build a better now, and if we indeed want something more, then we are reaching beyond ourselves to include others in order to maximize potential all around. Process like this is most effective and expansive ultimately as a shared experience.

---

[4] *FM Broadcast Translator Stations and FM Broadcast Booster Stations*, 47 C.F.R. Chapter I, Subchapter C, Part 74, Subpart L, § 74.1201 Definitions (2009), https://www.ecfr.gov/current/title-47/chapter-I/subchapter-C/part-74/subpart-L.

Author Ross Gay, in his brilliant 2019 book *The Book of Delights*, said, "My delight grows – much like love and joy – when I share it."[5] I love this idea. We don't ignore our own happiness. We embrace it. But we also share it. In doing so, we pass it along, and our own joy grows along with that process.

Now let's go deeper and take a look at *reverberation multipliers* and how you can be the very best relay possible.

Start with you.

Start with you. You are a reverberation multiplier.

I know, Simon Sinek famously wrote "Start with why," and who am I to argue with Simon after he was so kind for, perhaps I mentioned this, opening for me at TEDx? But I really do think that before starting with why, or before starting with anything else, we need to start with being centered and ready. Then we can ask all the why's we want to.

This book has been filled with ideas and ways to engage, especially ways to engage with others. We've talked about kindness, laughter, courage, relationships, and more. But let's remember that reference I made earlier about putting on your own mask when the plane is, let's say, unexpectedly descending or suddenly declining in altitude, or in other words, *rapidly landing poorly*. You get the idea. Putting on your own mask while prematurely arriving at a sudden unplanned destination prioritizes your well-being so that you can help others. But remember, too, that it also helps you. That's the point. It lets you start from a strong foundation so you can take action and be a solid relay for the ideas that come your way.

So, keep your mind clear and your body healthy. Do that however you choose, but do it. I mentioned eating vegan for the last few decades. Personally, I haven't had alcohol, drugs, tobacco, or caffeine in that time, either. That all helps me stay more focused mentally. But, you do

---

[5] Ross Gay, *The Book of Delights* (Chapel Hill, NC: Algonquin Books of Chapel Hill, 2019), xii.

you. The clearer your mind, the better you will show up for others and be able to amplify their ideas.

Taking the first step sets others up to be reverberation multipliers.

Take action. If you've got a big idea, bring it into reality. Ask yourself the two-word question: What...if? Speak the idea, make it real, and take the first step toward it. If you've embraced the ideas in this book, you have supportive concepts to help you through the step in the process that is by far the most difficult: the first. This is the action step. It is up to you to take it. Once you do, others will be inspired by what you have to share. But it has to start with you.

Taking action might be the catalyst for someone to have the gap bridged between what they have and what they want, or as we mentioned earlier, between what they imagine and what they actualize. But it can't happen unless you share that idea to start.

There's a huge difference, to use an example to which many can relate, between joining a gym and actually going. Showing your receipts at the end of the year to someone to prove that you've had a gym membership is not as impressive as them noticing your amazing changes on their own. And it's not as though you have to go with such total determination that going to the gym absorbs your entire life. Just get out the door that first time. The gym example is a metaphor for the first step in all things. It could be anything. Writing the first words of a story, sharing a concept for a video, rethinking how people communicate, developing new metrics for assessing performance. You name it. Put it motion and tell someone about it, and you'll inspire them to do the same.

Taking action **is very different from simply celebrating that you have a good idea.**

If you have shared copies of this book with the people you work with, you can be confident you have a safety net of people to support you in this process. Like I said earlier, you need to build a team of like-minded people who are committed to the concept of reverberation. That way, you can be relays for one another. You have to put your ideas into motion. Don't let them vanish from your mind or from being actualized because you were afraid to fashion them into words and then share those words with others. Let us not look back regretfully about what we haven't said or done. Put your idea into action.

John Greenleaf Whittier, in a few short, poetic lines over a century ago, put fuel to my fire with this couplet:

> For of all sad words of tongue or pen,
> The saddest are these: "It might have been!"[6]

That one always hurts to read. But there is still time to correct many of those things we haven't taken action on to prevent the "might have been" from referring to something we could have initiated but didn't. All is not lost. You can still turn things around.

However, in terms of that one person from way back when whom you thought was really cool, whom you were going to ask to dinner but didn't, and they later won the lottery and are living in a Swiss chalet on a mountaintop and posting on social media with their hair blowing in the breeze that they are happily married and in love, while you're sitting at home reading this book in your pajamas with your cat... is that an example of what might have been? Well, yeah. That one is on you. But thankfully, there's still time to take action on all the *other* impulses you've had.

You get the point. Let your ideas not go unspoken, and your motivations not acted upon. We get one life. Let's make it count. Ask that two-word question and let others hear it.

Keeping your mind clear and your sense of self intact are reverberation multipliers.

---

[6] John Greenleaf Whittier, *Yale Book of American Verse*, ed. Thomas R. Lounsbury (New Haven, CT: Yale University Press, 1912).

Keeping your mind clear will heighten your ability to share reverberations. One way to stay sharp is to not let your life get filled with other people's versions of you.

To start, let's stop fetishizing being busy. There is a difference between being busy out of obligation and responsibility, and being busy by choosing to take on too much. I couldn't possibly count the number of times people used to comment on how busy I was. I've definitely had times where I've been involved in too many projects. The problem is that being busy started to become my self-identity. In time, the way others see us begins to fold in on itself, meaning that we start to become the identity reflected back to us. Remember the Malones, whom I mentioned in Chapter 9, and how we become who we are by way of how others see us?

I would get increasingly and intentionally busy and say yes to more things to fulfill my destiny as people commented. This helped me build an identity as a busy person, which theoretically should have satisfied them. But then they would comment more, and as a result, I would get busier. You can see where this is going.

I finally reached a breaking point and stopped being that version of me. To be busy intentionally as an identity is self-destructive and unsustainable. The biggest problem with situations like that is the busy-ness then becomes more important than the action itself. Have you become the *intense* person? Or maybe the *busy* person? I'd rather be the active and engaged and focused person. Taking on too much makes you an ineffective relay.

Are you completely the description of you that others write? There has to be some agency here on your part. Being busy is oddly a choice at times. Yes, there are some things that require our attention. It is not like we can just stop feeding our kids or taking them to school. But heed the warning that we all too easily become driven by fulfilling an identity more than we are driven to fulfill the intention behind our tasks. We get to be proactive in our identity and claim at least some part of our it for ourselves. You get to focus on what matters the most to you. Make that choice, and let it be clear, so that your participation in reverberation is maximized.

I want to offer a few more concepts that will help you be an even more effective teammate and relay than you already are.

> **Improving communication is a reverberation multiplier.**

If you want to be a better relay, work to be a better communicator. Here are some solid ways you can do that to enhance your abilities as a teammate and improve your skills around working with other people.

Remember that it's OK when people ask questions. Assume the best. I recently told someone close to me to "skew to joy" rather than to sadness. What I meant was to assume the best and hope for the best because we might just get it. When someone asks a question, they might not be challenging you. They might just be trying to gain clarity and a deeper understanding of what you have to say.

Let yourself be a catalyst for sharing by remaining open to alternative points of view, even if those points of view differ from yours and especially if they challenge yours.

Be respectful even when in disagreement, because the goal of your communication is resolution, not continued conflict. Maintain a state of resolution as a goal.

If you want to become a better communicator, cultivate emotional courage. This seems at first glance like it might be in the wrong section, but it actually belongs right here. The internet has simultaneously created conditions where it seems necessary to post our every move on social media in a self-justification and virtue-signaling for the world in order to validate ourselves. At the same time, we've created the conditions where every person seeing those posts becomes judge, justice, and jury on equal par. We touched on this in Chapter 4.

We have set ourselves up for the potential for psychological disaster and targeted mistreatment. In the last few weeks of writing, I have listened to people from the following communities talk about how toxic their communities are: music, corporate photography, yoga, substance abuse/recovery, event-catering. You get the point from this wide cross-section of areas of interest. It's everywhere. We seem to love the ease and ability we have to cut one another down.

Resisting that reality requires a new way of being in the world (a reverberation in the force is felt from Chapter 6). If we intend to escape with our emotional well-being and our very psychological lives, we need to cultivate emotional courage. When we cultivate emotional courage, we solidify ourselves *in* ourselves and set ourselves up to be better relay towers for reverberating ideas that really matter rather than getting caught up in what doesn't.

Emotional courage looks like the focus we talked about in Chapter 5. It also takes the form of being committed to a process with a group of trusted people, and being willing to have our ideas heard even if we get feedback that shifts our perspective. Reverberation can do that. The original idea can change. But what if that idea is changed for the better? With emotional courage, we are ready for that possibility.

Cultivating emotional courage and developing a strong sense of self are two of the greatest actions we can take to ensure our communication remains clear and we are good relays for others. A good step toward developing emotional courage is to connect with someone you can talk to. Someone you trust. I prefer to do this in an analog, face-to-face way. But it is up to you. The next step is to actually share thoughts and inspirations, concerns and frustrations, with that someone who then knows to respond to you in a way that is supportive and connected. Step three is listening to their feedback if they choose to give it, and embracing the sharing as complete if they don't. The goal is literally to practice getting feedback. You want to solidify your sense of self in a trusted environment rather than throw yourself to the wolves of the world and then try to pick up the pieces as they tear your idea apart rather than serve as reverberation relays for you.

If we are not solid in our emotional state, grounded as the meaningful and vital individuals we are, we will be vulnerable to others and potentially reactionary. When we take time and do the necessary work to prioritize the clarity of our thinking, we bypass so much of the toxicity that makes its way toward, around, and through us on a daily basis. Reactions from emotionally unstable people are the worst kind of communication. We don't have to be that person. We can do better. A clear sense of self and maintaining focus on priorities are essential to being a good relay and to the success of *the reverberation effect.*

With the rise of AI, following in the footsteps of a generation of shifting to electronic communication in general, human connection has taken on new meaning, and is constantly being redefined. How we fit into a data-driven, social-media-consumed, reality-shifting, cancel-culture world is, in a sense, as yet unwritten. But the part that has been and continues to be written features us as the authors and drivers of ideas all along. The human emotional throughline, and the confidence that lets us be better relays, is consistent even if our role in the digital communicative chain is unclear at times.

Resist the inclination to react. Solidify your sense of self. You want something more than to have your *reactions* be the main vehicle for your communication and your presence in the world.

Technology, at the risk of sounding as if I am a Luddite or opponent to it (I am quite the opposite), is as invasive as it is supportive. It pushes us continually toward a place in which we sometimes are not sure of our own role in terms of human interaction.[7] Centering and taking time to reflect, process, and situate ourselves amidst the bits of data and critique will ground us and magnify our communicative potential to be a good relay and part of a solid team.

Speak passionately from your grounded place. Have your words be intentional and directed, heartfelt and honest. Be the communicator who reaches people intellectually as well as emotionally. If you've cultivated emotional courage, this will happen easier than you think. If it doesn't, get in touch, and we will work on it together.

Remember that human beings have far more in common with one another than we have differences. This opens up immense possibilities for us in terms of how we interact, share and listen to ideas, and approach one another. This is especially valuable when interacting with those who are seemingly different from we are, whether politically, socially, or ideologically. The divides today are immense and have been largely manufactured. They are part of the spectacle we discussed earlier.

Imagine the reverberation potential of people who are supportive of one another inherently and not looking to be critical of one another any chance they get. This is a culture that you can start to build. I want your team committed to the idea of reverberation and to elevating and expanding ideas to see where they can go. It starts

---

[7] Yuval Noah Harari, *21 Lessons for the 21st Century* (New York: Spiegel & Grau, 2018), 56.

by hearing an idea, developing it, sharing it in its new form, and then repeating that process to see how far it can expand. *What if…?*

Let's try to keep our minds open to alternative points of view.

Be sure as you are cultivating reverberation to listen intently and with patience. This is very difficult when connecting with those of alternative viewpoints. It doesn't mean saying yes to negativity, oppression, or a lack of compassion. But it does mean trying to see what we can learn from one another rather than letting ourselves be absorbed into the spectacle of conflict and thus being thrown off balance completely.

Practicing listening is the only way you will be a clear signal relay and not simply a point along the way in a game of telephone. That game is where the message is whispered from the first person, to the person next to them, around the room. It might start as something like, "Be like Cameron," and by the time it gets to the last person, it has morphed into something like, "The pizza guy is stammering." We have to practice our listening to be an effective part of the Reverberation Effect.

Reverberations let ideas expand beyond what they ever otherwise would have been. Your team can be a means by which that process happens regularly.

With reactions and intensity in mind, a helpful tool for boosting reverberation is to check your communication style and make sure it is *effective*, not *affective*. Are you impacting people in an encouraging way or in ways that elicit a response other than you intended? This often brings us back to what I said above: Are you the communicator, or are you the *way* you are communicating (intense, direct, busy, etc.) and not achieving the impact you want? You want to be the best relay possible, and you want those in your *reverberation* to be effective relays, too.

No one else's strength should diminish yours. Nor should yours diminish anyone else's.

If you are a team leader, a manager, a creative, or a member of what is an aspiring and effective reverberation team, work to ensure the way you communicate is in line with how, what, and why you communicate. If you want to check this, you can do the equivalent of someone reading the rough draft of a book. I'd recommend engaging people with questions about the effectiveness vs. the affectiveness of your communication style.

- Make a list of the aspects of your own communication style that you envision your team appreciates.
- Have each member of your team give constructive feedback to you of the communication style they see in you or that they interpret from you.

Then take a look at where there are similarities in those perspectives, or differences. This isn't easy to explore sometimes, but delivered supportively, it can be really helpful. This will take a thick skin, but that's where emotional courage comes in. The goal is to increase and improve your ability to be a reverberation multiplier, and a sharer of ideas that matter.

The responses should be areas where they think you are effective. It might also be areas where they would like for you to become *more* effective. The key is to not have this be a session where they tear you apart. This exploration should be about things they want you to improve to make your role as a communicator more impactful and the group more effective. The ultimate goal is for it to serve as a mirror for you, for things that are working, and for things that you can work on so that you can develop your identity and your potential impact as a reverberation relay.

When your communication is solid, you can be a means to amplify and then share ideas more effectively as a relay.

> **Building teamwork is a reverberation multiplier.**

Move forward with kindness in how you interact with people, both in the analog and digital world. The world needs less intensity.

Believe me, I understand intensity. I used to embrace it all the time. I have been the singer in punk bands, remember?

We need to believe in kindness as a transformative mechanism more than we rely on intensity to push our way through the world with our ideas. It might seem like it will take longer to get things done rather than just forcing your way, but I promise that believing in the kindness of others and responding to people with kindness first is absolutely the most effective approach to maximizing human dynamics.

If the goal is to most effectively share ideas and grow, then we can get there only through the buy-in of those we encounter. They might in time become relays for us, or us for them. It is important to be able to connect and strengthen our connection with those around us in order to solidify that reverberation potential.

Here is a good team-building activity if you want a way to strengthen your team, find approaches to problem-solving while having fun, and enjoy a bit of light-hearted chaos, too. Having fun is essential, and this is a good exercise with which to practice communication and help people be better relays. I like this exercise and use it from time to time as part of my reverberation trainings with groups.

Prepare paper bags with six marbles in each bag. Split your group into teams. It doesn't matter how many people are in each team as long as there are at least as many teams as you have bags of marbles for them. Give each team one of the paper bags with six marbles in it. The marble colors could be, for example, red, white, yellow, green, blue, and black. (Note: They don't have to be these exact colors as long as you have only six colors, repeating throughout all the teams).

Here is the catch: Not any one team gets all of the colors. Some teams get multiples of one color, other teams get multiples of another. Some teams have almost all the colors, but not quite.

Then you tell everyone that each team has ten minutes to put marbles in order on the table in front of them: red, white, yellow, green, blue, and black. The rules are: People can only whisper. No talking or screaming allowed. Then you start the timer. Don't answer any questions.

People will have to figure out other teams have different marbles and will have to make contact with the other teams through whispering. This prevents any one team from standing on a chair and asking the entire room who has a blue marble). It makes people have to engage, reverberate, and problem-solve together as they negotiate for the marbles they need.

Variations could be having each team be in a different corner of the room, or in different rooms. Or cutting out the whispering so people just go forth with whatever nonverbal style of communication works best for them. This exercise is really fun, and it's a great chance to practice rethinking how we communicate in order to effectively get our message shared and out into the world.

Effective team members, rooted in solid communication, make excellent reverberation relays.

A second teamwork concept for you to embrace so you build your reverberation network is simply to be willing to start small with your idea and build it from there. Asking that two-word question is a great launching point, but be ready to take a step back toward a simpler version of the original idea and then develop it outward. Remember from Chapter 7 that process isn't always linear.

I mentioned One Hundred for Haiti earlier. It is the 501(c)3 organization I launched in 2010. What I didn't mention is that the organization got its start after the earthquake in Haiti when some friends and I sailed to Haiti on a schooner with somewhere between 10,000 and 15,000 pounds of supplies and food for earthquake survivors. (We publicly said 10,000 pounds, but that was to satisfy Coast Guard regulations. It was more like 15,000 pounds, but you didn't hear that from me). We were at sea for eight days and nights, which was an adventure story of a lifetime. At times, the sea was as flat as a table and at other times, the waves were almost twenty feet high, and I thought for sure I was going to be swept overboard or find myself having to act out *Titanic* in real life.

As far as we know, we were the first private relief boat to make it to the southern coast of Haiti. In the aftermath of that sailing trip, I started One Hundred for Haiti as a nonprofit organization, which originally was designed to be a consortium of one hundred wealthier donors, individuals, or companies who would each donate $1,000 to Haitian relief, specifically with the intent of helping a medical doctor I knew in Haiti who was serving one of the poorest areas of

Port-au-Prince. I wanted to give him $100,000 toward helping people with medicine and medical care.

Why tell you this story?

Well, when I sent word out via social media about this ambitious plan, response was different from expected. I received exactly zero $1,000 donations. I heard instead from people who offered much smaller dollar amount donations. Messages started coming in from people who didn't have the requisite $1,000, but instead offered $2 or $5 or even just $1.

I decided to shift and pivot and accept those donations to start small and build from there. (I kept the name "One Hundred for Haiti" because it had a good ring to it but decided to expand the mission beyond just an elite hundred donors to anyone who wanted to participate.) We raised enough money to support that doctor, as well as help send another boat to Haiti with literally tons of rice and supplies.

Then we made the important shift from providing relief to supporting development. Today we support Haitians who are leading initiatives in the following areas. Together we have a lot of great things happening:

> We build houses and roofs for people with crumbling and dangerous earthen dwellings.
>
> We provide water systems to villages to help prevent cholera and other illnesses.
>
> We send dozens of kids to school for the duration of their K–12 scholastic existence.
>
> We help farmers plant crops to help feed an entire region.
>
> We provide internet to schools throughout the entire region we serve.
>
> We distribute food regularly for the hungriest families in that region.

None of those things were part of the primary mission/transmission, which was simply to sail to Haiti in response to Haitian need. Or the secondary one, which was to develop a system and network of relief and then development. We took a step back and started simply. That let us be part of a reverberation that amplified over time. In this particular situation, the original reverberation was the Haitian people and their clear communication. They expressed a desire to find partners with whom to work because they truly needed help in a dire time and wanted something more.

One Hundred for Haiti was simply a relay that answered a signal sent by a doctor asking for support. We thought we were set with that plan. But then we took a step back, started small with the donations, and built from there as relays for others. We were in the reverberation path for a group working on clean-water initiatives, so we took that on. We shared this as a signal boost with a group who was building roofs. They amplified our signal, and we took on and amplified theirs. We started building roofs too. Taking a step back and starting small let all of this happen. The original idea transformed, and the process to get there certainly wasn't linear.

In time, from the main primary signal, reverberation led to multiple groups, networking and connecting, helping and supporting one another, picking up the slack when others needed a break, and offering new ideas and approaches to taking action. The original message shifted, reverberated, and transformed into something bigger than it had been originally. The whole was far greater than the sum of its parts.

The Reverberation Effect allows for an idea or an action to grow organically and become bigger than itself in time. It inspires us to engage, listen, and respond to others because our ideas get enhanced, too. It gives us far more opportunities to interact and to develop ideas than we would have had on our own. But we need that solid team to make it happen. Cultivate engagement skills with the people around you. People will grow personally in their communicative skillsets, and the group will become stronger as a result.

Engage, listen, respond, and then reverberate and amplify.

Reverberation can help groups grow internally, too. It inspires a team to ask that all-important, two-word question.

When I thought of the phrase *"Engage, Listen, Respond"* and first used it in conjunction with the work being done with the volunteers of the Portland Mutual Aid Network, the dynamics of a new organization were challenging. We faced a lack of cohesion. We needed our focus to be refined. The slogan was a call for amplifying others' ideas as a primary directive.

The approach we'd taken up until that point was that of a ripple effect. Our ideas and energy rippled outward. This was limited and finite. Engaging, listening, and responding changed the game through solidifying the group's intentionality by way of others telling us what they needed.

Rather than sharing our own ideas and needs, we became a relay helping to amplify what other people needed. This was a major shift. Today, that group – like One Hundred for Haiti – is more than just the original idea, and in similar ways, larger than any one person involved in it. We truly became part of a reverberation, rather than seeing ourselves as the primary and only network itself. It started with this: Engage, listen, and respond. That process changed how the group interacted with the world, but thinking along the lines of reverberation also helped strengthen the group's internal communicative dynamics.

An important note is to embrace the change that can result from reverberation. The example above is a good one because it describes a group that found a shift in focus, a sharpened intentionality, and changed course from within. This is an important lesson in change management. We became better as a result of change. We developed, transformed, and expanded. We can't fear and condemn change because within it can reside as-yet-unseen possibilities for growth.

When we reverberate and amplify ideas, we put ourselves on track to build a better now.

There are lots of ways to better yourself as a relay. Enhancing your leadership skills is a reverberation multiplier. Educating yourself through studying trends and history is a reverberation multiplier. Being vulnerable is a reverberation multiplier. Expanding your skill set is a reverberation multiplier. Learning to love more deeply is a reverberation multiplier. Healing your wounds is a reverberation multiplier. Critical thinking is a reverberation multiplier. Taking care of others is a reverberation multiplier. Questioning systems and being willing to adapt or change them is a reverberation multiplier.

All of it helps us be better teammates, ready to do the work of reverberating and magnifying ideas that matter.

Welcome to the beginning. This is where we start.

We have arrived.

We reclaim the moment from the countless distractions that surround us in order to be centered and ready for action. We improve our skills as listeners to be more effective teammates. We ready ourselves to create and connect more effectively to bridge gaps between what we have and what we want. We send out reverberations of meaningful ideas to people who understand that focus matters and that change potentially means growth. We share ideas that get amplified, come back around, spread and grow. We do this to support others, to spread a mission statement, to achieve a goal, or a host of other valuable reasons. All of the work we have been exploring in this book is because you want something more, just as the people around you do, as well. And you can help them achieve it.

To see yourself as a world changer is one thing, but when you can see yourself as a relay and part of a reverberating team, it is far more generous and inspiring. This is where you can initiate change that manifests for others. Ultimately, this entire book is a step in that direction. Each of the strategies is, in its own way, a potential multiplier that lets us give back, uplift, and be a part of something more.

So, where do we go from here?

The goal of all of this is to create, elevate, and enhance potential. It is not to reclaim moments just for the sake of reclaiming moments or to build better nows for the sake of building better nows. If we take that route, it would be akin to creating art for the sake of creating art. We can do better than that. Let me illustrate this idea.

Let's say I take a moment for myself and set up a canvas and paint a sunset. It's my interpretation of the sunset. I take a step back and consider it. It's a cool painting. The colors are unusual. I'm actually colorblind, so I see sunsets differently. My painting looks like a half-asleep first grader grabbed a paint set. My artwork might not hang in a museum, but it's definitely a conversation starter!

You walk up. You look at the painting. You ponder it for a minute. You appreciate the colors. You like how I worked the clouds into the painting. Then you go off and buy an art set for yourself and copy my sunset. Your painting looks just like mine. You do this because you want to create art, too. And so, you do. What you paint is an exact copy.

Maybe someone else sees your painting and does the same with their own art set. And then someone else. In time, dozens of people or maybe even hundreds are jumping on the bandwagon, painting similar sunsets. My single art piece has helped to create myriad more painters creating an immense quantity of additional paintings.

Good, right? Not necessarily.

The purpose of art is not to create more art. The purpose of art is to create more life. Art elevates and inspires. It doesn't exist just to create copies of itself. We don't want to inspire people to be copies of us. We want people to thrive. That diverse and amplified team is the team I want to be a part of.

The purpose of art is not to have another, a dozen, or a million artists all creating exact copies of sunset paintings. The purpose of art, and specifically my artwork example of a sunset, is to have that painting inspire the next person who sees it so they see their next sunset differently and enjoy it more as a result. Perhaps that is you. The next time *you* see a real-life sunset of your own, maybe my painting will enhance and heighten your experience. Maybe you notice the colors of the real sunset differently. Maybe you notice the way the sun hides behind the clouds. Whatever it might be, in seeing the real sunset in a new way, because of my painting, the goal has been achieved: You have an enriched vision of the world to appreciate and enjoy. Art has created more life.

Then, let's say you take *that* vision, that perspective of a sunset and how it makes you feel, and you do something with it. Maybe you write something motivated by it. Maybe you call someone you haven't talked to in a while. Maybe you develop a new idea that you didn't think was possible before. Maybe you do something practical and draft a report you have been meaning to write for a while, and the sunset gets you inspired to do that.

That project or that phone call will inevitably impact or inspire someone else. Soon we have a grander vision of what a simple painting of a sunset could mean. Who knows what it could lead to? That's the meaning of the perspective shifts we've explored in this book. You're the painting, and you will inspire the people around you to experience life and their own potential differently.

What would we leave behind if we didn't paint that sunset in the first place, or share our idea, or take the initiative to lead a team, or tell someone how we feel, or try to develop an idea or innovation we've been mulling over for forever and a day?

Take this idea of enhancing experience and potential as the motivation behind this book. The purpose for improving your communication, teamwork, or leadership skills is not to create more communicators, teammates, or leaders. We don't want people just repeating our ideas back to us. The purpose of those actions is to create new perspectives and even more potential for all of us. When we reclaim the moment, we not only enhance our experience of life, but we set the stage to create opportunities for other people to do the same.

We increase our capacity for expansion when we build a better now and when we reclaim moments from the chaos of the world. What we then choose to do with that enhanced vitality and increased capacity is up to us.

Without the potential that comes from believing in the possibility of kindness, enhancing our focus, cultivating a revolutionary mindset, embracing the possibility of success, engaging with laughter, developing relationships, and being part of powerful reverberations we aren't fulfilling our responsibilities to the world as world changers. Moments are fleeting, and we could be absorbed into a world that would just as likely forget us as it could celebrate us.

We want something more, so let's do the work to bring that into reality. We can be that *new kind of human*. Let's change our world, or if you're so inspired and ambitious, *the* world. Ask that two-word question, and then take action on the next words that follow them.

> **What we want, we must create.**

Ultimately, when we build a better now, we find what we have been seeking. We create potential. That is the *more* we have been wanting all along. The potential for more experiences and connection, for more life, and for more space where new ideas can be shared and heard with more confidence. The space we create when we bring ourselves back to center and reclaim the moment is rich with possibility.

What will you bring into reality? How will your life be transformed when you bridge the gap between where you are and where you want to be?

Amidst that new possibility, what will you create? What innovation, idea, or relationship will you finally put into motion and develop now that you've created the space for it?

Please be in touch, and let me know.

Greg Bennick
Seattle, WA
April 2024
www.gregbennick.com

Acknowledgments

THANK YOU. FIRST and foremost, to the team at Wiley for believing in me.

Thank you too to a list of people who helped make this all possible...

Stephanie Witmer for having a thousand conversations with me about every single thing, and for expert proofreading

Richard Yonck for being there when I first uttered the words, "Build a Better Now."

John Kraljevich for the immense support from the moment I signed the contract

Brian Manowitz for being a constant source of creative inspiration

Jonathan Levit for reminding me to always keep creating

David Avrin for massive support, determination, and encouragement

Natalia Fidyka for inspiration about kindness

Pandit Dasa for helping to illuminate the path as a fellow Wiley author

Roy Hamrick and Stephen Carstens for decades of conversations

Cameron Collins for legal advice and playing Fortnite with me when I needed breaks

Shep Hyken for being a force to be reckoned with in the writing and speaking world

John Wilson for the books that changed my life and talks about the meaning of art

Dr. Heather Ashley Hayes for reminding me that completing big things is possible

Ross Haenfler and Skadi Snook for filling me with dinner

Tre Wideman for checking in all the time

Alina Kozarec for feeding me Thai food and treating me like gold

Charles Chaussinand for being wildly creative

Dave Whitson for being as solid as a rock intellectually

Ricardo Cozzolino for the continual accountability check-ins

Drew Wilkinson for the inspiration around sustainability

Shelli Gonshorowski for always encouraging me

Roberta Christensen for inspiring me to drive forward relentlessly

Erik Goldstein for normalizing being an expert on esoteric things

Magdalena Sky for encouraging me when I needed it most

Matt Miller for introducing me to the idea that punk rock is an art movement

Shealeigh Heindel for the delicious snacks that kept me nourished

Paul McKeever for conversations over Ethiopian food about how to build a better now

Marc Bennett for talks about the intersection of spirituality and business

Jake Conroy for discussing the difficulties of the permitting process

Shane Davis for always calling just to say hi

Eric Boehme for connecting with me about smart things

Jason Woodland for telling me, "All chips in. Deadly focus."

Veronica Viper for reminders about endurance

Melissa Broyles for getting your book done so I could see that it was possible

Dave Pak for extensive conversations about things that matter

Spencer Ackerman for being a spark that ignites many flames

One Set Studio in Oklahoma City for the incredible video work

Darryl Bennick for running over my foot but making up for it ever since

Mom and Dad for getting kicked out of the dance and thus making all of this possible

And for being by my side always: H, L, & S, BH, and S.

About the Author

GREG BENNICK IS in awe of the social, political, existential, and economic divides slicing through the modern day and how we are misguided and disempowered by them. His work focuses on ways to build bridges across these gaps if we are willing to work hard enough and look within to discover those solutions

When not at his keyboard, Greg is a keynote-speaking, Thai food-eating, knife-juggling global traveler from Seattle, Washington.

He spends his time connecting with audiences worldwide about ways to build a better now, researching and writing about rare coins, promoting compassion for elephants and other animals, and composing About the Author sections for himself.

This is his first book.

You can find out more about Greg at gregbennick.com or connect through LinkedIn or Instagram: @gregbennick.

Index

Ackerman, Spencer, 14–15
Allure of distraction, 87
Andaman Sea, xiii
Anxiety, response, 147–148
Art, purpose of, 225
Artificial intelligence (AI), 110, 148
Art of Intimacy, The (Malone), 194
Attention deficit hyperactive
      disorder (ADHD)
  diagnosis, 92
  preventative measure, 119
Authority, and Power, 49–51

Bailey, Wolfe, 13–14
Becker, Ernest, 52, 81, 156
Belonging, cultivating sense of
      meaning, 42, 188–189
Berger, Peter, 172
Big Wheel story, 70
Book of Delights, The
      (Ross Gay), 210
Bookstore story (Borders
      Books), 4–9

Bradbury, Ray, 96, 124
Bueller, Ferris, 161
Build a Better Now®, 16
Busy, fetishizing, 213

Catering, 214
Centering, and getting
      back to, 16
Change
  embracing, 80, 184
  management, 223
  ChatGPT, usage/impact,
      110, 148–149
Clients
  lessons to help with
      connection, 93
  solution to client-specific
      problems, 19–20
Climate change, xi
Coin collecting, 88–91
Confidence, 54, 93, 98
Conflict, 49, 162, 172
Connectedness, 169

Connection, 17–18, 21, 177–178
  strengthening, 180–181
Constructive feedback, 218
Consultation, humor, 161
Consultative standpoint (Chad
      Rapper), 187–188
Conversation, learning
      opportunity, 187
Costner, Kevin, 80–81
Courage
  emotional courage, cultivation,
      214–218
  finding, 139
  intimidation by Possibility of
      Success, 155
Creation, 53, 150, 156, 191, 196
Creative development, 142, 150
  strategies for world
      changers, xiv
Creativity, 46, 93, 139, 148, 157,
      159, 171, 193
  Sine Wave of, 10, 153–155, 154f
  teamwork and, 127, 174
Customers, 25, 31, 77, 82, 161

Dalai Lama, train before meeting
      him, 143–147
Darkness, leap, 10, 28, 63, 139, 153
Debord, Guy (The Society of the
      Spectacle), 108–110, 114
Deception of Defeat, The, 123
Deep breathing, impact, 120
Defeat, 9, 121
  Deception of, 123
Denial of Death, The
      (Becker), 52, 156
Diet, 26, 119
Disney train story, 55
Distraction, 224
  allure of and resistance to,
      87, 88, 108

DM/direct messages, 110
  inauthenticity, 6
Diversity, 183, 190
"Don't Be Afraid to Drop the Ball"
      (Bennick), 135
Double bind, 11, 171–173
Dynamite, Napoleon, 161

Elgee, Neil, 172–173
Emotional courage, 214–218
Empathic listening, practice, 84–85
Empowerment, 49–51, 66, 127, 156
Engage With Laughter, 161
Engagement, 135, 151, 163,
      168–169
  teams and, 170
Error, 198
  coins, 88–91
European Values Study, 23
Exercise, impact, 99–100, 119

FaceTime, and distraction, 110
Fahrenheit 451 (Ray Bradbury), 124
Failure, 66, 121
  amidst juggling, 102, 104
  fear of, 140, 150, 155
Flight from Death: The Quest
      for Immortality
      (documentary), 29
Floyd, George (death), 75
Focus, 1–227
  determination, 98
  keeping one's eyes on the
      knife, 87
  single mission, 118–119
Frankl, Victor, 161
Freud, Sigmund, 51, 72
Friends, and uplifting them with
      meaning, 53
  kindness to and with, 77
  process and contributions, 151

Gay, Ross (The Book of Delights), 210
Gender-inclusivity, 184
Generational divides, navigation, 20
Generational issues and bridging gaps, 113, 183, 189
  teams, 190
Generative creatures and the act of creation, 196
Goals and goal setting, 11, 34, 36, 113
  taking action and new approaches to, 140–141
Golden Rule, 189

Haiti, 30–31, 33, 95, 165, 185, 220–222
Hardy, Thomas, xiii
Hierarchies, 49, 197, 199
Hope, ix–xiv, 163
  possibility, 67, 72
Hopelessness, feeling, xi, 127
Human existence, double bind, 11, 171–173
Humor, group effectiveness, 163
  joyous risks, 164
  comedy, 132, 163
  customized, 168, 171

Ideas
  amplification of, 206
  creativity, 149
  new perspectives on, 18
  reverberation, 201
  revolutionary mindset, 123
Identity, 165, 181, 194
Ignition point, 47, 97, 128, 137
Images, impact of, 109, 111–113
Immediacy, juggling and focus, 98

Immobilization, 62, 135, 149, 152
  mistakes and, 121
Inclusion, value/support, 80, 190
India train story 143–148
Individualism, 183–184, 195
Influencer, 42, 58
Insecurities, 85–86
Instagram, 110, 115
Intention, ignition point, 97
Interactions, 83, 165, 171–172
Interdependency, 177–178
Internal voice, ignoring, 105
Intimacy, *The Art of Intimacy* (book), 194
Intimidation and possibility of success, 155
Isolation
  dread
    outsmarting, 179, 192, 197, 200
    soothing, 197
    threat of lonliness, 194

Joy, 43, 95, 133–134
  expectation, 143, 147
  soldiers on India train, 146
Juggling, 167
  ball dropping, not being afraid of, 101
  knife juggling story, 93
  learning to juggle in sixth grade, 90
  lesson, 97–107
  significance of, 93

Kafka, Franz, ix
Kiam, Victor, 166–168
  lessons learned from, 168
Kindness, The Possibility of, 69
Knife, Keep Your Eyes on, 87
Knife juggling story, 94

"Laughing at Death"
(Elgee), 172–173
Laughter, 161–178
courage, 177
customized comedy for corporate events, 31
engagement, 12, 20, 161–162, 168, 176
India train, 146–147
keynote speeches, 34
willingness, 164
Leadership
approaches to, 19, 177–178, 180–181
organizational, 18,48, 64–65, 87, 175
skills/development/enhancement, 223–224
Leg juggling story, 132
Life
force, offering (Becker), 156
perspective shifts, 20, 28, 42, 54, 171, 173
Lightheartedness, 164
Listening, 10, 19–20,
branding, 25
customer service, 187–188
bridging gaps, 22
in Haiti, 30, 185
to others, 30, 39, 150, 185
to ourselves, 24, 46
Loneliness, 186, 194, 196–197
Luckmann, Thomas, 172

Malone, Thomas Patrick
(Patrick Thomas), 194–195
Management, 36, 50, 190, 223
Martian Chronicles, The
(Bradbury), 96

Matter
distractions, goals, prioritization, 113, 117, 142
feeling that we, 21, 43, 45, 55, 151, 166
ideas that, 29, 32
instilling meaning in others, 39, 180–181, 187–188
moments and importance of, 11, 47
prioritization of tasks, 87, 213
relationships and people, 42, 63, 82, 151, 181
words and reverberation, 61, 201
work and feeling significant, 31, 57, 189, 192, 206
Meaning (also see Matter), 16, 20, 39, 156
art and, 225–226
connection to our work, 40, 180, 182–184, 198
craving a sense of, 27
human connection and, 215–216
identity and, 213
infusing in others, 42–43, 46, 50, 53, 175, 199
language and, 85
laughter, 172
striving for, 47, 54, 152, 159, 194, 198
Meditation, benefits, 120
Mentoring, 9, 189–190
Mind/mindset (see also Focus)
centering, deep breathing (impact), 120
clarity, 97, 119, 210–213
hopelessness, xi
humanity and rationality, 85
openness, 217
perspective, 105

revolutionary mindset, 9,
    16, 63, 123
saying yes before saying no,
    4, 74
shifting, 18
speaking one's, 31
Mistakes, approach, 87, 135
Morale
    increase, laughter (impact), 163
    team-based, 70, 73, 198
Moschen, Michael, 107, 157–158
Motivation, 29, 48, 155, 157, 180,
    203, 209, 212
Moto Logistics, 30
Music (see also *Punk Rock*), 32, 130

Naked Raygun, 1
News broadcasts and
    psychology, 162
Nickels, Greg, 37–38
Nietzsche, Friedrich, 174

Objective hierarchies, 197
One Hundred for Haiti, 220–223
Onstage experience, 15, 31, 41,
    93, 189, 193
Optimism and positivity, 168–169
Outcomes and forward thinking,
    80, 118, 140
Overcast Design, 13–14

Parents meeting story, 123
Parviainen, Duncan, 179
PayCompass, 187
People (see also *Meaning*)
    building relationships, 179, 189
    collaboration, 23, 82, 201
    isolation, 22, 179, 186, 192–194,
        196–197
    leadership in conjunction
        with, 21, 25

self help and critique of it, 3, 6–7
    team-building, 17, 20
    validating, 20, 26–27, 151 198
Perspective shifts, 20, 28, 42,
    54, 171, 173
Pessimism
    Big Wheel story, 69
    keynote speaking topic, 209
    kindness and, 69, 75, 79, 84
    origins in author, 71
    power and, 73
    Trap of, 73–74
Phones
    obsession with, 88
    putting down, 119
Plant Based on a
    Budget (Shapiro), 26
Portland Mutual Aid Network, 75–78
    origins and intent, 39
Positivity, 80, 128, 168–169
Possibility (See also Mind/
    mindset), x, 2, 16, 189
    creativity, 152–153
    envisioning change, 22
    future and, 47
    kickstarting, 201
    of dying on a banana peel, 44
    process 157–159
    success/intimidation, 150, 153
    The Possibility of Kindness, 69,
        73, 77
    "What if?" 202
Postcard story, 41
Power, 183
    authority, contrast, 49–51
    listening, 30
    presence, 49
Priorities, 95, 117, 215
Process
    exploration, 151
    high point, 152–155

Productivity, 12, 56–57, 87–88, 163, 175

Profitability, perspectives, 188

Progress, 53, 56, 61, 171, 179–180

Psychological equanimity, 113, 194

Psychological intervention due to news, 162–163

Pulitzer Prize, 15, 52, 156

Questioning
    defeat, 131
    systems, 224

Rank, Otto, 51–52, 72, 110, 193

Rapper, Chad, 187–188

Reign of Terror (Spencer Ackerman), 15

Relational transformation, need, 183

Relationships x, 16, 20, 46, 55, 65, 67, 82
    building, 63, 178, 179, 187, 192
    change, listening (impact), 186
    clarity/strengthening/ importance, 189
    clients, 77
    development, 16, 192–193, 199
    dynamics/values, 182–183
    enhancement, 165–166
    force multiplier, equivalence, 16, 195–196
    new, 69

Results, 17, 56, 93, 143 150

Reverberation
    amplification, 209
    multipliers, 211–212, 223–224
        function, 218
    potential, 216–217
    teams, 218

Reverberation Effect™, 204–205, 209, 217
    definition, 201–203

Revolutionary mindset, cultivation, 9, 63, 123, 132

Revolutionary thinking, 173

Ripple effect, 204

Risk/reward, decision (navigation), 108

Risk, 13, 42, 51, 108, 140, 149–150, 200
    creative, 16, 63
    joyous, 164, 177
    geopolitical, 22
    Trial lyric, 139

Roadblocks, 90, 130, 209

Robbins, Tony, 7–8

Rugged individualist (concept), 195

Russia tour, 38

Rustin, Bayard, 49

Sartre, Jean-Paul, 181

Say Yes! (concept), 4, 80–81, 98

Self-belief, revolutionary act, 125

Self-doubt, 40–41, 54, 121, 179

Self-esteem, 54, 131, 150–151, 166, 175–176

Shapiro, Toni Okamoto, 26–27

Shen, Patrick, 29

Sidran, Mark, 38

Sinek, Simon, 34, 210

Sine Wave of Creativity, 153–155, 154f

Sine wave, trajectory (concept), 155

Single mission (concept), 118–119

Sisyphus, 56–57, 64

Situationist International, 108, 110

Social awkwardness, 145

Social Construction of Reality, The (Berger/Luckmann), 172

Society of the Spectacle, The (Debord), 108

Speak truth to power (Rustin), 49

Spoken word touring, 38

Straight edge, 119
Success 12, 98, 120, 139, 150, 153
  chasing, 5, 28,
  trajectory, 153
Sustainability, 33, 150,
  183–184, 199
Systems, change from within, 36

Team
  connections, strengthening, 191
  creativity amidst disappointment,
    127, 150
  distractions, 98
  inspiration/motivation, 151
  intergeneralization, 190
  morale problems, experience, 73
  motivation, 180–181
  shared laughter, impact, 12
  variations on team activity, 220
Team-building, 219
  exercise, 170–171
Teamwork
  cultivation, 20
  essence, 191–192
  game-changing approach, 180
  importance of, 182
  improvement, purpose, 226
  positive reinforcement, 131
  psychology, 29, 39
  sustainability model, 150
TEDx, 34
Teen Dance Ordinance, 37
The Legacy Project
  co-founding, 35
  work, takeaway, 36
The Possibility of Kindness™,
  74–75, 79, 81, 84
TikTok, 110, 116, 152
Transformation, 31–32, 42, 53–54
  movement and courage
    combined, 159

laughter as catalyst, 173
Trauma of Birth, The (Rank), 51
Trial (band), 203–204, 207
True North Payment Solutions,
  187–188
Truth, 36, 85, 174, 183
  overwhelmed by, 111–112
  science and, 162
  speaking to power, 49
Tunnel
  metaphor, 158

Unrestrained (song lyrics),
  207–208

Vegan/veganism, 26, 210
Vision, 11, 26, 38, 170, 226
  leadership, 23
  management and, 64–65
  staying true to, 15, 184
Voice
  finding, 18, 34, 56, 59, 61, 64–65
  ignoring internal, 6, 11, 159
  power, 42, 46, 49
Vulnerability, 85–86, 177

Want, want not (contrast), 53
Weirdness, 28, 47, 52, 111,
  119, 161, 171
What if
  question, 203–206, 209, 217
  story 201
Whitson, Dave, 37
Whittier, John Greenleaf, 212
Wilkinson, Drew, 150
Work
  development and growth, 16
  focus and, 15
  improvement, 120–121
  problems at 19–20, 183–184
  stress (APA report), 24

Workforce, Gen Z representation, 199
World
  chaos, 226
  transformation, possibility, 127
  vision, 60
  weight, 161, 162
World changers, 17, 38, 40,
     53–54, 200
  management, 64

perspective, 224
  team trust, 197–198
Worry, 135, 144, 191
Writing, 149–150
  authenticity and, 4, 48
  near death of author, 1
  Rank, Otto, perspective, 110

YouTube videos, 34, 110, 114